Mike McGrath

Bash

in easy steps

In easy steps is an imprint of In Easy Steps Limited
16 Hamilton Terrace · Holly Walk · Leamington Spa
Warwickshire · United Kingdom · CV32 4LY
www.ineasysteps.com

In Easy Steps Limited supports The Forest Stewardship Council (FSC), the leading international forest certification organization. All our titles that are printed on Greenpeace approved FSC certified paper carry the FSC logo.

Printed and bound in the United Kingdom

ISBN 978-1-84078-809-9

Contents

Preface

The creation of this book has been for me, Mike McGrath, an exciting opportunity to demonstrate the powerful command-line shell functionality available with Bash. I sincerely hope you enjoy discovering the exciting possibilities of the command line and have as much fun with it as I did in writing this book. In order to clarify script code listed in the steps given I have adopted certain colorization conventions. Interpreter directives and comments are colored green; shell components are blue; literal string and numeric values are black; user-specified variable and function names are red. Additionally, a colored icon and a file name appears in the margin alongside the script code to readily identify each particular script:

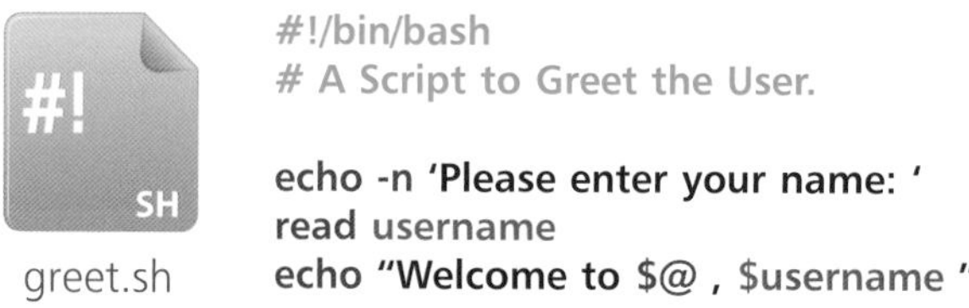
#!
SH
greet.sh
#!/bin/bash
A Script to Greet the User.
echo -n 'Please enter your name: '
read username
echo "Welcome to $@ , $username "

The screenshots that accompany each example illustrate the actual output produced by precisely executing the commands listed in the easy steps:

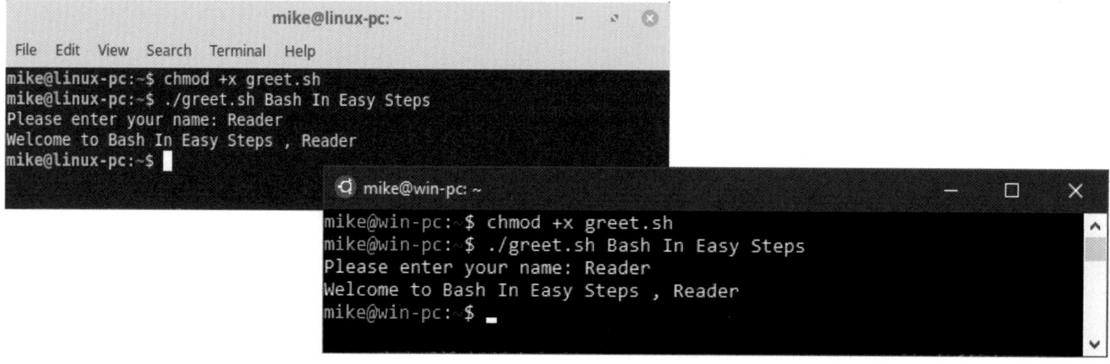
mike@linux-pc: ~
File Edit View Search Terminal Help
mike@linux-pc:~$ chmod +x greet.sh
mike@linux-pc:~$ ./greet.sh Bash In Easy Steps
Please enter your name: Reader
Welcome to Bash In Easy Steps , Reader
mike@linux-pc:~$
mike@win-pc: ~
mike@win-pc:~$ chmod +x greet.sh
mike@win-pc:~$ ./greet.sh Bash In Easy Steps
Please enter your name: Reader
Welcome to Bash In Easy Steps , Reader
mike@win-pc:~$

For convenience, I have placed source code files from the examples featured in this book into a single ZIP archive. You can obtain the complete archive by following these three easy steps:

1. Browse to **www.ineasysteps.com** then navigate to Free Resources and choose the Downloads section

2. Find Bash in easy steps in the list, then click on the hyperlink entitled All Code Examples to download the archive

3. Now, extract the contents to any convenient location, such as your home directory

1 Getting Started

This chapter introduces the Bash command interpreter shell and demonstrates essential basic commands.

Introducing Bash

BASH
THE BOURNE-AGAIN SHELL

GNU Bash logo

Computer operating systems include a command-line interpreter that allows the user to communicate directly with the system by typing text commands at a waiting prompt. The command-line interpreter is a "shell" facility that will process the input command and produce an appropriate output response.

An early shell facility was created for the Unix operating system by Stephen Bourne at Bell Labs way back in 1979. This early "Bourne shell" (**sh**) proved to be very popular as it was both a command-line interpreter and a scripting language that supported most features needed to produce structured programs.

The GNU Project is a free-software mass collaboration project. You can discover more at **gnu.org/gnu/thegnuproject.en.html**

Ten years later, in 1989, a free software replacement for the Bourne shell was created by Brian Fox for the GNU Project. Recognizing its ancestry, the replacement shell was named "Bash" – an acronym for the phrase **B**ourne-**a**gain **sh**ell. The Bash command syntax is a superset of that in the Bourne shell, but incorporates many extensions that are lacking in the Bourne shell. Bash can efficiently process commands typed at a prompt and execute shell program scripts that have been saved as text files.

Today Bash is the default shell for most Linux operating systems, for Apple's macOS operating system (formerly OS X), and for the Solaris Unix operating system.

The Bash command-line processor typically runs in a text window. This is similar to the Command Prompt window found in the Windows operating system in which users can type commands to be interpreted by the Windows Command Processor.

Microsoft has recognized the power and popularity of Bash by introducing support for "WSL" (**W**indows **S**ubsystem for **L**inux) in the Windows 10 operating system. This allows users to run a Linux environment directly on Windows so they can issue Bash commands at a shell prompt, create and execute Bash shell scripts, and run Linux command-line applications.

This book describes and demonstrates how to utilize the power of Bash with examples that can be run natively in a "Terminal" text window on a Linux operating system and within a (WSL) Linux environment on the Windows 10 operating system.

Discovering the Shell

When you open a new Terminal window on a Linux operating system, a command prompt appears indicating that a shell process has been started for you automatically. This shell will typically be the Bash shell facility.

Linux Terminal

The name of the shell in use can be seen in information about the current Terminal process by issuing a **ps $$** command. The output from this command should confirm Bash as the current shell under its "COMMAND" heading. If another shell is listed you can switch to the Bash shell simply by issuing a **bash** command if it is available. In the event that the Bash program is not already available it must be installed by you or the system administrator.

Once you have confirmed that Bash is the current shell you can see its version information by issuing a **bash --version** command:

1. Launch a Terminal window, then at the prompt exactly type **ps $$** and hit **Return** to discover the current shell

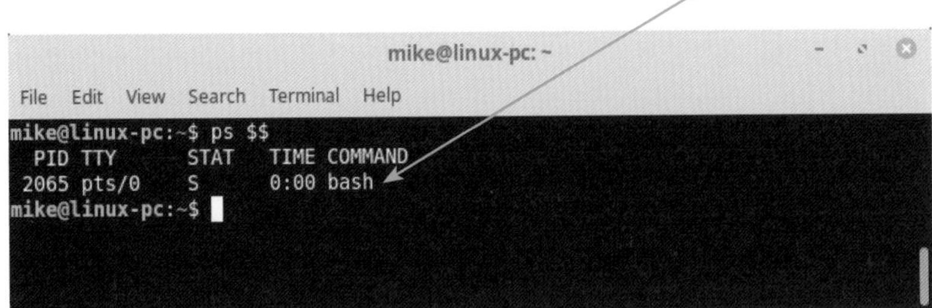

Bash is case-sensitive so the commands MUST be capitalized exactly as listed. For example, the **ps** command must use only lowercase letters.

2. Next, type a **clear** command and hit **Return** (or press **Ctrl** + **L** keys) to clear the Terminal window to a prompt

3. Now, exactly type **bash --version** then hit **Return** to discover the current Bash version

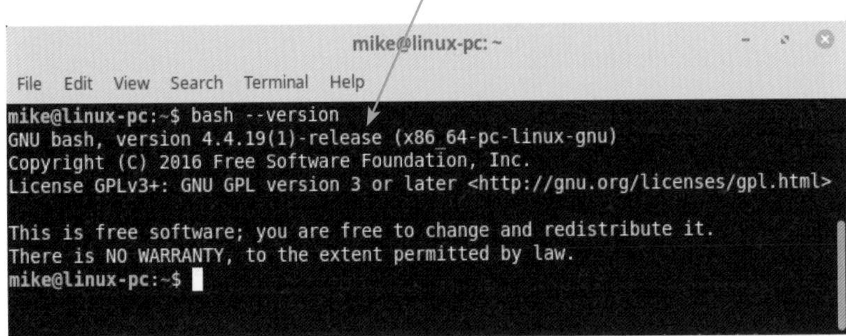

Installing Linux on Windows

The Windows Subsystem for Linux (WSL) allows you to install a variety of Linux distributions ("distros") from the Windows Store. Before any distro can be installed you must, however, first enable the optional WSL feature on your Windows 10 system:

This happy penguin is "Tux" – the friendly mascot of the Linux operating system.

1. Right-click the "Windows PowerShell" item on the Start menu, then choose **Run as Administrator** – to open a PowerShell window with Administrator privileges

2. In PowerShell, precisely type this command:
Enable-WindowsOptionalFeature -Online -FeatureName Microsoft-Windows-Subsystem-Linux

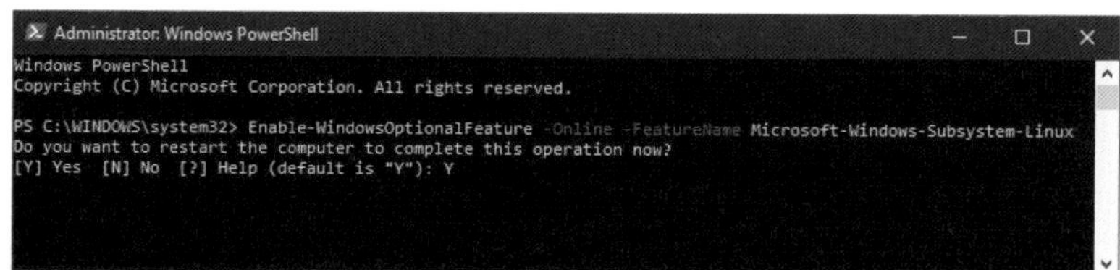

You will need your PC to have an internet connection to download a Linux distro.

3. Hit **Return** to execute the command, then type **Y** and hit Return once more – to restart the operating system

4. Next, click the **Microsoft Store** item on the Start menu, then search for "WSL" to find the available Linux distros

You cannot install Ubuntu Linux on the Windows 10 S version of the operating system.

5. Select your preferred Linux distro, such as the **Ubuntu** distro that is used to demonstrate WSL in this book

6. Click the **Get** button to download the chosen Ubuntu distro onto your PC

If installation fails with error **0x8007007e** your system doesn't support Linux from the store – ensure you are running Windows 10 build 16215 or later; the Windows Subsystem for Linux is enabled; and that you have restarted your PC.

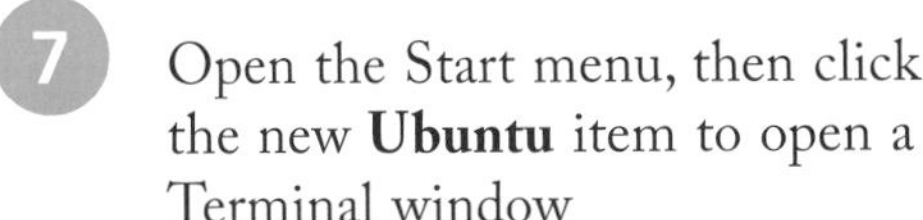

7. Open the Start menu, then click the new **Ubuntu** item to open a Terminal window

8. Wait while the distro's files are decompressed and installed – this takes a while, but only happens once

9. Finally, enter a username and password of your choice to set up a Linux user account

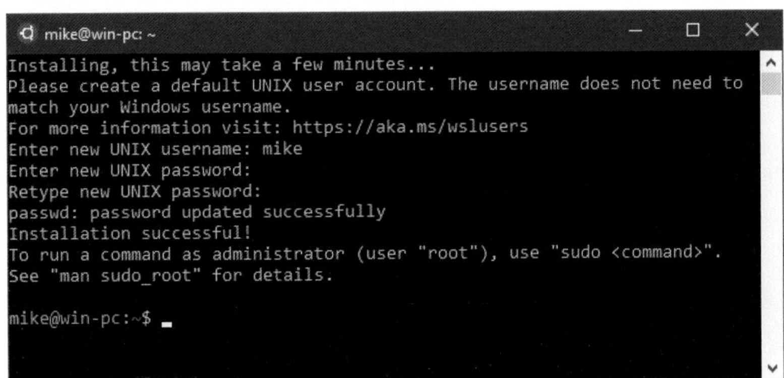

Record your username and password in a safe place where you can easily find them – you will need them to perform some Bash shell operations later.

Initializing the Distro

Advanced Package Tool

Following installation of a Linux distro in WSL, as described on page 11, it is recommended that you update the distro.

The Linux operating system consists of separate "packages" that are indexed in a catalog, which can be updated by the system's package manager. In the Ubuntu distro the package manager is the Advanced Package Tool (**apt**). This package manager can update the package catalog with the command **apt update** and can upgrade the packages with the command **apt upgrade**.

Changes to the system require administrator privileges so each of these commands must therefore be preceded by a **sudo** command:

1. Click Start, **Ubuntu** to open a Terminal window
2. At the prompt, type this command, then hit **Return**
   sudo apt update
3. Now, enter the password you chose for your Linux account, then hit **Return** to update the catalog

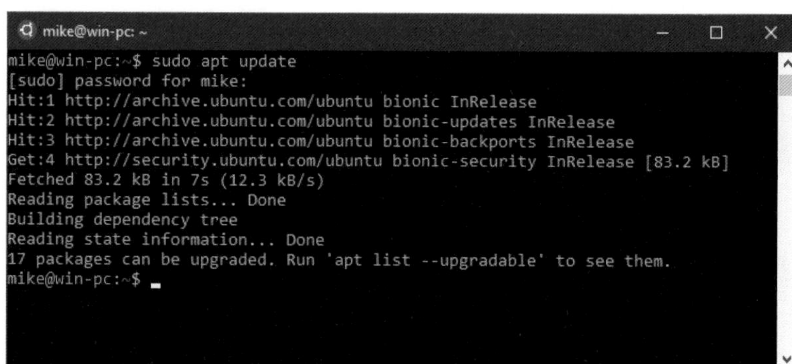

mike@win-pc: ~
mike@win-pc:~$ sudo apt update
[sudo] password for mike:
Hit:1 http://archive.ubuntu.com/ubuntu bionic InRelease
Hit:2 http://archive.ubuntu.com/ubuntu bionic-updates InRelease
Hit:3 http://archive.ubuntu.com/ubuntu bionic-backports InRelease
Get:4 http://security.ubuntu.com/ubuntu bionic-security InRelease [83.2 kB]
Fetched 83.2 kB in 7s (12.3 kB/s)
Reading package lists... Done
Building dependency tree
Reading state information... Done
17 packages can be upgraded. Run 'apt list --upgradable' to see them.
mike@win-pc:~$

4. Type a **clear** command and hit **Return** (or press **Ctrl** + **L** keys) to clear the Terminal window to a prompt
5. At the prompt, type this command, then hit **Return**
   sudo apt upgrade
6. Read the summary of available upgrades, then type **Y** and hit **Return** to continue

You can discover more about the **sudo** command on page 82.

```
mike@win-pc:~$ sudo apt upgrade
Reading package lists... Done
Building dependency tree
Reading state information... Done
Calculating upgrade... Done
The following packages will be upgraded:
  apt apt-utils base-files cloud-init console-setup console-setup-linux
  keyboard-configuration libapt-inst2.0 libapt-pkg5.0 liblxc-common liblxc1
  libmspack0 libxml2 lshw open-iscsi python3-distupgrade
  ubuntu-release-upgrader-core
17 upgraded, 0 newly installed, 0 to remove and 0 not upgraded.
Need to get 6200 kB of archives.
After this operation, 38.9 kB of additional disk space will be used.
Do you want to continue? [Y/n] Y
```

7. See the available replacement packages now get downloaded and unpacked to upgrade your system

```
Preparing to unpack .../04-open-iscsi_2.0.874-5ubuntu2.1_amd64.deb ...
Unpacking open-iscsi (2.0.874-5ubuntu2.1) over (2.0.874-5ubuntu2) ...
Preparing to unpack .../05-libxml2_2.9.4+dfsg1-6.1ubuntu1.2_amd64.deb ...
Unpacking libxml2:amd64 (2.9.4+dfsg1-6.1ubuntu1.2) over (2.9.4+dfsg1-6.1ubuntu1) ..
Preparing to unpack .../06-lshw_02.18-0.1ubuntu6.18.04.1_amd64.deb ...
Unpacking lshw (02.18-0.1ubuntu6.18.04.1) over (02.18-0.1ubuntu6) ...
Preparing to unpack .../07-ubuntu-release-upgrader-core_1%3a18.04.24_all.deb ...
Unpacking ubuntu-release-upgrader-core (1:18.04.24) over (1:18.04.21) ...
Preparing to unpack .../08-python3-distupgrade_1%3a18.04.24_all.deb ...
Unpacking python3-distupgrade (1:18.04.24) over (1:18.04.21) ...
Preparing to unpack .../09-liblxc-common_3.0.1-0ubuntu1~18.04.2_amd64.deb ...
Unpacking liblxc-common (3.0.1-0ubuntu1~18.04.2) over (3.0.1-0ubuntu1~18.04.1) ...
Preparing to unpack .../10-liblxc1_3.0.1-0ubuntu1~18.04.2_amd64.deb ...
Unpacking liblxc1 (3.0.1-0ubuntu1~18.04.2) over (3.0.1-0ubuntu1~18.04.1) ...
Preparing to unpack .../11-libmspack0_0.6-3ubuntu0.1_amd64.deb ...
Unpacking libmspack0:amd64 (0.6-3ubuntu0.1) over (0.6-3) ...
Preparing to unpack .../12-cloud-init_18.3-9-g2e62cb8a-0ubuntu1~18.04.2_all.deb ...

Progress: [ 64%] [##############################################.................]
```

8. Type a **clear** command and hit **Return** (or press **Ctrl** + **L** keys) to clear the Terminal window to a prompt

9. Now, exactly type **bash --version** then hit **Return** to discover the current Bash version – identical to that on the Linux system illustrated on page 9

```
mike@win-pc:~$ bash --version
GNU bash, version 4.4.19(1)-release (x86_64-pc-linux-gnu)
Copyright (C) 2016 Free Software Foundation, Inc.
License GPLv3+: GNU GPL version 3 or later <http://gnu.org/licenses/gpl.html>

This is free software; you are free to change and redistribute it.
There is NO WARRANTY, to the extent permitted by law.
mike@win-pc:~$
```

For further help with installation of Linux in the WSL you should refer to the Troubleshooting page online at **docs.microsoft.com/en-us/windows/wsl/troubleshooting**

The Bash versions are identical on this Windows 10 PC and the Linux PC, so the vast majority of examples in this book can run on either PC. Most screenshots illustrate Bash in WSL on Windows but would appear identical in a Linux Terminal. There are, however, a few examples that are illustrated in a Linux Terminal as these require a graphical Linux interface or a multi-user Linux environment.

Understanding Commands

When the user hits the Return key after typing a command at a shell prompt it adds a final invisible newline character. This denotes the end of the command and indicates to the shell that it should then attempt to interpret that command. The Bash interpreter first reads the command line as "standard input" (stdin) and splits it into separate words broken by spaces or tabs. Each of these words is known as a "token". The interpreter next examines the first token to see if it is one of the shell's "built-in" commands or an executable program located on the file system.

Don't forget

Each program can accept standard input and can produce standard output and standard error messages.

When the first token is recognized as a built-in shell command the interpreter executes that command; otherwise, it searches through the directories on a specified path to find a program of that name. The interpreter will then execute a recognized built-in command or recognized program and display any result in the Terminal as "standard output" (stdout). Where neither is found the interpreter will display an error message in the Terminal as "standard error" (stderr).

The Bash **type** command can be used to determine whether a token is recognized as a built-in shell command or the location of a recognized program, or to display a message if none can be found:

1. At a command prompt type **type clear** then hit **Return** to see the location of the **clear** program on the filesystem

2. Next, type the command **type exit** then hit **Return** to discover that **exit** is in fact a built-in shell command

3. Now, type **type nosuch** then hit **Return** to see this token cannot be found to match a built-in command or program name

You can also use the built-in command **hash** to see a list of your recently issued program commands and the number of times executed (hits).

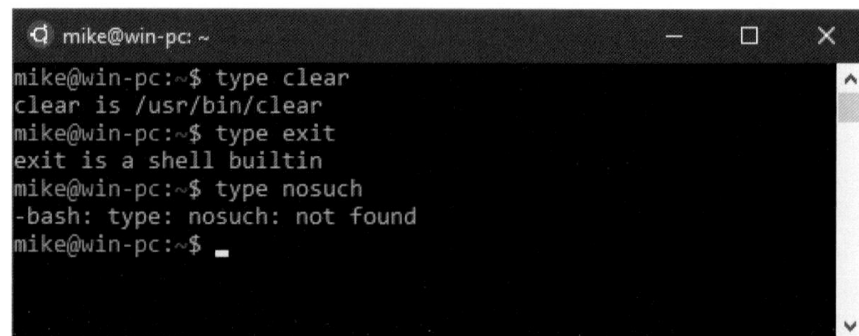

The Bash built-in **echo** command simply reads all following tokens from standard input then prints them as standard output – unless they are recognized as a command "option". Many built-in commands and programs accept one or more options that specify how they should be executed. Typically, an option consists of a dash followed by a letter. For example, the **echo** command accepts an **-n** option that denotes it should omit the newline character that it automatically prints after other output:

You will often want to suppress the automatic newline with **echo -n** when printing a request for user input.

4. At a prompt, type **echo** followed by some text then hit **Return** to see that text printed with an added newline

5. Now, type **echo -n** followed by some text then hit **Return** to see that text printed without an added newline

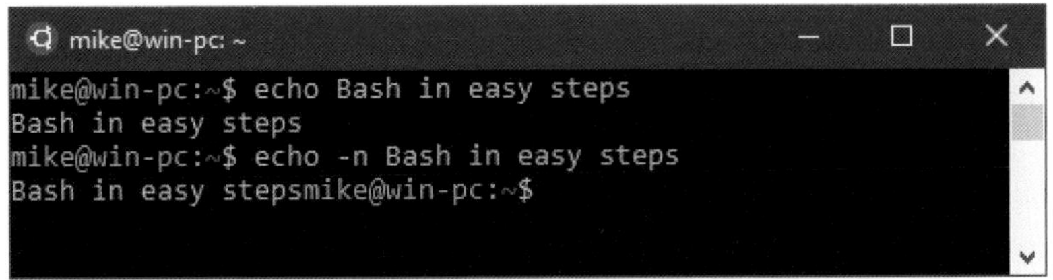

mike@win-pc: ~
mike@win-pc:~$ echo Bash in easy steps
Bash in easy steps
mike@win-pc:~$ echo -n Bash in easy steps
Bash in easy stepsmike@win-pc:~$

In addition to the built-in shell commands the Bash shell also contains a number of built-in shell variables. These are named "containers" that each store a piece of information, and their names use all uppercase characters. To access the information stored within a variable its name must be prefixed with a **$** dollar sign:

You can also use the command **echo $PATH** to discover which directories the Bash shell searches when you issue any command.

6. At a prompt, enter **echo $SHELL** to see the location of the Bash interpreter program on the filesystem

7. Now, enter **echo $BASH_VERSION** to see the version number of the Bash shell interpreter

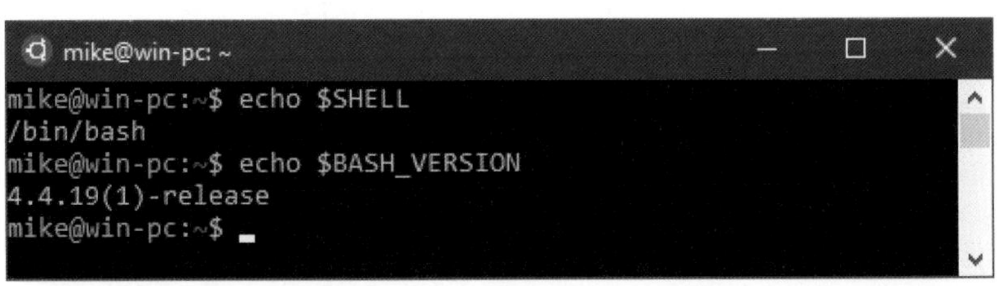

Navigating the File System

The Linux filesystem is arranged in a tree-like hierarchy of directories and files, with the "root" directory at its base:

- The root directory is simply addressed by a **/** forward slash.
- Sub-directories in the root directory are addressed by appending their directory name to the forward slash. For example, the "home" directory has the address **/home**.
- Directories in sub-directories are addressed by appending another forward slash and their name. For example, a "user" directory in the "home" directory has the address **/home/user**.
- Files in directories are addressed by appending another forward slash and the filename, such as **/home/user/filename**.

This hierarchical address system can therefore easily describe the "absolute path" of any directory or file from the / root base. Additionally, contents of the current directory and its sub-directories can be addressed by name using their "relative path". For example, a sub-directory named "user" within **/home** can be addressed from **/home** simply as **user**, and a file within that sub-directory can be addressed as **user/filename**.

As Linux is case-sensitive the names of directories and files in addresses must be correctly capitalized.

When you launch a Terminal window you are located in your home directory – a directory bearing your username that is located in **/home**, such as **/home/mike**. You can see your current location at any time with the **pwd** (print working directory) command and list the contents of that directory with the **ls** command. Contents of sub-directories can be listed simply by specifying their address to the **ls** command:

1. Launch a Terminal, then enter **pwd** at the prompt to see the absolute path address of your current location

2. Next, enter **ls /** to see the contents of the root directory

```
mike@win-pc:~$ pwd
/home/mike
mike@win-pc:~$ ls /
bin   dev  home  lib    media  opt   root  sbin  srv  tmp  var
boot  etc  init  lib64  mnt    proc  run   snap  sys  usr
mike@win-pc:~$
```

Here, listed directories are colored blue, executable files are colored green, and other writables are colored black-on-green.

3. Now, enter **ls /bin** to see the many executable binary files you can run from the command line

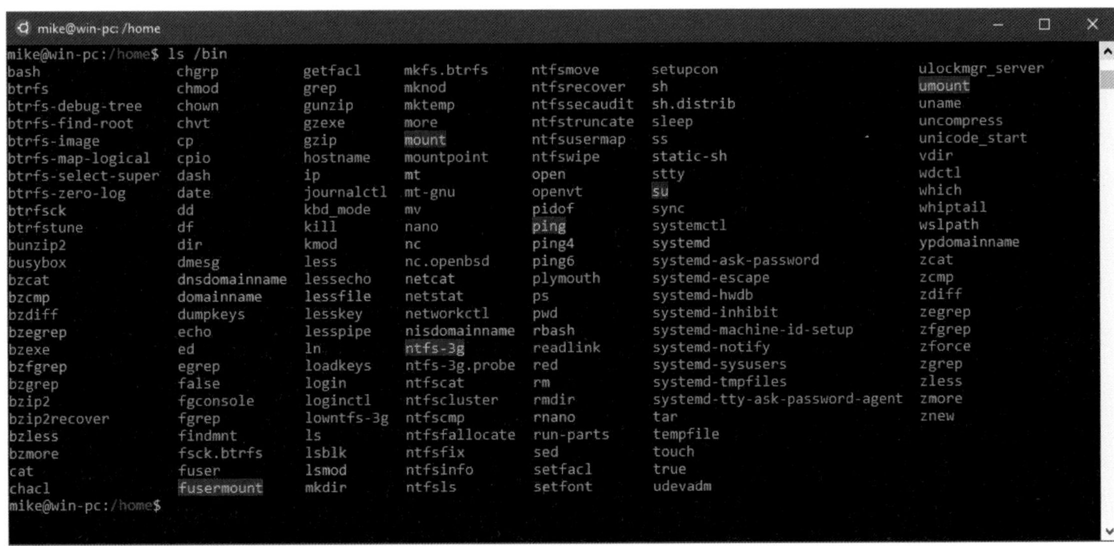

mike@win-pc: /home
mike@win-pc:/home$ ls /bin
bash chgrp getfacl mkfs.btrfs ntfsmove setupcon ulockmgr_server
btrfs chmod grep mknod ntfsrecover sh umount
btrfs-debug-tree chown gunzip mktemp ntfssecaudit sh.distrib uname
btrfs-find-root chvt gzexe more ntfstruncate sleep uncompress
btrfs-image cp gzip mount ntfsusermap ss unicode_start
btrfs-map-logical cpio hostname mountpoint ntfswipe static-sh vdir
btrfs-select-super dash ip mt open stty wdctl
btrfs-zero-log date journalctl mt-gnu openvt su which
btrfsck dd kbd_mode mv pidof sync whiptail
btrfstune df kill nano ping systemctl wslpath
bunzip2 dir kmod nc ping4 systemd ypdomainname
busybox dmesg less nc.openbsd ping6 systemd-ask-password zcat
bzcat dnsdomainname lessecho netcat plymouth systemd-escape zcmp
bzcmp domainname lessfile netstat ps systemd-hwdb zdiff
bzdiff dumpkeys lesskey networkctl pwd systemd-inhibit zegrep
bzegrep echo lesspipe nisdomainname rbash systemd-machine-id-setup zfgrep
bzexe ed ln ntfs-3g readlink systemd-notify zforce
bzfgrep egrep loadkeys ntfs-3g.probe red systemd-sysusers zgrep
bzgrep false login ntfscat rm systemd-tmpfiles zless
bzip2 fgconsole loginctl ntfscluster rmdir systemd-tty-ask-password-agent zmore
bzip2recover fgrep lowntfs-3g ntfscmp rnano tar znew
bzless findmnt ls ntfsfallocate run-parts tempfile
bzmore fsck.btrfs lsblk ntfsfix sed touch
cat fuser lsmod ntfsinfo setfacl true
chacl fusermount mkdir ntfsls setfont udevadm
mike@win-pc:/home$

You can change location into a directory using the **cd** command. Additionally, your home directory can be addressed using a tilde ~ alias, and the parent of the current directory can be addressed using a .. alias. The Bash prompt string typically displays the current directory just before the **$** sign:

4. Enter **cd /bin** to see the prompt change to display the subdirectory location

5. Enter **cd** .. then hit **Return** to move to the parent directory, and see the prompt string change once more

6. Finally, enter **cd** ~ to return to your home directory, and see the prompt string change again

Here, all listed files are executable but those colored white-on-red set the user ID when run, and those colored light blue are (symbolic) links to the actual location. You can learn more about links on pages 32-33.

You can also use the command **cd -** to return to the previous directory you were located in.

Dealing Wildcards

The **ls** command, introduced on pages 16-17, will list all files and folders in the current or specified directory except special hidden files whose names begin with a . period (full stop) character. Typically these are system files, such as a **.bashrc** hidden file in your home directory containing the shell configuration details. Hidden files can be included in the list displayed by the **ls** command by adding an **-a** option, so the command becomes **ls -a**.

Don't forget

If you wish to delete a directory remember that it may contain hidden files – use the **ls -a** command to check the directory's contents.

Optionally, a filename pattern can be supplied to the **ls** command so it will list only filenames matching the specified pattern. Special "wildcard" characters, described in the table below, can be used to specify the filename pattern to be matched:

Wildcard:	Matches:
?	Any single character
*	Any string of characters
[*set*]	Any character in *set*
[!*set*]	Any character not in *set*

The **?** wildcard is used to specify a pattern that matches filenames where only one single character may be unknown. For example, where the **ls** command lists **file.a**, **file.b**, and **file.exe** the command **ls file.?** would list only **file.a** and **file.b** – not **file.exe**.

You can include a hyphen in the *set* pattern by placing it first or last in the list within the square brackets.

More usefully, the * wildcard is used to specify a pattern that matches filenames where multiple characters may be unknown. For example, where **ls** lists **img.png**, **pic.png**, and **pic.jpg** the command **ls *.png** would list only **img.png** and **pic.png** – not **pic.jpg**.

The [*set*] wildcard construct is used to specify a pattern that matches a list or a range of specified characters. For example, where the **ls** command lists **doc.a**, **doc.b**, **doc.c**, and **doc.d** the command **ls doc.[ac]** would list only **doc.a** and **doc.c** – as this pattern specifies a list of two possible extensions to be matched. In the same directory the command **ls doc.[a-c]** would, however, list **doc.a**, **doc.b**, and **doc.c** – as the pattern specifies a range of three possible extensions to be matched. Placing an exclamation mark at the start of a *set* pattern lists files not matched. For example, here the command **ls doc[!a-c]** would list only **doc.d**.

In executing commands containing wildcards the shell first expands the wildcard matches and substitutes them as a list of "arguments" to the command. So, the command **ls doc.[a-c]** might in effect become **ls doc.a doc.b doc.c** before the list gets printed. This is apparent in the error message that gets displayed when no matches are found. For example, **ls non*** might produce the error message **non*: No such file or directory** – as **non*** is the argument:

1. Type **ls** at the prompt, then hit **Return** to see all unhidden files in a current **/home/Documents** directory

2. Next, enter **ls doc.?** to see all files named "doc" that have a single-letter file extension

3. Now, enter **ls *.c** to see all files of any name that have a ".c" file extension

4. Enter **ls *.[a-c]** to see all files of any name that have a ".a", ".b" or ".c" file extension

5. Now, enter **ls *.[!a-c]** to see all files of any name that do not have a ".a", ".b" or ".c" file extension

6. Finally, enter **ls non*** to see an error message reporting that no matches have been found

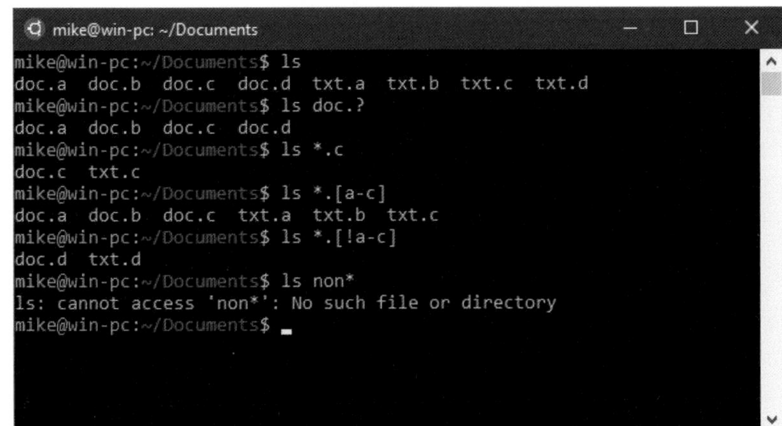

mike@win-pc: ~/Documents
mike@win-pc:~/Documents$ ls
doc.a doc.b doc.c doc.d txt.a txt.b txt.c txt.d
mike@win-pc:~/Documents$ ls doc.?
doc.a doc.b doc.c doc.d
mike@win-pc:~/Documents$ ls *.c
doc.c txt.c
mike@win-pc:~/Documents$ ls *.[a-c]
doc.a doc.b doc.c txt.a txt.b txt.c
mike@win-pc:~/Documents$ ls *.[!a-c]
doc.d txt.d
mike@win-pc:~/Documents$ ls non*
ls: cannot access 'non*': No such file or directory
mike@win-pc:~/Documents$

The process of pattern matching with wildcards demonstrated here is commonly known as "globbing" – a reference to global wildcard expansion.

Wildcards can also be used for pathname expansion when specifying addresses – for example, **ls ~/D***.

Recognizing Metacharacters

Just as the special wildcard characters **? * [ ]** can be used to perform pathname expansion, plain strings can be expanded using **{ }** brace characters. These may contain a comma-separated list of substrings that can be appended to a specified prefix or prepended to a specified suffix, or both, to generate a list of expanded strings. The brace expansions can also be nested for complex expansion. Additionally, brace expansion can produce a sequence of letters or numbers by specifying a range separated by .. between the braces:

There must be no spaces within the braces, or between the braces and each specified prefix and suffix.

1. At a prompt, type **echo b{ad,oy}** then hit **Return** to see two expanded strings – appended to the specified prefix
2. Next, enter **echo {ge,fi}t** to see two expanded strings – prepended to the specified suffix
3. Now, enter **echo s{i,a,o,u}ng** to see four expanded strings – both appended and prepended
4. Enter **echo s{tr{i,o},a,u}ng** to see four complex expanded strings – appended and prepended
5. Next, enter **echo {a..z}** to see an expanded letter sequence of the lowercase alphabet
6. Finally, enter **echo {1..20}** to see an expanded numeric sequence from 1 to 20

Bash version 4 introduced zero-padded brace expansion so that **echo {001..3}** produces 001 002 003.

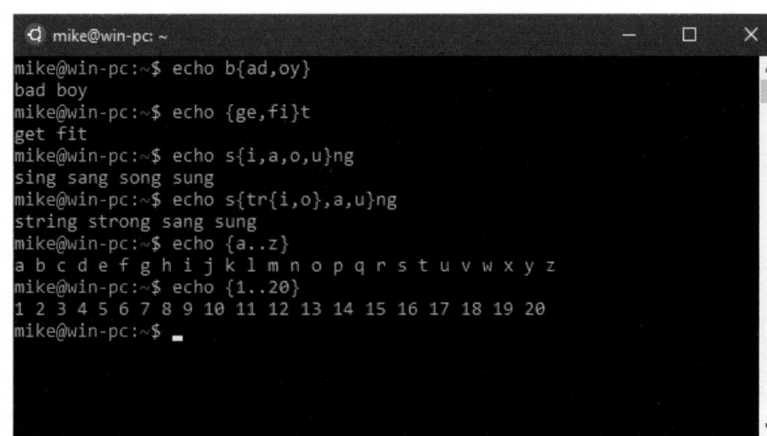

mike@win-pc: ~
mike@win-pc:~$ echo b{ad,oy}
bad boy
mike@win-pc:~$ echo {ge,fi}t
get fit
mike@win-pc:~$ echo s{i,a,o,u}ng
sing sang song sung
mike@win-pc:~$ echo s{tr{i,o},a,u}ng
string strong sang sung
mike@win-pc:~$ echo {a..z}
a b c d e f g h i j k l m n o p q r s t u v w x y z
mike@win-pc:~$ echo {1..20}
1 2 3 4 5 6 7 8 9 10 11 12 13 14 15 16 17 18 19 20
mike@win-pc:~$

The wildcards ? * [ ] and braces { } are just some examples of "metacharacters" that have special meaning to the Bash shell. The table below lists all metacharacters that have the special meaning described when used in commands at a shell prompt only – the same characters can have other meanings when used in other situations, such as in arithmetical expressions.

Metacharacter:	Meaning:
~	Home directory
`	Command substitution (old style)
#	Comment
$	Variable expression
&	Background job
*	String wildcard
(	Start of subshell
)	End of subshell
\	Escape next character
|	Pipe
[	Start of wildcard set
]	End of wildcard set
{	Start of command block
}	End of command block
;	Pipeline command separator
'	Quote mark (strong)
"	Quote mark (weak)
<	Redirect input
>	Redirect output
/	Pathname address separator
?	Single-character wildcard
!	Pipeline logical NOT

Some of the metacharacters in this table have been introduced already but others are described later in this book.

Notice that the semi-colon ; character allows two commands to be issued on the same line. For example, type **echo {a..z} ; echo {1..9}** then hit Return.

Quoting Phrases

The metacharacters that have special meaning to the Bash shell can be used literally, without applying their special meaning, by enclosing them within a pair of ' ' single-quote characters to form a quoted phrase. For example, to include the name of a shell variable in a phrase without interpreting its value:

Always enclose phrases you want to use literally within single quotes to avoid misinterpretation.

1. At a prompt, type **echo Processed By: $SHELL** then hit **Return** to see the shell variable get interpreted in output

2. Now, enter **echo 'Processed By: $SHELL'** to see the shell variable printed literally in output

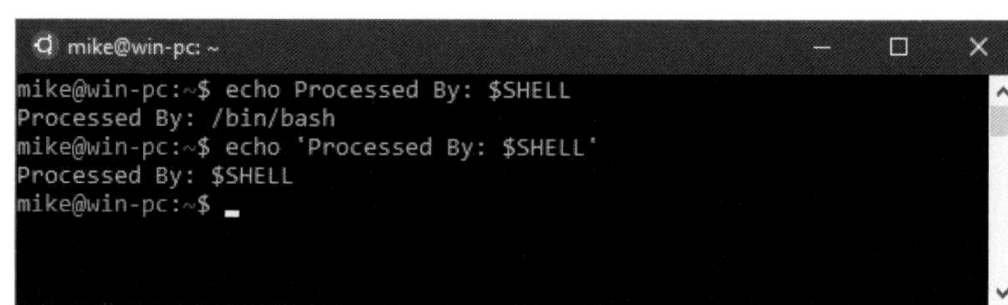

Alternatively, the significance of the leading **$** metacharacter of a shell variable can be ignored if preceded by a \ backslash character to "escape" it from recognition as having special meaning:

The newline **\n** and tab **\t** sequences can be included in phrases if preceded by a backslash – for example, **echo \\nNEWLINE \\tTAB**.

3. At a prompt, type **echo Processed By: $SHELL** then hit **Return** to see the shell variable get interpreted in output

4. Now, enter **echo Processed By: \$SHELL** to see the shell variable printed literally in output

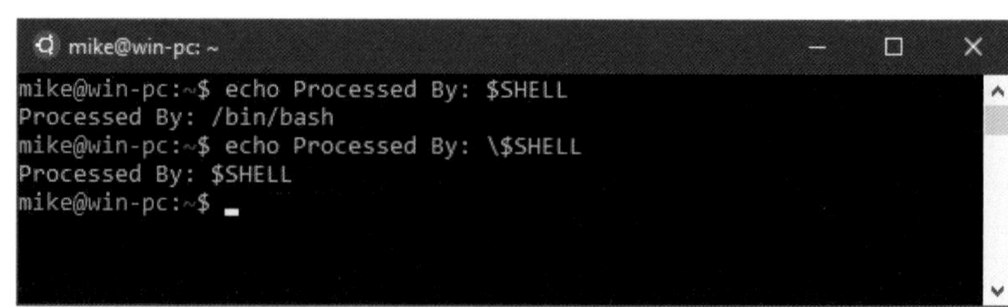

It is necessary to precede a single-quote character with a \ backslash when it is used as an apostrophe, so it is not interpreted as an incomplete quoted phrase. An incomplete quoted phrase or a \ backslash at the end of a line allows a command to continue on the next line as they escape the newline when you hit Return:

5. At a prompt, enter **echo It\'s escaped** to see the apostrophe appear in output

6. Next, type **echo Continued ** then hit **Return**, type **text written along ** then hit **Return**, and type **several lines** then hit **Return** to see the continued phrase in output

Notice that the shell prompt string changes to a **>** to indicate it is awaiting further input.

```
mike@win-pc: ~
mike@win-pc:~$ echo It\'s escaped
It's escaped
mike@win-pc:~$ echo Continued \
> text written along \
> several lines
Continued text written along several lines
mike@win-pc:~$
```

Double-quote marks " " are regarded as weak by the Bash shell as they do allow the interpretation of shell variables they enclose. They can, however, be useful to print out a quoted string if the entire string (and its double quotes) are enclosed in single quotes:

7. Type **echo "Interpreted With $SHELL"** then hit **Return** to see the shell variable get interpreted in unquoted output

8. Now, enter **echo '"Interpreted With $SHELL"'** to see the shell variable printed literally in quoted output

You could alternatively escape double-quote characters with a backslash to print them in output – for example, **echo \"With \$SHELL\"**.

```
mike@win-pc: ~
mike@win-pc:~$ echo "Interpreted With $SHELL"
Interpreted With /bin/bash
mike@win-pc:~$ echo '"Interpreted With $SHELL"'
"Interpreted With $SHELL"
mike@win-pc:~$
```

Getting Help

Bash includes an online help system for its built-in commands. Information on all its built-in commands can be displayed using the **help** command, and **help | more** can be used to display just one screen at a time. A command name can be specified to discover information about that particular command:

The **|** character is a "pipe" that allows output to be redirected – here output is sent to the **more** command. Pipelines are described in more detail on pages 48-49.

1. At a prompt, type **help | more** then hit **Return** to see all built-in Bash commands and their options

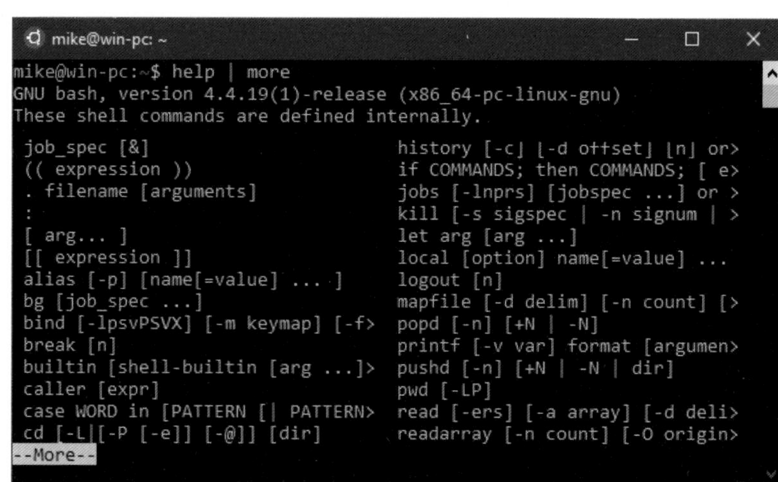

mike@win-pc: ~
mike@win-pc:~$ help | more
GNU bash, version 4.4.19(1)-release (x86_64-pc-linux-gnu)
These shell commands are defined internally.
job_spec [&]   history [-c] [-d offset] [n] or>
((expression))   if COMMANDS; then COMMANDS; [e>
. filename [arguments]   jobs [-lnprs] [jobspec ...] or >
:   kill [-s sigspec | -n signum | >
[arg...]   let arg [arg ...]
[[expression]]   local [option] name[=value] ...
alias [-p] [name[=value] ...]   logout [n]
bg [job_spec ...]   mapfile [-d delim] [-n count] [>
bind [-lpsvPSVX] [-m keymap] [-f>   popd [-n] [+N | -N]
break [n]   printf [-v var] format [argumen>
builtin [shell-builtin [arg ...]>   pushd [-n] [+N | -N | dir]
caller [expr]   pwd [-LP]
case WORD in [PATTERN [| PATTERN>   read [-ers] [-a array] [-d deli>
cd [-L|[-P [-e]] [-@]] [dir]   readarray [-n count] [-O origin>
--More--

2. Hit **Return** to scroll down the screen one line at a time, or type **q** and hit **Return** to quit help and return to a shell prompt

Bash version 4 introduced two new help options: **help -d** displays a short description and **help -m** displays information in a man page-like format.

3. Now, enter **help echo** to display information about the Bash shell built-in **echo** command

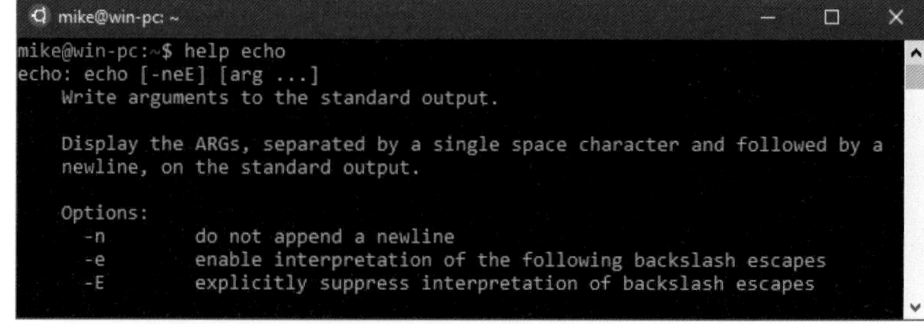

mike@win-pc: ~
mike@win-pc:~$ help echo
echo: echo [-neE] [arg ...]
Write arguments to the standard output.
Display the ARGs, separated by a single space character and followed by a newline, on the standard output.
Options:
-n   do not append a newline
-e   enable interpretation of the following backslash escapes
-E   explicitly suppress interpretation of backslash escapes

Information about all commands, both shell built-in commands and those other commands that are actually programs located on the file system, can be found on any Linux operating system in the famous Manual pages. The name of any command can be specified to the **man** command to display the Manual page describing that command and its options. Alternatively, an **-f** option can be used to display a brief description of a command:

4. At a prompt, type **man ps** then hit **Return** to see the Manual page for the **ps** command automatically paginated

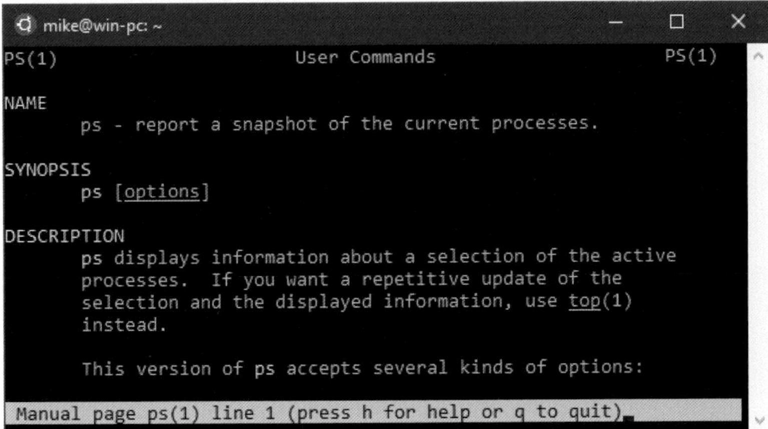

```
PS(1)                     User Commands                     PS(1)

NAME
       ps - report a snapshot of the current processes.

SYNOPSIS
       ps [options]

DESCRIPTION
       ps displays information about a selection of the active
       processes.  If you want a repetitive update of the
       selection and the displayed information, use top(1)
       instead.

       This version of ps accepts several kinds of options:

 Manual page ps(1) line 1 (press h for help or q to quit)
```

5. Hit **Return** to scroll down the screen one line at a time, or type **q** and hit **Return** to return to a shell prompt

6. Now, enter **man -f ps** to display the "what is" description of the **ps** command

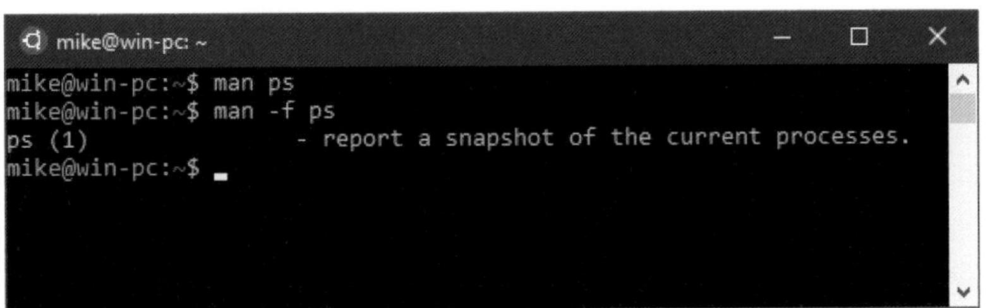

```
mike@win-pc:~$ man ps
mike@win-pc:~$ man -f ps
ps (1)               - report a snapshot of the current processes.
mike@win-pc:~$
```

You can use the **type** command, described on page 14, to discover whether a command is a shell built-in or its file system location.

You can also use the **info** command as an alternative to **man**.

Summary

- Bash is a command interpreter shell that enables the user to interact with the kernel of a Linux operating system.
- The command **ps $$** displays the current process information and can be used to confirm Bash as the current shell.
- Usernames and hostnames can be displayed with the **whoami** and **hostname** commands.
- A Terminal window can be cleared using the **clear** command and closed using the **exit** command.
- The **type** command can be used to determine whether a token is a built-in shell command or a recognized program.
- Standard input can be printed on standard output using the shell built-in **echo** command.
- Shell variables **$SHELL** and **$BASH_VERSION** store the filesystem location and version number of the Bash program.
- The **pwd** command displays the current working directory address and the **ls** command can be used to list its contents.
- Absolute and relative addresses, or ~ and .. aliases, can be specified to the **cd** command to change directory location.
- Wildcards **?** , * , and **[ ]** can be used to specify filename patterns to match a single character, a string, or a set.
- Brace expansion combines each item in a comma-separated list within **{ }** characters to a specified outer prefix and suffix.
- Brace expansion can also produce a sequence of letters or numbers from a range separated by .. within **{ }** characters.
- Wildcards **?** , * , **[ ]** and braces **{ }** are just some examples of metacharacters that have special meaning to the Bash shell.
- Enclosing with single quotes **' '** or prefixing with a backslash **** allows metacharacters to be displayed literally.
- Surrounding phrases with weak **" "** double-quote characters allows the shell to perform interpretation.
- Online help can be found for any command using the **man** or **info** commands and for built-ins using the **help** command.

2 Managing Files

This chapter demonstrates how to manipulate directories and files.

Creating Folders

It is sometimes useful to be able to extract the name of a file, program, or directory from the end of a path address using the **basename** command. Conversely, you can use the **dirname** command to remove the final part of the path address to a file.

A new directory can be created in the current working directory by specifying a directory name of your choice to the **mkdir** command, or elsewhere by specifying an absolute path:

The **basename** and **dirname** commands simply display a part of the path address – they do not actually implement any action.

1. At a prompt, enter the command **echo $SHELL** to display the absolute path address location of the **bash** program
2. Next, issue a **basename $SHELL** command to extract the program name from the path address
3. Now, issue a **dirname $SHELL** command to extract the parent directory of the **bash** program name from the path
4. Enter the command **ls Docs** to display the contents of a directory named "Docs" – to see it only contains a directory named "Text" in this example
5. Now, enter the command **mkdir Docs/Pdf** to create a new directory named "Pdf" within the "Docs" directory
6. Finally, issue the **ls Docs** command once more – to see it now contains directories named "Pdf" and "Text"

The "Docs", "Pdf" and "Text" directories are not standard default directories – here they have been created for demonstration purposes.

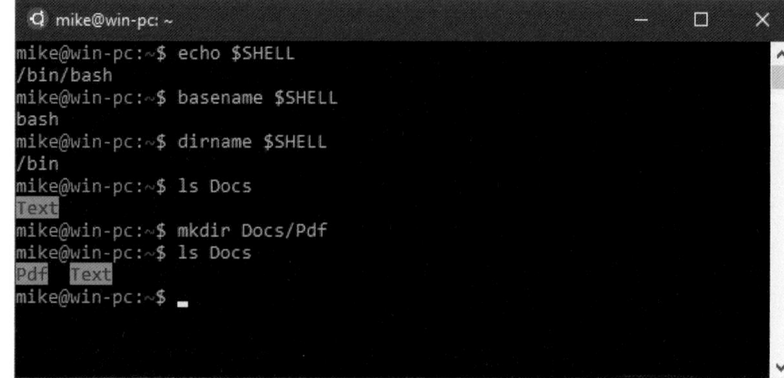

Directories can be removed in the shell using the **rmdir** command. This command takes the directory name as its argument and will instantly remove an empty directory, but will simply warn you that the directory is not empty if it contains any files.

Having to delete files manually, one by one, may provide safeguards but can be tedious. An intelligent alternative is available by using the recursive interactive **-ri** option of the **rm** command. This steps inside the directory and examines every file – requesting your confirmation before deleting each file. When all files have been deleted it asks if you want to delete the directory:

Some versions offer an **-v** option for both the **rmdir** command and the **rm** command to produce verbose output – describing what is happening.

7. Enter an **rmdir Docs/Pdf** command to remove the "Pdf" directory that you have just created

8. Issue the command **ls Docs** – to see the "Docs" directory only contains a directory named "Text" once more

9. Now, issue the command **rmdir Docs/Text** to attempt to remove the "Text" directory to see a warning

10. Enter the command **rm -ri Docs/Text** to interactively delete the files within the "Text" directory, and remove the directory itself by replying **Y** (yes) to each question

11. Finally, issue the command **ls Docs** once again to see the "Docs" directory is now completely empty

If you are feeling brave, and are absolutely certain the directory contains nothing you will miss, you can use the **rm** command with just an **-r** option to instantly delete a directory and its entire contents – use with care!

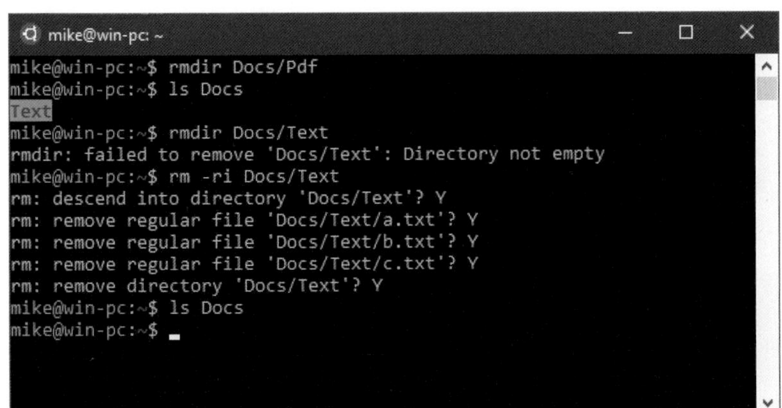

mike@win-pc: ~
mike@win-pc:~$ rmdir Docs/Pdf
mike@win-pc:~$ ls Docs
Text
mike@win-pc:~$ rmdir Docs/Text
rmdir: failed to remove 'Docs/Text': Directory not empty
mike@win-pc:~$ rm -ri Docs/Text
rm: descend into directory 'Docs/Text'? Y
rm: remove regular file 'Docs/Text/a.txt'? Y
rm: remove regular file 'Docs/Text/b.txt'? Y
rm: remove regular file 'Docs/Text/c.txt'? Y
rm: remove directory 'Docs/Text'? Y
mike@win-pc:~$ ls Docs
mike@win-pc:~$

Arranging Files

The shell **mv** command lets you easily move files around your filesystem from the command line. This command requires two arguments stating the name of the file to be moved and the destination to which it should be moved:

1. Launch a Terminal then enter an **ls** command to list the contents of your home directory – see it contains a file named "alpha.txt" and a "Documents" sub-directory

2. Next, issue a **mv alpha.txt Documents** command to move the file "alpha.txt" to the "Documents" sub-directory

3. Now, issue an **ls** command once more, to see the file is no longer in your home directory, then issue an **ls Documents** command – to confirm the file has moved to within the "Documents" sub-directory

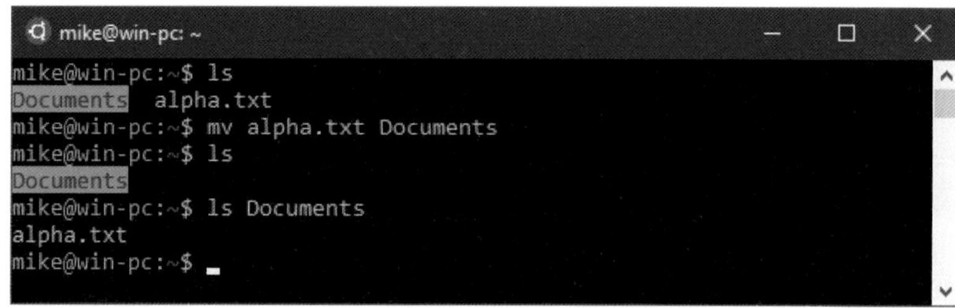
mike@win-pc: ~
mike@win-pc:~$ ls
Documents alpha.txt
mike@win-pc:~$ mv alpha.txt Documents
mike@win-pc:~$ ls
Documents
mike@win-pc:~$ ls Documents
alpha.txt
mike@win-pc:~$

Interestingly, the **mv** command can also be used to rename a file by stating its current name and a new name as its two arguments:

4. Enter a **cd Documents** command, to move into the "Documents" sub-directory, then issue the command **mv alpha.txt zebra.txt** to rename the file just moved

5. Now, issue an **ls** command once more – to confirm the file has been renamed

```
mike@win-pc: ~/Documents
mike@win-pc:~$ cd Documents
mike@win-pc:~/Documents$ mv alpha.txt zebra.txt
mike@win-pc:~/Documents$ ls
zebra.txt
mike@win-pc:~/Documents$
```

Beware

The **mv** command will by default overwrite a file of the same name in the new location without any warning.

Hot tip

In WSL you can find your Windows folders at **/mnt/c/Users/*username***. For example, your Windows "Music" folder might be found at **/mnt/c/Users/mike/Music**.

Hot tip

You can use the **-i** interactive option with the **mv** command to prompt you before overwriting a file of the same name.

If you wish to copy, rather than move, a file to a new location the **cp** command can be used. This command can accept one or more files to be copied as its arguments, stating the destination as the final argument:

6. Enter a **cp zebra.txt** ~ command to copy the file in the Documents directory to your home directory – using the tilde ~ alias for the home directory address

7. Then, issue **ls ; ls** ~ commands to list the contents of both directories to confirm a copy of the file is now in both

The semi-colon ; character is a command separator that allows two commands to be issued on the same line.

```
mike@win-pc: ~/Documents
mike@win-pc:~/Documents$ cp zebra.txt ~
mike@win-pc:~/Documents$ ls ; ls ~
zebra.txt
Documents  zebra.txt
mike@win-pc:~/Documents$ _
```


The **rm** command can be used to delete one or more files named as its arguments. The * wildcard can also be used to delete all files in a directory – if you are absolutely certain none are needed:

8. Enter the command **rm** * to remove all files in the "Documents" sub-directory

9. Now, issue a **rm ../zebra.txt** to remove the file copied into the parent directory – your home directory in this case

10. Finally, issue **ls ; ls** ~ commands once more to confirm the file has been removed from both directories

The wildcard * "all" metacharacter should be used with caution as you may inadvertently remove hidden files.

```
mike@win-pc: ~/Documents
mike@win-pc:~/Documents$ rm *
mike@win-pc:~/Documents$ rm ../zebra.txt
mike@win-pc:~/Documents$ ls ; ls ~
Documents
mike@win-pc:~/Documents$ _
```

Adding Links

Text contained within a plain text file can be displayed on standard output, in the Terminal screen, simply by specifying the filename to a **cat** (con**cat**enate) command:

1. Enter an **ls** command to discover a text file named "sample.txt" in the current directory, then issue the command **cat sample.txt** to display its text contents

```
mike@win-pc: ~/Documents
mike@win-pc:~/Documents$ ls
sample.txt
mike@win-pc:~/Documents$ cat sample.txt
Here is some sample text.
mike@win-pc:~/Documents$ _
```

The full path address of the file must be specified if it is not in the current directory.

A link to any file can be created by specifying the target filename and a link filename as two arguments to the **ln** command. This allows the name of the link to be specified to the **cat** command:

2. Enter an **ln sample.txt sample.hardlink** command then issue an **ls** command to see a link file has been created

3. Now, issue the command **cat sample.hardlink** to display text contents via the link

```
mike@win-pc: ~/Documents
mike@win-pc:~/Documents$ ln sample.txt sample.hardlink
mike@win-pc:~/Documents$ ls
sample.hardlink  sample.txt
mike@win-pc:~/Documents$ cat sample.hardlink
Here is some sample text.
mike@win-pc:~/Documents$ _
```

Links are created as individual files that are not automatically deleted when their target gets deleted.

By default the **ln** command creates a "hard" link but a symbolic "soft" link can be created using that command's **-s** option:

4. Enter an **ln -s sample.txt sample.softlink** command then issue an **ls** command to confirm another link file has been created alongside the text file

5. Now, issue the command **cat sample.softlink** to display text contents via the second link

```
mike@win-pc:~/Documents$ ln -s sample.txt sample.softlink
mike@win-pc:~/Documents$ ls
sample.hardlink  sample.softlink  sample.txt
mike@win-pc:~/Documents$ cat sample.softlink
Here is some sample text.
mike@win-pc:~/Documents$
```

To understand the difference between hard and soft links it is important to recognize that on Linux the files comprise two parts – the filename and the actual data. The filename is allocated an "inode" that points to the data. Hard links are allocated the same inode as their target so both point to the data. Soft links, on the other hand, are allocated a different inode that merely points to the target file. This means that a hard link will continue to point to the data when the original file is removed but a soft link will not. The numeric inodes that point to data can be seen by specifying an **-i** option to the **ls** command, and the target file stored in a soft link can be seen using a **readlink** command:

Don't forget

The inode maintains an internal count of how many filenames are pointing to its data – so the data only gets deleted when that count reaches zero.

6. Enter an **ls -i** command to display the file inodes – see the hard link has the same inode as the original text file

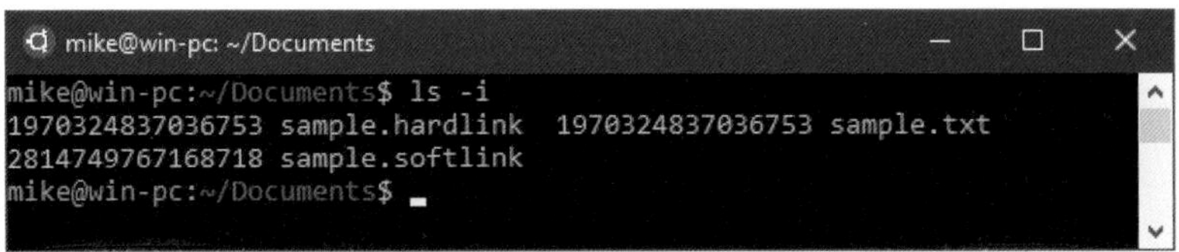
mike@win-pc: ~/Documents
mike@win-pc:~/Documents$ ls -i
1970324837036753 sample.hardlink 1970324837036753 sample.txt
2814749767168718 sample.softlink
mike@win-pc:~/Documents$

7. Next, enter an **rm sample.txt** command then issue an **ls -i** command to confirm removal of the original text file

8. Now, enter **cat sample.hardlink** and **cat sample.softlink** commands to attempt to display the text data again

Hot tip

Notice that the "orphaned" soft link gets colored red here. You can use **readlink** to identify the missing target file. For example, here use the command **readlink sample.softlink**.

```
mike@win-pc:~/Documents$ rm sample.txt
mike@win-pc:~/Documents$ ls -i
1970324837036753 sample.hardlink  2814749767168718 sample.softlink
mike@win-pc:~/Documents$ cat sample.hardlink
Here is some sample text.
mike@win-pc:~/Documents$ cat sample.softlink
cat: sample.softlink: No such file or directory
mike@win-pc:~/Documents$
```

Examining Properties

Several commands can be used to examine attributes of any file. The most comprehensive is the **stat** command that lists every important attribute of the file stated as its argument including its actual byte size, number of allocated 512-byte blocks, inode number, access permissions, and history.

The **wc** word count command is useful to quickly discover how many lines, words, and bytes a text file contains and the **file** command reports what type of file it is:

You can also use the **du** command to examine disk usage, demonstrated on page 40.

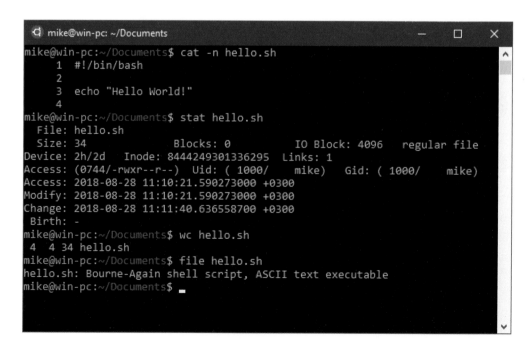

1. Enter a **cat -n hello.sh** command to display the text content of a file named "hello.sh" – so the **-n** option will add line numbers to the output for clarity
2. Next, issue a **stat hello.sh** command to discover comprehensive attributes of the file
3. Now, issue a **wc hello.sh** to discover that file's line count, word count, and byte count
4. Finally, issue a **file hello.sh** command to discover what type of file this is

mike@win-pc: ~/Documents

```
mike@win-pc:~/Documents$ cat -n hello.sh
     1  #!/bin/bash
     2
     3  echo "Hello World!"
     4
mike@win-pc:~/Documents$ stat hello.sh
  File: hello.sh
  Size: 34              Blocks: 0          IO Block: 4096   regular file
Device: 2h/2d   Inode: 8444249301336295  Links: 1
Access: (0744/-rwxr--r--)  Uid: ( 1000/    mike)   Gid: ( 1000/    mike)
Access: 2018-08-28 11:10:21.590273000 +0300
Modify: 2018-08-28 11:10:21.590273000 +0300
Change: 2018-08-28 11:11:40.636558700 +0300
 Birth: -
mike@win-pc:~/Documents$ wc hello.sh
 4  4 34 hello.sh
mike@win-pc:~/Documents$ file hello.sh
hello.sh: Bourne-Again shell script, ASCII text executable
mike@win-pc:~/Documents$ _
```

A new empty file can be created simply by specifying a new filename to the **touch** command. The **touch** command also introduces some interesting possibilities as it can change the Last Accessed and Last Modified timestamp attributes of a file. Used alone it simply updates these to the present time but used with an **-t** option it allows you to specify a date and time in the format MMDDhhmm.ss. Alternatively, used with an **-d** option it allows you to specify a date and time in the format YYYY-MM-DD hh:mm:ss enclosed within quote marks:

5. Enter **touch -t 12011200.00 hello.sh** to backdate the timestamps of a file named "hello.sh" to that time

6. Next, issue a **stat hello.sh** command to confirm the Access and Modify timestamps have been updated

7. Now, enter **touch -d "2020-01-01 15:00" hello.sh** to update its timestamps to that date and time

8. Finally, issue a **stat hello.sh** command once more to confirm the timestamps have been updated again

The specific date format required for the **touch** command can vary on different systems. Use the command **man touch** to check the Manual page for details.

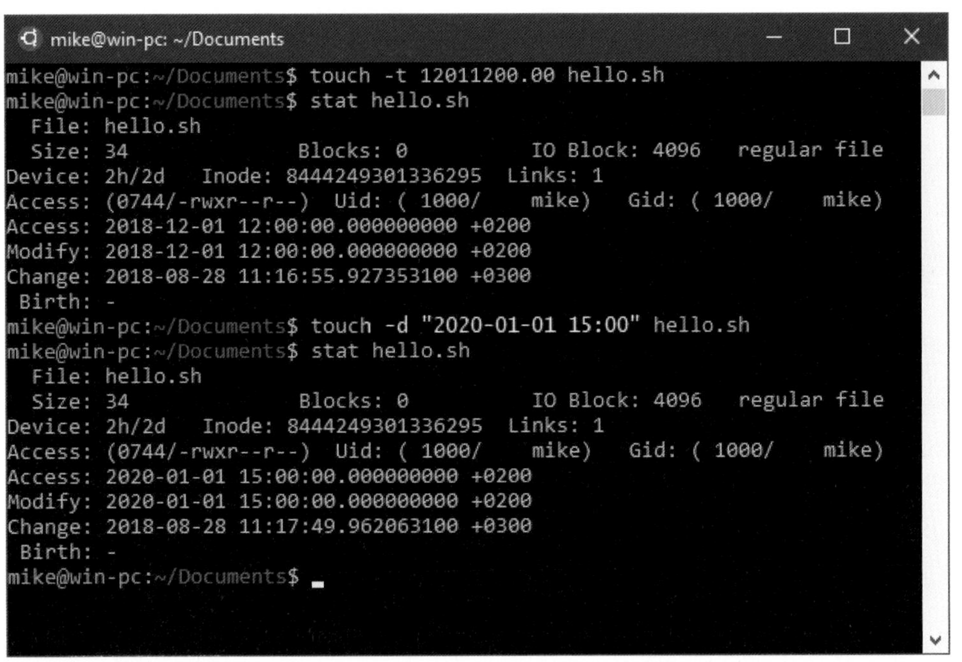

Comparing Files

The Bash shell provides several ways to compare two files. You can check to see if two files are identical with the **cmp** command. If they are indeed identical the command reports nothing, but if they differ it reports the location of the first difference.

Text files can be compared line by line with the **comm** command. Its output is slightly unusual as it creates three columns to indicate lines that match in each file:

- **Column 1** – lines found in the first file, but not the second.
- **Column 2** – lines found in the second file, but not the first.
- **Column 3** – lines found in both files.

Hot tip

The **cmp** command can also be used to compare binary files – such as image files.

1. Enter a **cat -n abc.txt** command to display the content of a file named “abc.txt”, containing three lines “Alpha”, “Bravo”, and “Charlie”, then enter a **cat -n acd.txt** command to display the content of a file named “acd.txt”, containing three lines “Alpha”, “Charlie”, and “Delta”
2. Next, issue a **cmp abc.txt acd.txt** command to discover where the first difference occurs between these two files
3. Now, issue a **comm abc.txt acd.txt** command to see a line-by-line comparison

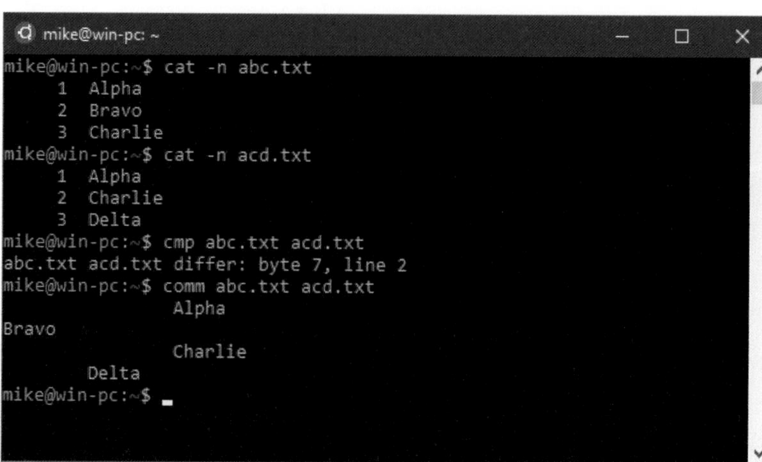

mike@win-pc: ~
mike@win-pc:~$ cat -n abc.txt
1 Alpha
2 Bravo
3 Charlie
mike@win-pc:~$ cat -n acd.txt
1 Alpha
2 Charlie
3 Delta
mike@win-pc:~$ cmp abc.txt acd.txt
abc.txt acd.txt differ: byte 7, line 2
mike@win-pc:~$ comm abc.txt acd.txt
Alpha
Bravo
Charlie
Delta
mike@win-pc:~$

Here “Bravo” is unique to the first file, “Delta” is unique to the second file, but “Alpha” and “Charlie” are common to both files.

The **diff** command offers an alternative to the **comm** command for comparison of text files. It too compares file content line by line and it produces a detailed report showing any unique lines. It can also be used to compare two directories to reveal unique files.

Files may also be compared using checksum numbers to verify their integrity. Checksum numbers are often found on internet download pages so the user can ensure that a downloaded file is intact – typically, the checksum is made using the MD5 algorithm.

The **md5sum** command produces a 32-byte checksum for the file specified as its argument and should exactly match that stated by the originator if the file is indeed intact.

An alternative checksum can be created in much the same way by the **cksum** command. This generates a CRC (Cyclic Redundancy Check) value and includes the file's byte size in the output.

The **comm** command has options to suppress column output. For example, **-12** suppresses the first two columns to show only common text.

4. Enter a **diff abc.txt acd.txt** command to discover those lines that are unique to each file

5. Now, issue a **md5sum abc.txt** command to create a checksum number for that file

6. Finally, issue a **cksum abc.txt** command to create another checksum number for that file

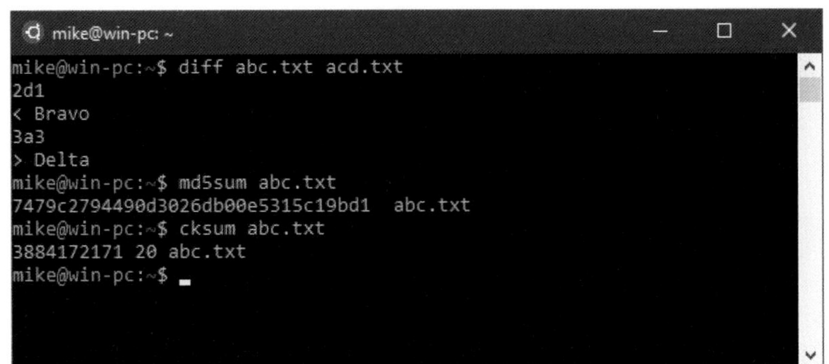

You can discover more about the **diff** command output by using **man diff**.

Finding Files

Locating a file on your system can be achieved from a shell prompt using the **find** command. This is a very powerful command, with over 50 possible options, but it has an unusual syntax. Possibly the one most used looks like this:

find *DirectoryName* **-type f -name** "*FileName*"

The directory name specifies the hierarchical starting point from which to begin searching. If you know the file exists somewhere in your home directory structure you can begin searching there by specifying that with the ~ tilde home directory alias. In this case the **-type f** option specifies that the search is for a file ("f") and the **-name** option specifies a filename search is to be made:

1. Enter the command **find ~ -type f -name "hello*"** to seek all files in your home directory structure whose name begins with the string "hello"

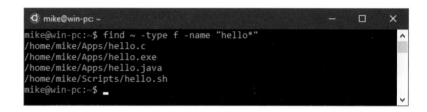

```
mike@win-pc: ~
mike@win-pc:~$ find ~ -type f -name "hello*"
/home/mike/Apps/hello.c
/home/mike/Apps/hello.exe
/home/mike/Apps/hello.java
/home/mike/Scripts/hello.sh
mike@win-pc:~$
```

By default the **find** command will only report the location of actual files, but you can also have it include symbolic links in the report by adding an **-L** option as its very first argument:

2. Enter the command **find ~ -type f -name "*jaguar*"** to seek all files within your home directory structure whose name contains the string "jaguar"

3. Now, repeat the command adding an **-L** option to also report the location of any soft links to the files

```
mike@win-pc: ~
mike@win-pc:~$ find ~ -type f -name "*jaguar*"
/home/mike/Pictures/jaguar.jpg
mike@win-pc:~$ find -L ~ -type f -name "*jaguar*"
/home/mike/Desktop/jaguar-pic.softlink
/home/mike/Pictures/jaguar.jpg
mike@win-pc:~$
```

Don't forget

Remember to enclose the file name within quotes to protect it from expansion by the shell.

Use the wildcard * with the file name when you know the name but not the extension.

You can specify **-type d** to the **find** command to seek directories.

The results of a search made with the **find** command can be filtered by comparison of their timestamps with an **-newer** option. This specifies the name of a file against which the results of the search should be compared. Only the results of files modified later than the specified comparison file will be displayed. Usefully, the **touch** command can be used to create a temporary file bearing a specified timestamp, for comparison against search results:

4. Enter a **touch -t 12021230 temp** command to create a file named "temp" bearing a December 2 12:30 timestamp

5. Next, issue a **find Apps -type f -name "hello*" -newer temp** command to seek all files within a directory named "Apps" whose name begins with the string "hello" and whose timestamp is after the specified time of 12:30

6. Now, enter **rm temp** to remove the temporary file

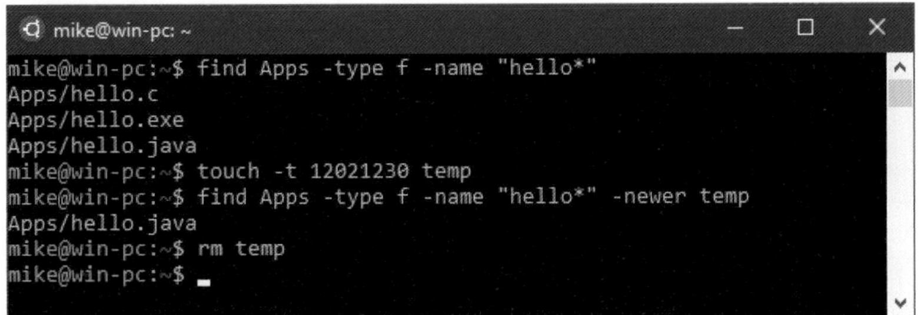

mike@win-pc: ~
mike@win-pc:~$ find Apps -type f -name "hello*"
Apps/hello.c
Apps/hello.exe
Apps/hello.java
mike@win-pc:~$ touch -t 12021230 temp
mike@win-pc:~$ find Apps -type f -name "hello*" -newer temp
Apps/hello.java
mike@win-pc:~$ rm temp
mike@win-pc:~$

You can use an **-iname** option to the **find** command instead of **-name** if you want to make a case-insensitive search.

An action can be performed on each file result using an **-exec** option with the **find** command. This can be a command followed by **{}** braces and terminated by an escaped semi-colon character:

7. Enter **find ~ -type f -name "dino*" -exec file {} \;** to seek all files in your home directory structure whose name begins with the string "dino" and display their **file** type

```
mike@win-pc: ~
mike@win-pc:~$ find ~ -type f -name "dino*" -exec file {} \;
/home/mike/Documents/dino.pdf: PDF document, version 1.7
/home/mike/Music/dino.mp3: Audio file with ID3 version 2.3.0
/home/mike/Pictures/dino.jpg: JPEG image data
/home/mike/Videos/dino.mp4: ISO Media, MP4 v2 [ISO 14496-14]
mike@win-pc:~$
```

When using the **-exec** option there must be space on either side of the **{}** braces, but no space between them.

Compressing Files

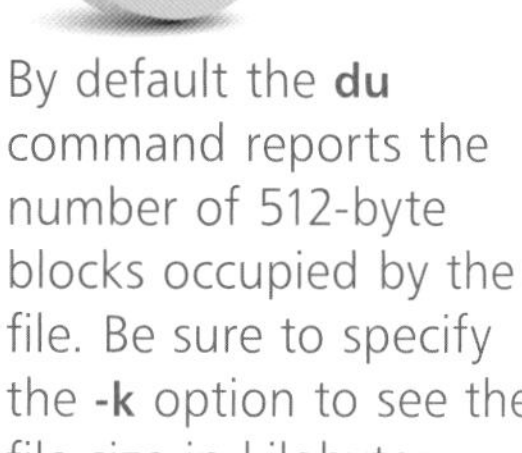

The traditional GNU zip file compression tool in Linux uses the **gzip** command to compress one or more files, stated as its arguments, into a single compressed file – adding a ".gz" file extension and replacing the original files. Conversely, its companion **gunzip** command can be used to extract files from an archive created with **gzip** – replacing the compressed file.

1. Enter the command **du -k ballad.txt** to learn the kilobyte size of a text file named "ballad.txt"

2. Next, enter **gzip ballad.txt** to create a compressed version of that file – named with an added ".gz" file extension

3. Now, issue a further **du -k ballad*** command to compare the file size of the compressed **gzip** file to the original

By default the **du** command reports the number of 512-byte blocks occupied by the file. Be sure to specify the **-k** option to see the file size in kilobytes.

```
mike@win-pc: ~
mike@win-pc:~$ du -k ballad.txt
96      ballad.txt
mike@win-pc:~$ gzip ballad.txt
mike@win-pc:~$ du -k ballad*
24      ballad.txt.gz
mike@win-pc:~$
```

4. Enter **gunzip ballad.txt.gz** to extract the original file – being sure to include the added ".gz" file extension

Notice that the size of the files in this example compresses 96KB down to 24KB – and the uncompressed version is the same as the original file.

```
mike@win-pc: ~
mike@win-pc:~$ gunzip ballad.txt.gz
mike@win-pc:~$ du -k ballad*
96      ballad.txt
mike@win-pc:~$
```

If you simply want to compress and decompress smaller files the **gzip** and **gunzip** tools are probably what you should use.

The more modern **bzip2** compression tool can sometimes achieve better compression than **gzip** but is less widely used – distributing **bzip2** files may not find universal acceptance. It works just like the **gzip** tool but adds a ".bz2" file extension, and also has a companion **bunzip2** uncompressor.

5. Issue a command **du -k ballad*** to learn the kilobyte size of any local files whose names begin "ballad" – in this example there's just one, named **ballad.txt**

6. Enter **bzip2 ballad.txt** to create a compressed version of that file – named with an added ".bz2" file extension

7. Issue a further **du -k ballad*** command to compare the file size of the compressed **bzip2** file to the original file

```
mike@win-pc: ~
mike@win-pc:~$ du -k ballad*
96      ballad.txt
mike@win-pc:~$ bzip2 ballad.txt
mike@win-pc:~$ du -k ballad*
32      ballad.txt.bz2
mike@win-pc:~$
```

Notice that the size of the files in this example compresses 96KB down to 32KB – but the uncompressed version is larger than the original file.

8. Enter **bunzip2 ballad.txt.bz2** to extract the original file – being sure to include the added ".bz2" file extension

```
mike@win-pc: ~
mike@win-pc:~$ bunzip2 ballad.txt.bz2
mike@win-pc:~$ du -k ballad*
128     ballad.txt
mike@win-pc:~$
```

You can use an **-c** option with **gunzip** and **bunzip2** to display the contents of compressed text files on standard output.

The **bzip2** and **bunzip2** tools can add overhead to the compression process so are better suited for large files – experiment to see which compression tool best suits your needs.

Making Backups

Linux provides many tools to archive your data and back up your system onto a tape drive, CD, remote machine or other location.

The **cpio** command can be used to copy output to an archive or copy input from an archive. It must always employ an **-i <** input option or an **-o >** output option to specify direction of data flow. The result of an **ls** command can be directed to the **cpio** command using a **|** pipeline to easily archive all contents of a directory:

Hot tip

The metacharacters > < and | are used for redirection and are described more fully in the next chapter.

1. Enter an **ls** command to list the current directory files

2. Next, issue a **ls | cpio -o > ../archive.cpio** command to pipe the list of current directory files to **cpio** for output to a new archive it will create in the parent directory

3. Now, enter **rm * ; ls** to delete all files in the current directory and to confirm it is now empty

4. Finally, restore all files by input from the backup location with the command **cpio -i < ../archive.cpio** – then issue another **ls** command to confirm success

```
mike@win-pc: ~/Music
mike@win-pc:~/Music$ ls
rain.mp3  storm.mp3  thunder.mp3
mike@win-pc:~/Music$ ls | cpio -o > ../archive.cpio
43544 blocks
mike@win-pc:~/Music$ rm * ; ls
mike@win-pc:~/Music$ cpio -i < ../archive.cpio
43544 blocks
mike@win-pc:~/Music$ ls
rain.mp3  storm.mp3  thunder.mp3
mike@win-pc:~/Music$
```

Arguably, **tar** is less efficient than **cpio** but it offers simpler syntax and is widely used – the choice is simply a matter of personal preference.

The **tar** tape archive command is an alternative backup facility with an **-cf** option to create files and an **-xf** option to extract files.

5. Issue an **ls** command to list the current directory files, then archive all files to a backup location in the parent directory **tar -cf ../archive.tar ***

6. Enter **rm * ; ls** to delete all files in the current directory and to confirm it is now empty

7. Restore all files by extracting from the backup location with the command **tar -xf ../archive.tar** – then issue another **ls** command to confirm success

```
mike@win-pc: ~/Music
mike@win-pc:~/Music$ ls
rain.mp3  storm.mp3  thunder.mp3
mike@win-pc:~/Music$ tar -cf ../archive.tar *
mike@win-pc:~/Music$ rm * ; ls
mike@win-pc:~/Music$ tar -xf ../archive.tar
mike@win-pc:~/Music$ ls
rain.mp3  storm.mp3  thunder.mp3
mike@win-pc:~/Music$ _
```

You can use **cpio -it** or **tar -tf** to retrieve a table of contents from a backup archive.

The **tar** command can also incorporate an **-z** option that calls upon **gzip** and **gunzip** to work with compressed "tarball" archives:

8. Issue an **ls** command to list the current directory files, then archive all files to a backup location in the parent directory **tar -czf ../archive.tar.gz ***

9. Enter **rm * ; ls** to delete all files in the current directory and to confirm it is now empty

10. Restore all files by extracting from the backup location with the command **tar -xzf ../archive.tar.gz** – then issue another **ls** command to confirm success

```
mike@win-pc: ~/Music
mike@win-pc:~/Music$ ls
rain.mp3  storm.mp3  thunder.mp3
mike@win-pc:~/Music$ tar -czf ../archive.tar.gz *
mike@win-pc:~/Music$ rm * ; ls
mike@win-pc:~/Music$ tar -xzf ../archive.tar.gz
mike@win-pc:~/Music$ ls
rain.mp3  storm.mp3  thunder.mp3
mike@win-pc:~/Music$ _
```

A tarball is a compressed **tar** archive and typically has a file extension **.tar.gz** or **.tgz**. Tarballs are used for source code packages.

Summary

- The **basename** and **dirname** commands extract parts of a path address, and directories are created by the **mkdir** command.
- Directories are removed by the **rmdir** command and files are removed by the **rm** command.
- The **mv** command can be used to move a file to a specified location or rename the file.
- Another copy of a file is created at a specified location by the **cp** command.
- Contents of a plain text file can be displayed on standard output by specifying the filename to the **cat** command.
- The **ln** command will by default create a hard link to a specified file that is allocated the same inode as that file.
- A soft link created with an **ln -s** command stores the path to the target file and can be read using the **readlink** command.
- The **stat** command provides comprehensive file attribute information and **du -k** displays file size in kilobytes.
- The **wc** command reveals the word count within a specified text file and the **file** command reports the type of a file.
- The **touch** command can be used to create a new empty file or modify the timestamp of an existing file.
- File content can be compared for similarity by the **cmp**, **comm**, and **diff** commands.
- Checksums can be created and verified using the **md5sum** command or the **cksum** command.
- A file can be found on the filesystem by specifying a search stating directory, type, and filename to the **find** command.
- The **find** command can accept an **-newer** option to filter by timestamp or an **-exec** option to specify an action to perform.
- Files can be compressed by the **gzip** or **bzip2** commands and compressed contents extracted by **gunzip** or **bunzip2**.
- Archives can be created using the **cpio** or **tar** commands.

3 Handling Text

This chapter demonstrates how to manipulate text.

Reading and Writing

The most basic Bash utility for handling text input and output within the Terminal is the **cat** concatenate (join) command, which simply reads text input then writes it as output. Where one or more text filenames are specified to the **cat** command the text content is read as input then written as standard output in the Terminal. Spacing and indentation are preserved in the output so each line of output is identical to each line within the text file input. Optionally, each line can be numbered in the output by specifying an **-n** option to the **cat** command:

Multiple text files can be specified to the **cat** command as a space-separated list for successive display on standard output.

1. Type a **cat** command and specify the name of a text file as its argument then hit **Return** – see input read from the text file get written as standard output

2. Next, repeat the command with an added **-n** option to see line numbers inserted at the start of each line of output

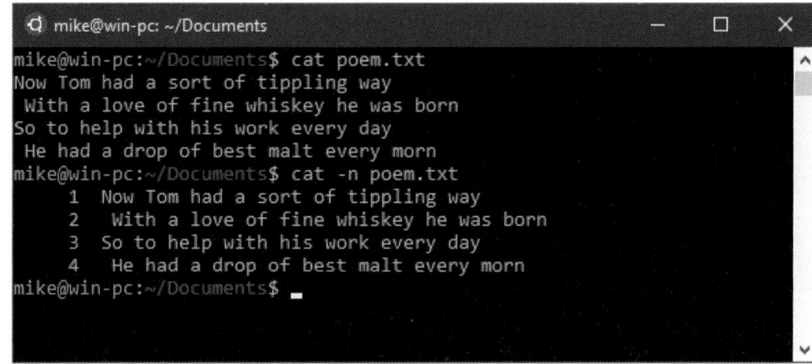

mike@win-pc: ~/Documents
mike@win-pc:~/Documents$ cat poem.txt
Now Tom had a sort of tippling way
 With a love of fine whiskey he was born
So to help with his work every day
 He had a drop of best malt every morn
mike@win-pc:~/Documents$ cat -n poem.txt
     1 Now Tom had a sort of tippling way
     2   With a love of fine whiskey he was born
     3 So to help with his work every day
     4   He had a drop of best malt every morn
mike@win-pc:~/Documents$

Where no filename is supplied to the **cat** command it will await standard input to be typed in the Terminal, which will be read then written as standard output when you hit Return. The **cat** command then awaits further standard input to repeat the cycle. The cycle can be ended by pressing the Ctrl + D keyboard keys to return to a normal prompt string.

The filename argument specified to **cat** implies a **<** input redirection operator. For example, a command **cat log** implies **cat < log**.

3. Issue a **cat** command then hit **Return** to see the Terminal awaiting input

4. Type lines of text then hit **Return** to see your input repeated on standard output, then press **Ctrl** + **D** to finish

```
mike@win-pc:~/Documents$ cat
Here is a line of standard input
Here is a line of standard input
And here is another line
And here is another line
mike@win-pc:~/Documents$
```

The **echo** command, which by default simply reads standard input then writes it on standard output, can write that input text into a file instead by specifying a filename after a **>** redirection operator. Multiple lines of text can be typed by escaping the Return key with the \ backslash character at the end of each line. Then, when you hit Return, the prompt changes to indicate the command is awaiting further input. Tab **\t** and newline **\n** characters can also be inserted into the text by escaping with a \ backslash character and using an **-e** escape option with the **echo** command:

5. Enter the command **echo Stored! > stored.txt** to write "Stored!" into a file named "stored.txt"

6. Next, issue an **echo -e ** command then hit **Return** to see the prompt change to await input

7. Now, enter **Here is a \\nNewline ** then hit **Return**

8. Then, enter **and a \\tTab > saved.txt** to write the lines of standard input into a file named "stored.txt"

9. Finally, issue a **cat saved.txt stored.txt** command to write the preserved text from both files onto standard output

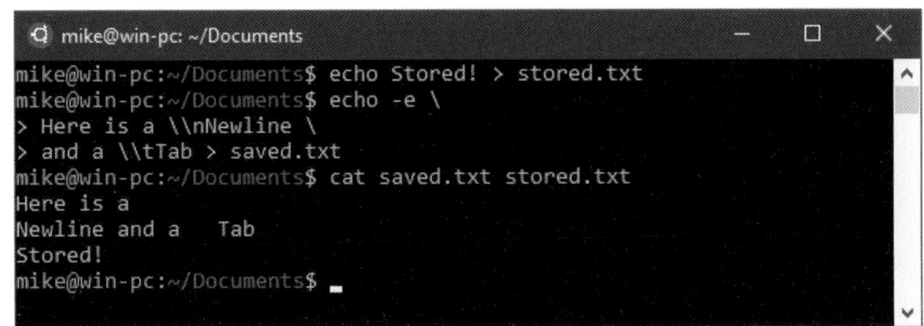

mike@win-pc: ~/Documents
mike@win-pc:~/Documents$ echo Stored! > stored.txt
mike@win-pc:~/Documents$ echo -e \
> Here is a \\nNewline \
> and a \\tTab > saved.txt
mike@win-pc:~/Documents$ cat saved.txt stored.txt
Here is a
Newline and a   Tab
Stored!
mike@win-pc:~/Documents$

You can also use **cat** to write a new file combining content read from existing files – for example, with this: **cat file1 file2 > file3**.

Text directed to a file with the **>** operator will overwrite any existing text. Use a **>>** operator if you prefer to append to existing text instead.

Redirecting Output

The output of a command can be redirected to become input for another command using the | pipe operator. A command line containing two or more commands connected by pipes is known as a "pipeline". Output from the first command at the prompt is sent to the following command along the pipeline for processing. The most common use of pipelines is to display the text content on standard output one line and screen at a time, rather than have it immediately scroll to the very end, with the **more** command – for example, to display the contents of your home directory line by line with the commands **ls ~ | more**. The output can then be scrolled forward one line at a time or by one screen at a time:

Pipelines can be combined with other redirection operators – for example, with **cat log | tail > endlog**.

1. Enter the command **cat ballad.txt | more** to pipe the output from the **cat** command, read from a file named "ballad.txt", to the **more** command for display

2. Now, repeatedly hit **Return** to scroll forward line by line, or hit the **Spacebar** to scroll forward screen by screen, or hit the **Q** key to quit the **more** facility

The **more** facility only allows you to scroll forwards, not backwards through the display.

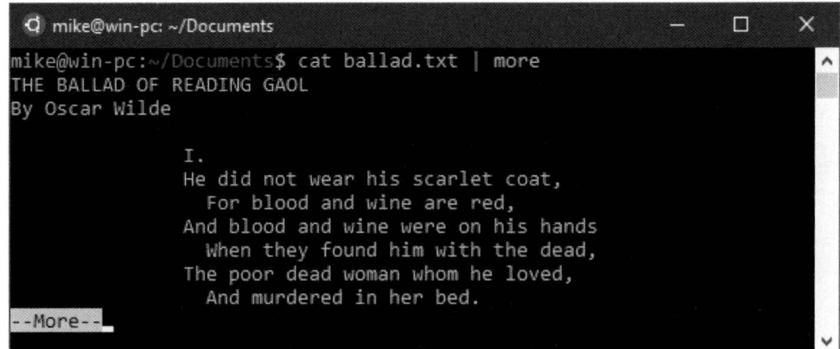

The **less** command is similar to the **more** command but is more flexible as it lets you scroll forward and backward:

3. Enter the command **cat ballad.txt | less** to pipe the output from the **cat** command to **less** for display

4. Press **Up** or **Down** arrow keys to scroll line by line, or hit **Spacebar** or **B** key to scroll by screen, or **Q** key to quit

```
mike@win-pc: ~/Documents
    In a suit of shabby grey;
  A cricket cap was on his head,
    And his step seemed light and gay;
  But I never saw a man who looked
    So wistfully at the day.

  I never saw a man who looked
    With such a wistful eye
  Upon that little tent of blue
    Which prisoners call the sky,
  And at every drifting cloud that went
    With sails of silver by.
:
```

Another common use of pipelines is to display a number of lines from the beginning of a text file with **head** command or from the end of a text file with the **tail** command. By default each command will display 10 lines – for example, to display the final entries appended to a log with the commands **cat log | tail** . The number of lines to be displayed can be specified by an ***-n*** option, where ***n*** should be replaced by the required number of lines:

You can also use the Left and Right arrow keys to scroll horizontally with the **less facility**.

5. Enter the command **cat -b ballad.txt | head -6** to pipe the output from the **cat** command to **head** – numbering all non-empty lines, but displaying just the first six

6. Enter the command **cat -b ballad.txt | tail -6** to pipe the output from the **cat** command to **tail** – numbering all non-empty lines, but displaying just the final six

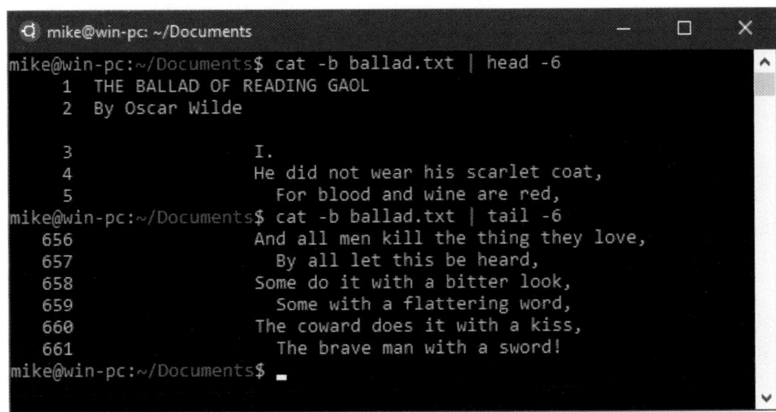

mike@win-pc: ~/Documents
mike@win-pc:~/Documents$ cat -b ballad.txt | head -6
1 THE BALLAD OF READING GAOL
2 By Oscar Wilde
3 I.
4 He did not wear his scarlet coat,
5 For blood and wine are red,
mike@win-pc:~/Documents$ cat -b ballad.txt | tail -6
656 And all men kill the thing they love,
657 By all let this be heard,
658 Some do it with a bitter look,
659 Some with a flattering word,
660 The coward does it with a kiss,
661 The brave man with a sword!
mike@win-pc:~/Documents$

Pipelines allow multiple actions to be performed on output without the need for temporary files.

Seeking Strings

The **grep** command is one of the most useful and can be used to seek a given string within a specified text file. Without supplying any options the **grep** command simply displays each line where the string is found:

Enter a command **grep 'sword' ballad.txt** , to seek the string "sword" within a local text file named "ballad.txt", then hit **Return** to see all lines containing that string

```
mike@win-pc: ~/Documents
mike@win-pc:~/Documents$ grep 'sword' ballad.txt
                 The brave man with a sword!
               For, right within, the sword of Sin
                 The brave man with a sword!
mike@win-pc:~/Documents$
```

You can omit the quote marks around the string in the **grep** commands if it is a single word but strings containing spaces must be enclosed in single quotes.

Usefully, the **grep** command has an **-n** option that adds the number of the line within the file where the string is found to the display:

Issue the command **grep -n 'sword' ballad.txt** then hit **Return** to see all numbered lines containing that string

```
mike@win-pc: ~/Documents
mike@win-pc:~/Documents$ grep -n 'sword' ballad.txt
52:                 The brave man with a sword!
319:              For, right within, the sword of Sin
780:                The brave man with a sword!
mike@win-pc:~/Documents$
```

You can suppress the file names in the results when searching multiple files with **grep** by using an **-h** option.

Multiple files can be searched for a string specified to the **grep** command and the output then displays the name of each file where the string is found, together with the line where it appears:

Enter a command **grep 'best' *.txt** , to seek the string "best" within all local text files then hit **Return** to see all filenames and lines containing that string

```
mike@win-pc: ~/Documents
mike@win-pc:~/Documents$ grep 'best' *.txt
ballad.txt:                    For the best man and the worst.
poem.txt: He had a drop of best malt every morn
mike@win-pc:~/Documents$
```

When you prefer just to know the name of each file containing a given string an **-l** option can be specified to the **grep** command so it will not display each line where the string is found:

4. Enter a command **grep -l 'best' *.txt** then hit **Return** to see the names of all files containing that string

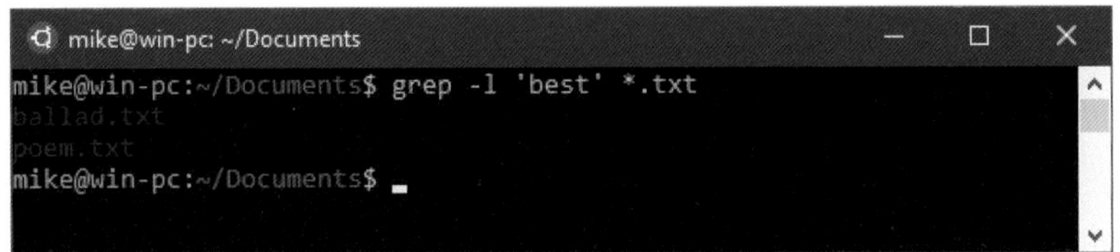

You can invert a **grep** search using an **-v** option – to display all results where the specified string is not found.

It is often useful to incorporate the **grep** command in a pipeline so it can seek a string within output supplied by another command. For example, the **ls** * command, which returns a list of all directories and files in the current directory and its sub-directories, can be searched for files with a particular extension:

5. Enter the command **ls * | grep -c '.sh'** to discover how many shell script files are within the current hierarchy structure with a file extension of ".sh"

6. Now, enter the command **ls * | grep '.sh'** to see a list of shell script file names within the current hierarchy

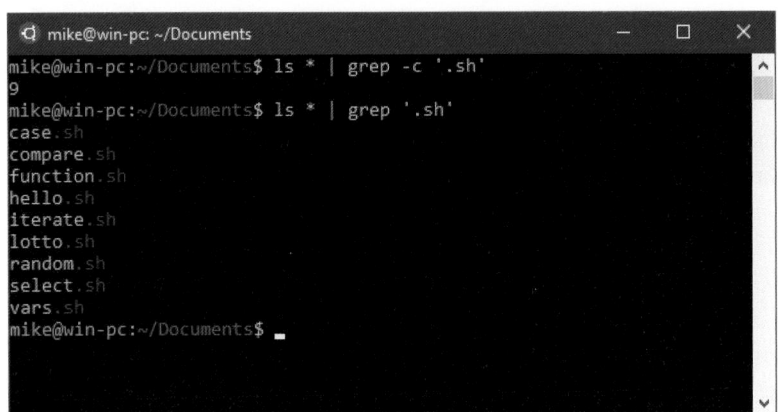

The search is case-sensitive but can be made insensitive by adding an **-i** option to the **grep** command.

Sorting Order

You can check if a file has lines in sorted order by stating the file name to a **sort -c** command.

Lines of text contained within a text file can easily be arranged in alphanumerical order using the **sort** command. This can be used alone or in a pipeline to sort output produced by a previous command. Comparisons are made of each line, with emphasis upon the first character in each line. General sort priority order is spaces, then digits, then letters. Alphabetically, the lines are grouped with uppercase words before lowercase words:

1. Enter a command **cat names.txt** to display a text file named "names.txt" containing lines that begin with a space, digits, uppercase letters, and lowercase letters

2. Now, issue a **sort names.txt** command to display that file's lines sorted alphanumerically

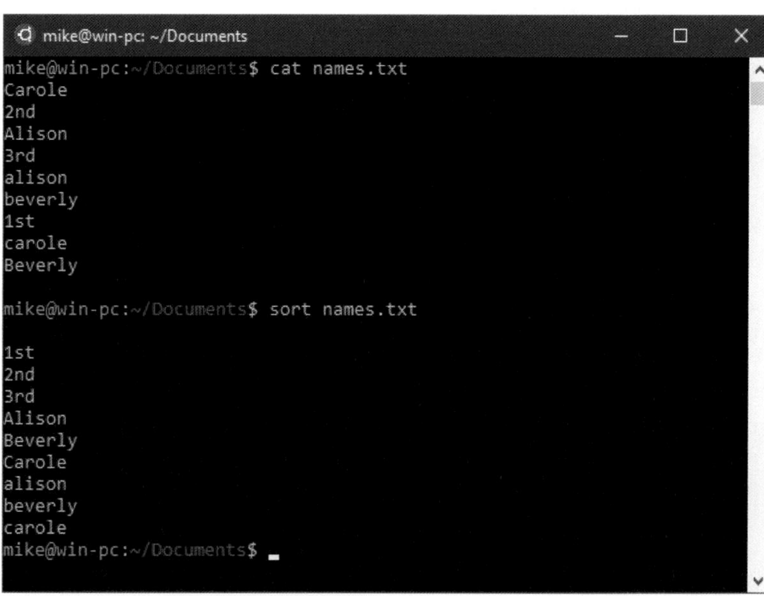

In this example the final line in the unsorted file contains a space, so gets sorted to the beginning in the output.

Lines of text from multiple files can also be merged into a sorted display simply by specifying their filenames as a space-separated list. For example, **sort names.txt fruit.txt** merges two files. Sorted output can be directed into a file, instead of getting displayed in the Terminal, by specifying a filename after an **-o** option to the **sort** command. Alternatively, it can be piped to a **tee** command to be both displayed and stored in a file:

3. Enter a command **sort fruit.txt | tee sorted.txt** to display lines of a file "fruit.txt" sorted and to also get stored

4. Now, issue **cat fruit.txt** and **cat sorted.txt** commands to display the unsorted and sorted file content

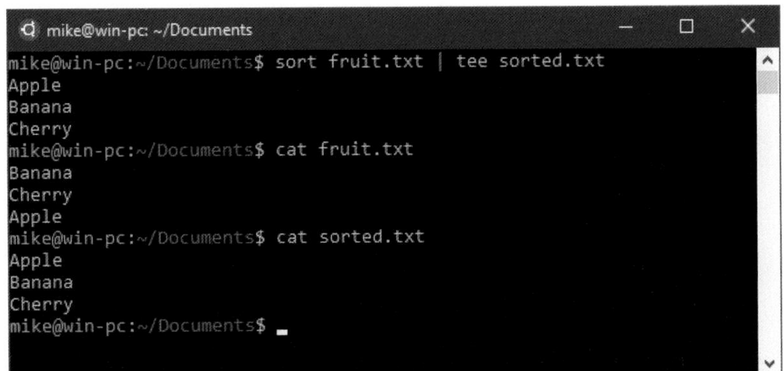

You can reverse the sorting order with a **sort -r** command.

Duplicate sorted lines can be removed by specifying an **-u** option to the **sort** command:

5. Enter a command **grep 'sword' ballad.txt** to display all lines of text from the file "ballad.txt" that contain the word "sword" and see two duplicate lines

6. Now, enter a **grep 'sword' ballad.txt | sort -u** command to display only unique lines of text containing "sword"

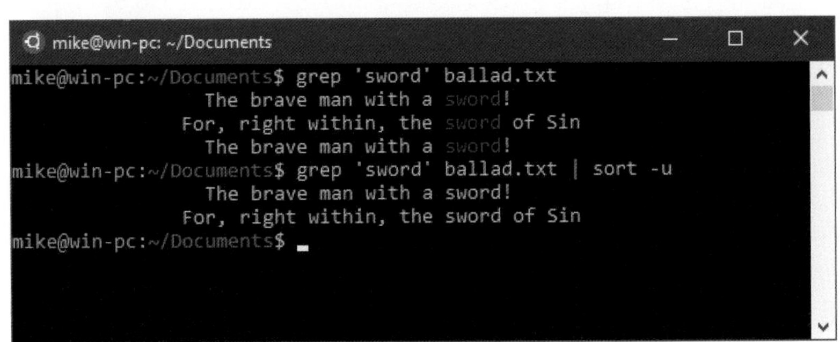

You may also use pipe to the **uniq** command to eliminate duplication – try **man uniq** for details.

Arranging Columns

The shell **cut** and **paste** commands may not be what you might expect. The **paste** command arranges lines of text into columns that are, by default, delimited by an invisible Tab character. Each column is regarded as a numbered "field" that can be selected by specifying its field number to an **-f** option of the **cut** command:

Don't forget

By default the columns are separated (delimited) by an invisible Tab character.

1. Enter a **cat abc.txt def.txt ghi.txt** command to display the content of three files that each contain one word on three lines – see the lines get displayed in succession
2. Next, issue a **paste abc.txt def.txt ghi.txt** command to see the lines get displayed in columns
3. Now, issue a **paste abc.txt def.txt ghi.txt | cut -f2** command to see only the second field get displayed
4. Finally, issue a **paste abc.txt def.txt ghi.txt | cut -f1,3** command to see the first and third fields get displayed

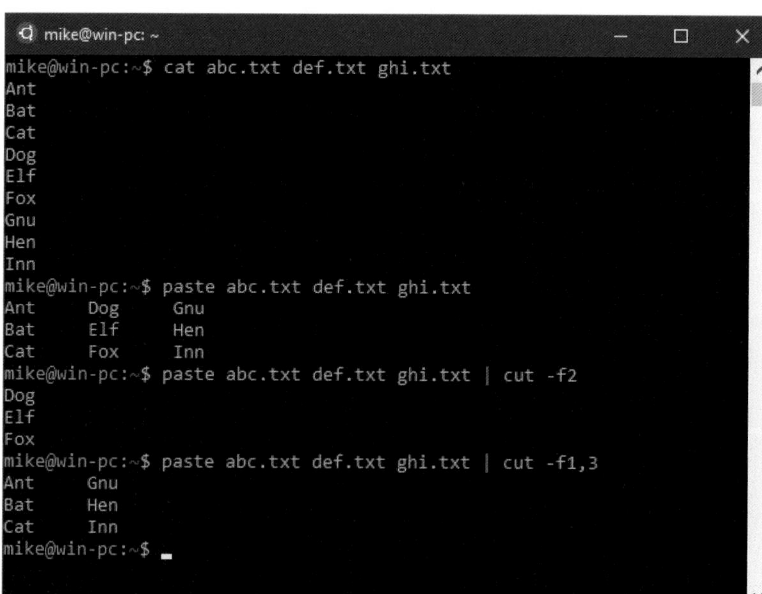
mike@win-pc: ~
mike@win-pc:~$ cat abc.txt def.txt ghi.txt
Ant
Bat
Cat
Dog
Elf
Fox
Gnu
Hen
Inn
mike@win-pc:~$ paste abc.txt def.txt ghi.txt
Ant Dog Gnu
Bat Elf Hen
Cat Fox Inn
mike@win-pc:~$ paste abc.txt def.txt ghi.txt | cut -f2
Dog
Elf
Fox
mike@win-pc:~$ paste abc.txt def.txt ghi.txt | cut -f1,3
Ant Gnu
Bat Hen
Cat Inn
mike@win-pc:~$

Hot tip

A range of fields can also be selected, such as the command **cut f1-3**.

This arrangement places the first lines of each text file on the first row, the second lines on the second row; and so on.

Lines from text files can alternatively be arranged in sequence along each row by specifying an **-s** option to the **paste** command. This arrangement places the first lines of each text file in the first column, the second lines in the second column; and so on:

5. Enter a **paste -s abc.txt def.txt ghi.txt** command to see the lines get displayed in columns

6. Now, issue a **paste -s abc.txt def.txt ghi.txt | cut -f2** command to see only the second field get displayed

```
mike@win-pc: ~
mike@win-pc:~$ paste -s abc.txt def.txt ghi.txt
Ant     Bat     Cat
Dog     Elf     Fox
Gnu     Hen     Inn
mike@win-pc:~$ paste -s abc.txt def.txt ghi.txt | cut -f2
Bat
Elf
Hen
mike@win-pc:~$
```

Arranging the columns using **paste -s** produces a different set of lines in each column field to those of the default arrangement.

The columns can be delimited by a different character, and selected by that character, by specifying an alternative delimiting character to an **-d** option of both the **cut** and **paste** commands:

7. Enter a **paste -d: abc.txt def.txt ghi.txt** command to see the lines get displayed in columns separated by a colon

8. Now, issue a **paste -d: abc.txt def.txt ghi.txt | cut -f1,3 -d:** command to see the first and third fields get displayed

```
mike@win-pc: ~
mike@win-pc:~$ paste -d: abc.txt def.txt ghi.txt
Ant:Dog:Gnu
Bat:Elf:Hen
Cat:Fox:Inn
mike@win-pc:~$ paste -d: abc.txt def.txt ghi.txt \
> | cut -f1,3 -d:
Ant:Gnu
Bat:Hen
Cat:Inn
mike@win-pc:~$
```

The **cut** command is useful to select fields from a file of comma-separated values – for example, by a command **cut -f2 -d, csv.txt**.

Matching Expressions

All occurrences of an individual character in a string can be replaced with a specified alternative character by stating the characters as arguments to the **tr** (translate) command. The first argument specifies the character to be replaced and the second is the replacement character. Additionally, the arguments can map several characters to several alternatives.

Arguments to the **tr** command can also specify a range expansion of characters to be replaced. Commonly, this is used to change all alphabet letters between lowercase (**'[a-z]'**) and uppercase (**'[A-Z]'**):

The **tr** command can easily translate a whole file to uppercase – for example, by a command **cat x.txt |tr '[a-z]' '[A-Z]'**.

1. Enter a command **echo Simple Clip | tr 'i' 'a'** to replace all occurrences of a single letter in output
2. Next, issue an **echo String Up | tr 'ti' 'pa'** command to replace all occurrences of two letters in output
3. Now, issue an **echo Sit On | tr '[a-z]' '[A-Z]'** command to convert all alphabet letters to uppercase in output

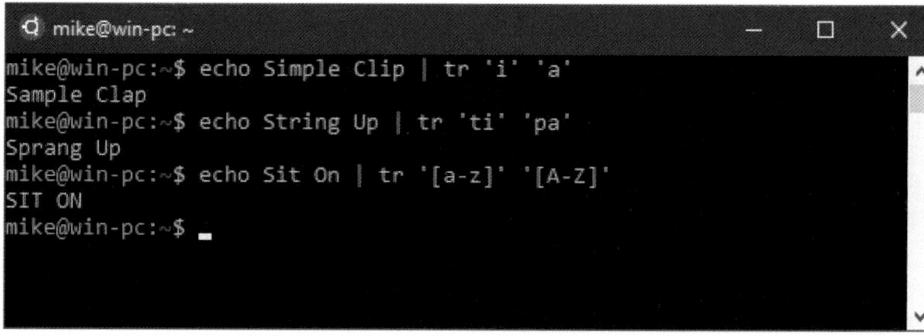

mike@win-pc: ~
mike@win-pc:~$ echo Simple Clip | tr 'i' 'a'
Sample Clap
mike@win-pc:~$ echo String Up | tr 'ti' 'pa'
Sprang Up
mike@win-pc:~$ echo Sit On | tr '[a-z]' '[A-Z]'
SIT ON
mike@win-pc:~$

Occurrences of a particular string can be replaced with a specified alternative string by stating the strings in a substitution editing command to the **sed** (stream editor). This has three parts delimited by default by a forward slash **/** character. The first part simply requires the letter **s** to denote substitution as the type of edit, the second part is the string to be replaced, and the third part is the replacement string – for example, **'s/old/new/'**.

The **/** slash delimiter in the **sed** editing command can be changed to anything you prefer – for example, a colon with **'s:old:new:'**.

By default a **sed** substitution editing command will only replace the first occurrence of the string on each line. It is unlike the **tr** command, which maps characters to alternatives, as the characters must be arranged in the specified string order to match:

4. Enter a command **echo good day | sed 's/day/night/'** to replace the string "day" with the string "night" in output

5. Next, issue an **echo day day | sed 's/day/night/'** to see only the first occurrence of "day" get replaced

6. Now, issue an **echo yad day | sed 's/day/night/'** to see only the correctly ordered characters "day" get replaced

```
mike@win-pc:~$ echo good day | sed 's/day/night/'
good night
mike@win-pc:~$ echo day day | sed 's/day/night/'
night day
mike@win-pc:~$ echo yad day | sed 's/day/night/'
yad night
mike@win-pc:~$
```

Strictly speaking, the strings do not need to be enclosed within quotes unless they include metacharacters, but it is considered good practice to enclose them.

The first occurrence of any lowercase string on each line can be matched using the expression **[a-z]***. As the exact string may be unknown in this case, the editing command allows an ampersand **&** to represent the string in the replacement string specification. All lowercase strings can be matched on each line by appending a letter **g** at the end of the editing command to denote "global":

7. Enter a command **echo hot day | sed 's/[a-z]*/(&)/'** to add parentheses around the first lowercase string only

8. Next, issue an **echo hot day | sed 's/[a-z]*/(&)(&)/'** to replace the first string with two parenthesized versions

9. Now, issue an **echo hot day | sed 's/[a-z]*/(&)/g'** to add parentheses around each lowercase string globally

```
mike@win-pc:~$ echo hot day | sed 's/[a-z]*/(&)/'
(hot) day
mike@win-pc:~$ echo hot day | sed 's/[a-z]*/(&)(&)/'
(hot)(hot) day
mike@win-pc:~$ echo hot day | sed 's/[a-z]*/(&)/g'
(hot) (day)
mike@win-pc:~$
```

The expression **[a-z]*** matches one or more lowercase characters, **[A-Z]*** matches one or more uppercase characters, and **[0-9]*** matches one or more digits.

Editing Text

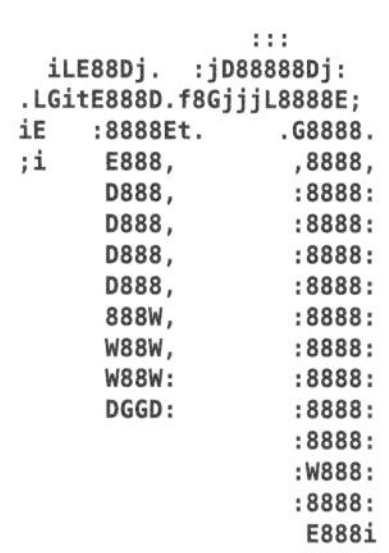

Nano logo

A popular Linux shell program for creating and editing text files is the easy-to-use "Nano" program that runs within a Terminal:

1. Type **nano** at a prompt then hit **Return** to open the Nano text editor in the shell window

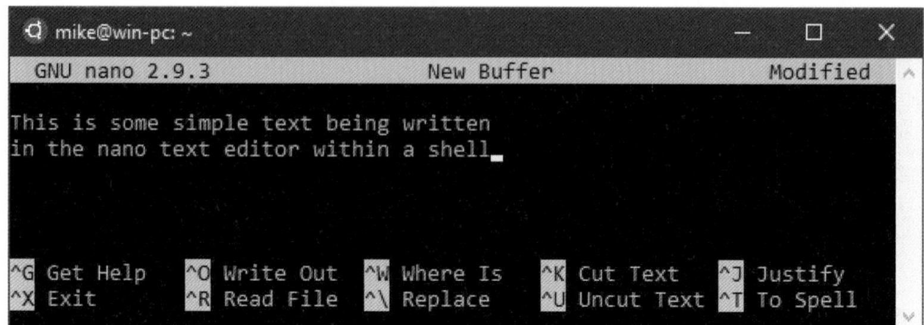

The Nano editor has a title bar displaying version number, file name ("New Buffer" until named), and whether recently modified. A blinking cursor appears below the title bar where you can type and edit text. The bottom of the editor lists Control key shortcuts, with the Control key represented by the ^ character.

The Nano editor makes extensive use of the **Ctrl** key – you need to press it to execute its commands.

2. Press **Ctrl** + **G** keys to open the online Help system, then press **Ctrl** + **X** keys to close online Help
3. Now, type some text into the Nano editor – use the arrow keys to navigate around the text as required
4. Next, press **Ctrl** + **O** keys to see a status bar appear above the shortcut list requesting a file name to write
5. Type a name for the text file; say, **sample.txt**

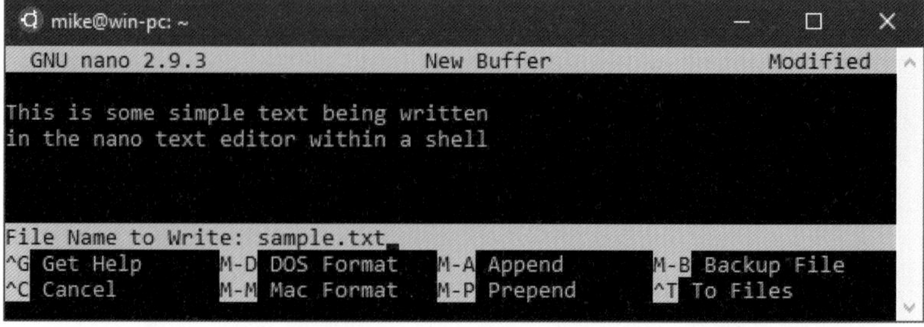

You can launch Nano in "expert mode" by typing **nano -x** at a prompt if you prefer not to see the shortcuts list.

6. Next, hit the **Return** key to write the file, in your home directory by default – see the title bar now display the given file name and the status bar display a confirmation

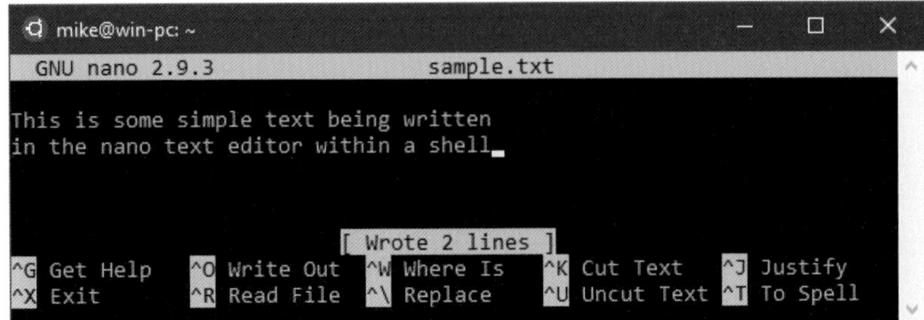

You can press the **Ctrl** + **C** keys to cancel any Nano operation.

7. Now, press **Ctrl** + **X** keys to close the Nano text editor and return to a regular shell prompt

8. Then, issue the command **cat sample.txt** to read the contents of the text file you have just created

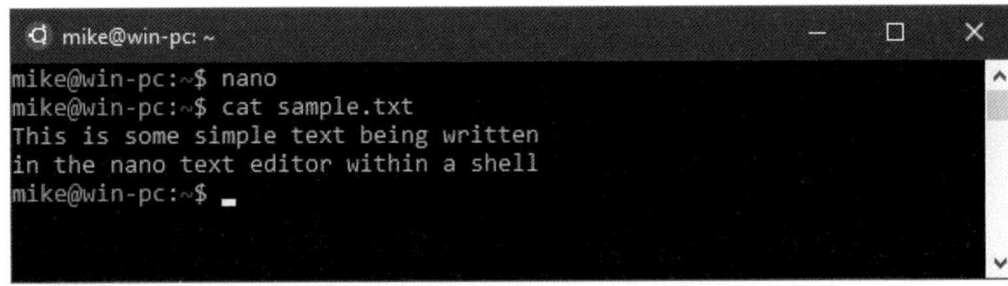

With Nano open, press **Esc** twice then type a 3-digit number 000-255 to print the character of that character value.

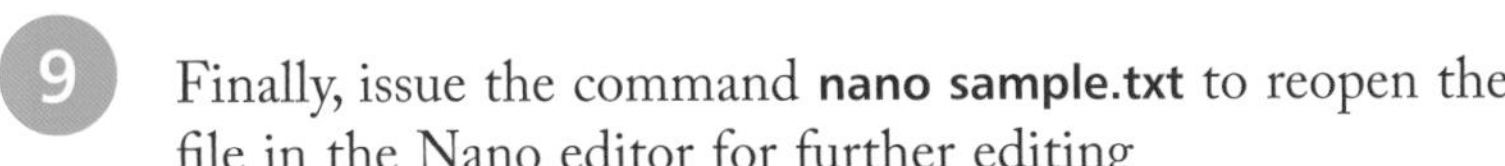

9. Finally, issue the command **nano sample.txt** to reopen the file in the Nano editor for further editing

Inserting Text

Vi IMproved (VIM) logo

The classic Linux shell program for creating and editing text files is the compact "Vi" (Visual) program that runs within a Terminal:

Type **vi** at a prompt then hit **Return** to open the Vi text editor in the shell – see "Vi IMproved" (VIM) appear

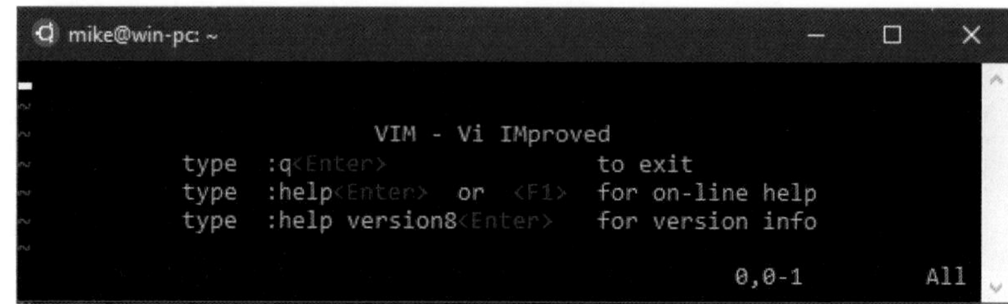

The Vi editor makes extensive use of the : colon key – you need to include it by typing **:help** for online help.

The Vi editor displays a tilde character at the beginning of each empty line. You cannot enter any text initially as Vi opens in "Command Mode" where it will attempt to interpret anything you type as an instruction:

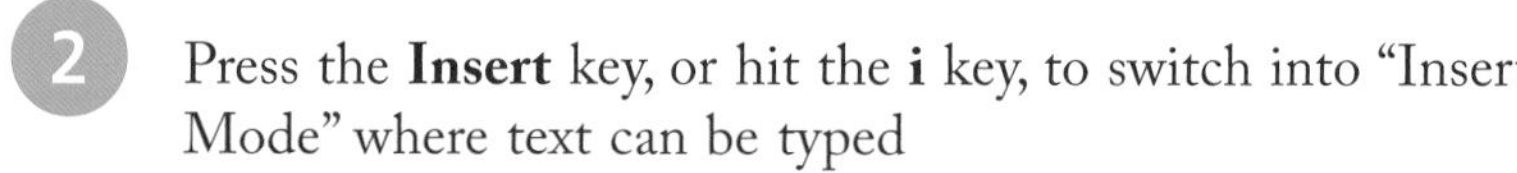

Press the **Insert** key, or hit the **i** key, to switch into "Insert Mode" where text can be typed

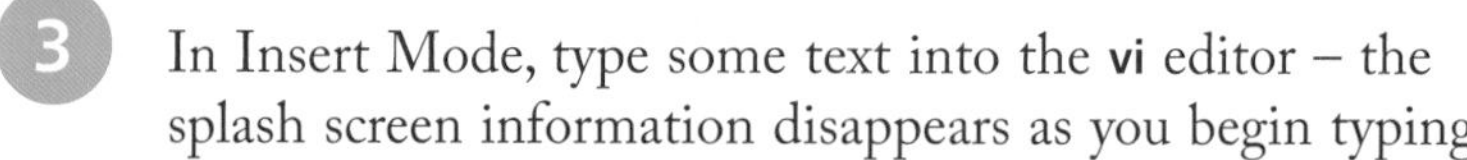

In Insert Mode, type some text into the **vi** editor – the splash screen information disappears as you begin typing

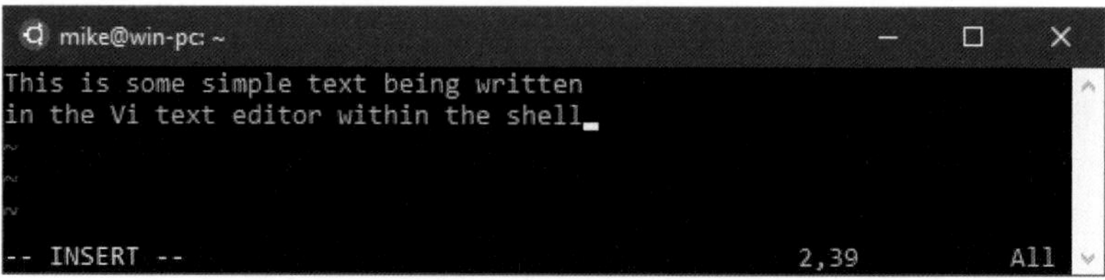

The Vi editor does not have automatic word wrap at line ends – it will wrap mid-word unless you hit **Return** to wrap a word manually.

There are a number of special key combinations listed in the Vi **man** pages that let you navigate to different locations in the text, but most recent Linux systems use the enhanced VIM version that lets you use the arrow keys on your keyboard for this purpose.

To save your text as a file, first hit the **Esc** key to exit Insert Mode – switching back into Command Mode

5. Next, type a : colon to begin a Vi command – a colon character appears at the bottom-left corner of the editor

6. Now, type a lowercase **w** (for "write") followed by a space and a name for the text file; say, **simple.txt**

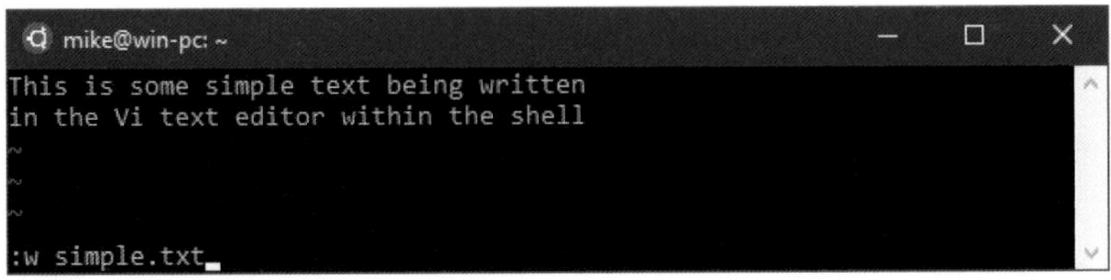

Using Vi needs a little practice – you may prefer the Nano text editor described on the previous pages 58-59.

7. Then, hit the **Return** key to write the file – in your current directory by default

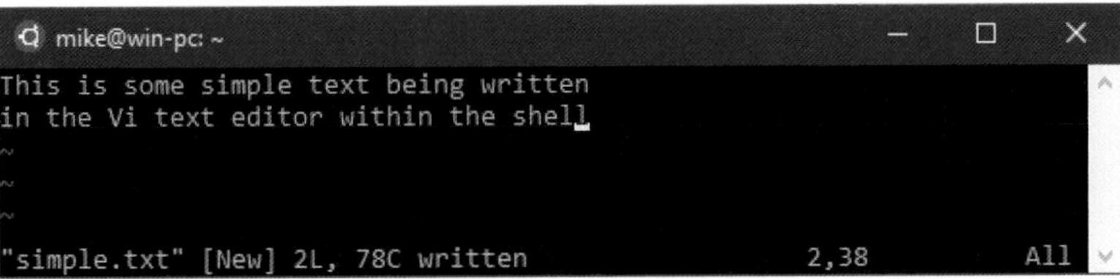

8. Finally, type a **:q** command then hit **Return** to close Vi and return to a regular shell prompt

You can now issue the command **cat simple.txt** to read the contents of the text file you have just created or launch Vi once more to open the file for further editing:

9. Issue the command **vi simple.txt** to reopen the file you have just created in the Vi editor

To edit a file opened in Vi you first need to hit the **Insert** key to switch into Insert Mode.

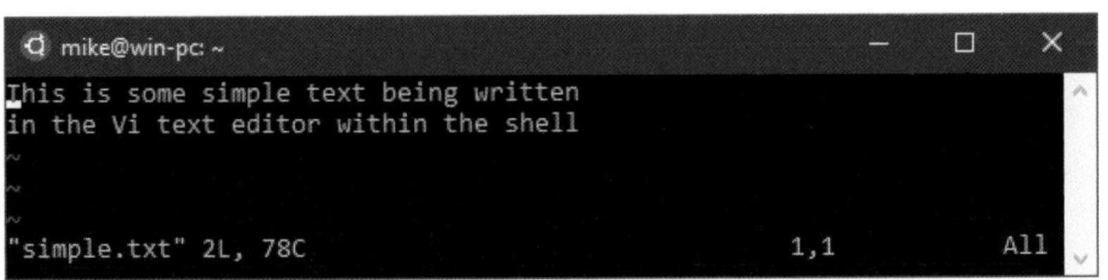

Summary

- The **cat** command can read one or more specified text files and write that content as standard output in the Terminal.
- Text can be written or overwritten in a file specified to the **>** redirection operator and appended to an existing file specified to the **>>** redirection operator.
- Output produced by one command can be sent as input to another command by the **|** pipe operator.
- Commands producing lengthy output can be piped to the **more** or **less** command for viewing one screen at a time.
- The **head** command displays only the beginning of a text file whereas the **tail** command displays only the end of a text file.
- The **grep** command can seek a given string within specified text files or within input passed to it in a pipeline.
- Lines of a text file can be listed as standard output in alphanumerical order by the **sort** command.
- Sorted content can be piped to the **tee** command to be both displayed as standard output and stored in a text file.
- The **paste** command can arrange lines of text into columns that are delimited by an invisible **\t** tab character.
- Individual column fields arranged by **paste** can be selected for display as standard output when piped to the **cut** command.
- All occurrences of an individual character in a string can be replaced by an alternative specified to the **tr** command.
- The case of all characters in a text stream can be changed by specifying **[a-z]** and **[A-Z]** expressions to the **tr** command.
- Occurrences of a string in a text stream can be substituted by an alternative specified in a **sed** editing command.
- The **nano** program is a user-friendly text editor that requires extensive use of the **Ctrl** Control key to implement commands.
- The **vi** program has Command and Insert modes that require extensive use of the : colon key to implement commands.

4 Editing Commands

This chapter demonstrates how to modify and recall commands at the prompt.

Amending Characters

Emacs word editing

Commands typed at a Bash prompt can be edited to remove characters by using the ← and → arrow keys to position the cursor to the right of characters to be removed, then pressing the ⌫ **Backspace** key to remove characters to the left of the cursor. Additionally, a Bash Terminal has two command-editing modes; namely "Emacs" (**E**diting **mac**ro**s**) mode and "Vi" (**Vi**sual) mode. Typically, Bash will start in Emacs mode as its default, or you can switch to Emacs mode at any time using a **set -o emacs** command. Emacs mode allows you to perform command-editing functions by pressing various key combinations, like these basic functions:

Keys:	Function:
Ctrl + **F**	Move the cursor Forward one character
Ctrl + **B**	Move the cursor Back one character
Ctrl + **D**	Delete one character at the cursor

1. Enter **echo 1 2 3 | sed 's/[0-9]*/(&)/g'** to enclose each individual number in parentheses – but see the result fail

mike@win-pc: ~
mike@win-pc:~$ echo 1 2 3 | sed 's/[0-9]*/(&)/g'
(1 2 3)

2. Press **Ctrl** + **B** to move the cursor ***Back*** to the space between **[** and **0**, then press **Ctrl** + **D** to ***Delete*** the space

mike@win-pc: ~
mike@win-pc:~$ echo 1 2 3 | sed 's/[_0-9]*/(&)/g'

3. Press **Ctrl** + **F** to move the cursor ***Forward*** to the space between **9** and **]**, then press **Ctrl** + **D** to ***Delete*** the space

4. Now, hit **Return** to see the edited command succeed

mike@win-pc: ~
mike@win-pc:~$ echo 1 2 3 | sed 's/[0-9]*/(&)/g'
(1) (2) (3)

Beware

The **Ctrl** + **D** key combination is also the Terminal exit command shortcut – using this on an empty command line will exit the Terminal.

Emacs mode also recognizes these keys that allow you to perform command editing of entire words:

Keys:	Function:
Esc F	Move the cursor Forward one word
Esc B	Move the cursor Back one word
Esc D	Delete the word after the cursor
Esc Backspace	Remove the word before the cursor
Ctrl + **Y**	Yank (retrieve) the words last deleted

Don't forget

In this case a word is defined as a sequence of alphanumeric characters – so all other characters, such as **<** or **&**, are treated as a word break.

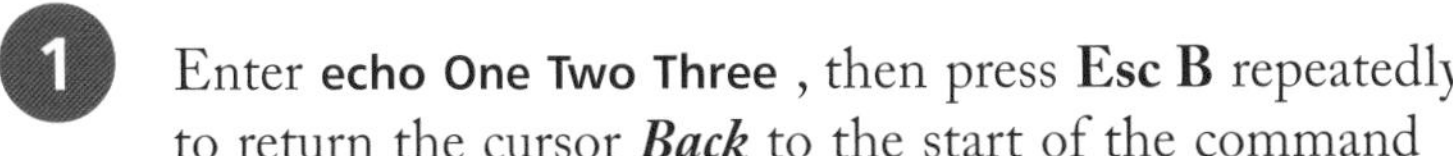

1. Enter **echo One Two Three** , then press **Esc B** repeatedly to return the cursor ***Back*** to the start of the command

mike@win-pc: ~
mike@win-pc:~$ echo One Two Three

2. Next, press **Esc F** repeatedly to move the cursor ***Forward*** to be between the words "Two" and "Three"

mike@win-pc: ~
mike@win-pc:~$ echo One Two Three

3. Now, press **Esc D** to ***Delete*** the next word "Three", then press **Esc Backspace** to remove the previous word "Two"

mike@win-pc: ~
mike@win-pc:~$ echo One

Beware

Functions that use the **Ctrl** key are combinations so both keys must be pressed together, whereas functions that use the **Esc** key are sequences so they must be pressed individually.

4. Finally, hit **Return** to execute the edited command then press **Ctrl** + **Y** to ***Yank*** back the words last deleted

mike@win-pc: ~
mike@win-pc:~$ echo One
One
mike@win-pc:~$ Two Three

Changing Lines

Emacs mode recognizes these key combinations that allow you to perform editing of entire command lines:

Emacs line editing

Keys:	Function:
Ctrl + **A**	Place the cursor At the start of the line
Ctrl + **E**	Move the cursor to the End of the line
Ctrl + **K**	Kill (remove) all from cursor to the line end
Ctrl + **U**	Remove all from the line start Up to the cursor
Ctrl + **Y**	Yank (retrieve) the words last deleted

1. Enter **echo 1 2 3 | sed 's/[0-9]*/(&)/g'** , then press **Ctrl** + **A** to place the cursor ***At*** the start of the command line

mike@win-pc: ~
mike@win-pc:~$ echo 1 2 3 | sed 's/[0-9]*/(&)/g'

2. Press **Ctrl** + **F** to move the cursor ***Forward*** to the pipe

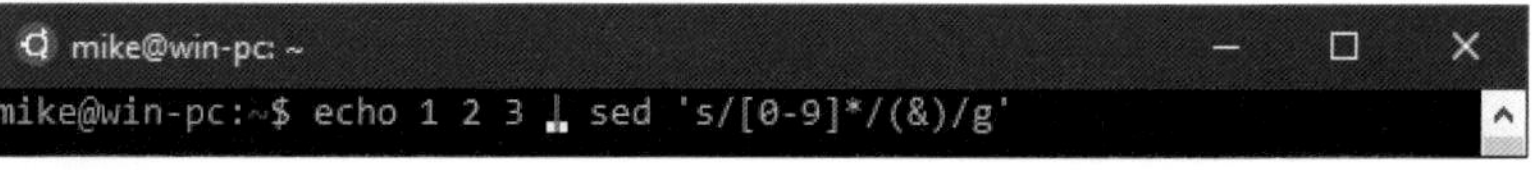
mike@win-pc: ~
mike@win-pc:~$ echo 1 2 3 | sed 's/[0-9]*/(&)/g'

3. Now, press **Ctrl** + **K** to ***Kill*** everything up to the line end

mike@win-pc: ~
mike@win-pc:~$ echo 1 2 3

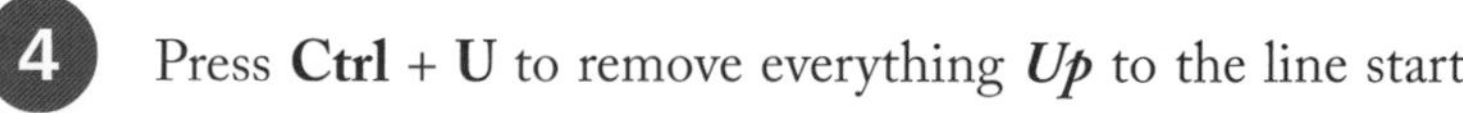

4. Press **Ctrl** + **U** to remove everything ***Up*** to the line start

mike@win-pc: ~
mike@win-pc:~$

5. Finally, press **Ctrl** + **Y** to ***Yank*** back the words last deleted

mike@win-pc: ~
mike@win-pc:~$ echo 1 2 3 | sed 's/[0-9]*/(&)/g'

Hot tip

With the cursor mid-line you can hold down **Ctrl** then press **E U** or **A K** to remove an entire line.

Recalling history

Emacs mode also recognizes these key combinations that allow you to recall from history commands you have previously issued:

Keys:	Function:
Ctrl + P	Scroll back to Previous command in history
Ctrl + N	Scroll forward to Next command in history
Ctrl + R	Make a Reverse-intelligent-search in history

Hot tip

You can alternatively use the ↑ and ↓ arrow keys to scroll back and forward through the command history.

1. Enter commands of **whoami** and **hostname** then press **Ctrl** + **P** twice to scroll back two ***Previous*** commands – recalling the **whoami** command to the prompt

mike@win-pc: ~
mike@win-pc:~$ whoami
mike
mike@win-pc:~$ hostname
win-pc
mike@win-pc:~$ whoami

2. Press **Ctrl** + **N** once to scroll forward to the ***Next*** command – recalling the **hostname** command to the prompt

mike@win-pc: ~
mike@win-pc:~$ whoami
mike
mike@win-pc:~$ hostname
win-pc
mike@win-pc:~$ hostname

Don't forget

After recalling any command from history just hit Return to execute that command.

3. Finally, press **Ctrl** + **U** to empty the command line then press **Ctrl** + **R** to enter ***Reverse***-intelligent-search mode – then type "wh" to recall the **whoami** command

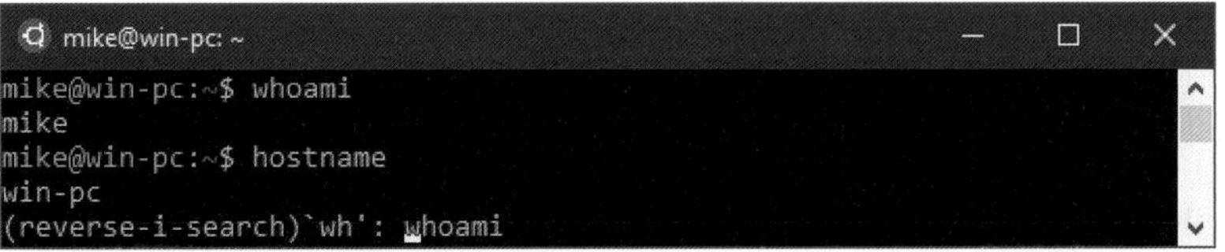
mike@win-pc: ~
mike@win-pc:~$ whoami
mike
mike@win-pc:~$ hostname
win-pc
(reverse-i-search)`wh': whoami

Completing Commands

Emacs command editing

Emacs mode recognizes these keys that allow you to perform textual completion of a string typed at the prompt:

Keys:	Function:
Tab	Attempt general completion
Esc ?	Display a list of possibilities
Esc /	Attempt filename completion
Ctrl + X /	Display a list of possible filenames
Esc ~	Attempt username completion
Ctrl + X ~	Display a list of possible usernames
Esc $	Attempt variable name completion
Ctrl + X $	Display a list of possible variable names
Esc @	Attempt hostname completion
Ctrl + X @	Display a list of possible hostnames
Esc !	Attempt command name completion
Ctrl + X !	Display a list of possible command names

1. Enter the command **ls De**, then hit **Tab** to see a "Desktop" directory name get completed if it exists

mike@win-pc: ~
mike@win-pc:~$ ls Desktop/

Beware

The **Esc ?** list of possibilities will not include filenames unless there are no function or command name possibilities – use **Esc /** for filenames.

2. Press **Ctrl** + **U** to clear the command line then type **ls Do** and hit **Tab** to see no completion take place
3. Now, hit **Tab** once more to see a list of possibilities
4. Finally, type **c**, appending it to **ls Do**, then hit **Tab** to see a "Documents" directory get completed if it exists

mike@win-pc: ~
mike@win-pc:~$ ls Do
Documents/ Downloads/
mike@win-pc:~$ ls Documents/

Utilities

Emacs mode also recognizes these keys that provide various command-editing utility functions:

Keys:	Function:
Ctrl + **L**	Clear screen placing current line at top
Ctrl + **M**	Hit Return (also possible with **Ctrl** + **J**)
Ctrl + **T**	Transpose current and previous characters, then move the cursor forward one character
Esc C	Capitalize the word at or next after the cursor
Esc U	Uppercase the word at or next after the cursor
Esc L	Lowercase the word at or next after the cursor
Esc .	Insert last word of previous command

As filenames are often the last word on a command line the **Esc .** function (and a similar **Esc _** function) is especially useful if you want to use several commands on a file that has a long filename.

1. Enter the command **echo Pool**, then press **Ctrl** + **M** to execute the command

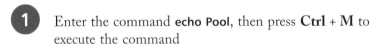

mike@win-pc: ~
mike@win-pc:~$ echo Pool
Pool
mike@win-pc:~$

2. Next, press **Ctrl** + **L** to clear the screen, then type an **echo** command – including a trailing space character

3. Now, press **Esc .** to recall the string "Pool", then press **Ctrl** + **T** to transpose its last two characters, into "Polo"

4. Finally, press **Ctrl** + **J** to execute the edited command

The **Ctrl** + **M** keys actually produce the same ASCII character as Return whereas **Ctrl** + **J** produces a linefeed character – that Unix also recognizes as Return.

Adjusting Characters

Vi word editing

As an alternative to the typical default Emacs command-editing mode some Bash users prefer to use Vi command-editing mode as it recognizes commands similar to those of the Vi text editor. Switching the Terminal to Vi command-editing mode is simply achieved by issuing a **set -o vi** command at the prompt.

Like the Vi text editor, Vi command-editing mode has two modes of its own – an "Input Mode" and a "Control Mode". Normally, the command line will be in Input Mode where commands can be typed. Switching to Control Mode allows the command line to be edited and previous commands to be recalled from history. Control Mode is entered when you hit the **Esc** key and Input Mode can be resumed by pressing the **A** key.

In Input Mode commands can be edited to remove characters by using the ← and → arrow keys to position the cursor to the right of characters to be removed, then pressing the ⌫ Backspace key to remove characters to the left of the cursor. Additionally, the key combination **Ctrl** + **W** deletes the entire word left of the cursor.

In Control Mode the following keys provide basic functions to easily move around the command line:

You must hit **Esc** to enter Control Mode before using the keys to move around the command line.

Keys:	Function:
H	Move left one character
L	Move right one character
B	Move to the start of current word; or if at a word start, move to the start of the word to the left
W	Move to the start of the word to the right
E	Move to the end of the current word
0 (zero)	Move to the start of the line
$	Move to the end of the line

All except the last two functions listed above can be prefixed by a number to specify how many times its action should be repeated. For example: in Control Mode, 3 L moves right three characters. This also applies to the arrow keys so that in Control Mode pressing the 3 then the → key also moves right three characters.

By default Vi command-editing mode defines a word to be any sequence of alphanumeric characters or the _ underscore character. If you wish its definition to include all other characters such as the . period (full stop) and / slash characters when moving to the start or end of a word, hold down Shift then press W, B, or E keys:

1. Enter a **set -o vi** command to use Vi command-editing and enter into its Input Mode
2. Now, enter a **cat Documents/in_easy_steps** command to see the cursor at the end of the line as usual

3. Next, hit **Esc** to enter Control Mode and see the cursor move one character left – onto the end of the command

4. Now, press **B** to move the cursor to the start of the word and see the word break around the / slash character

5. Then, press **$** to move back to the end of the line

6. Press **Shift** + **B** to move the cursor to the start of the word and see the word now break around the space character

The **Ctrl** + **L** key combination can be used to clear the screen only when in Control Mode – from Input Mode you need to press an **Esc Ctrl** + **L** key sequence.

In Control Mode you can exit to Input Mode and place the cursor at the line end by pressing a **$ A** key sequence.

Inserting Text

Vi line editing

Vi command-editing mode provides several different exit functions from Control Mode. These allow you to return to Input Mode ready to insert text at your preferred position on the command line and are provided by these keys:

Keys:	Function:
I	Insert text before the current character
A	Append text after the current character
Shift + I	Insert text at the start of the line
Shift + A	Append text at the end of the line
Shift + R	Overwrite existing text at the current position

1. Enter a **set -o vi** command to use Vi command editing then enter a **grep 'sword' ballad.txt** command for edit

mike@win-pc: ~
mike@win-pc:~$ grep 'sword' ballad.txt

2. Next, hit **Esc** to enter Control Mode and see the cursor move one character left – onto the end of the line

mike@win-pc: ~
mike@win-pc:~$ grep 'sword' ballad.txt

3. Now, press **5 B** to move the cursor to the start of the quoted word search term that is to be replaced

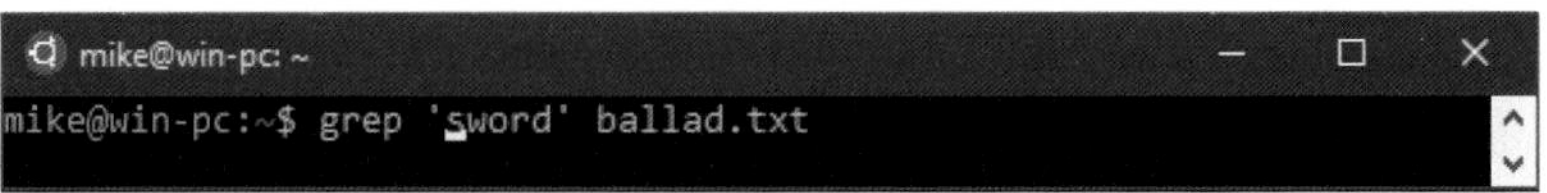
mike@win-pc: ~
mike@win-pc:~$ grep 'sword' ballad.txt

4. Press **Shift + R** to exit Control Mode and type **flame** to overwrite the previous search term – completing the edit

mike@win-pc: ~
mike@win-pc:~$ grep 'flame' ballad.txt

Hot tip

The key combination **Shift** + **I** is a shortcut for the **0 I** key sequence. Similarly, **Shift** + **A** is a shortcut for **$ A**.

Deleting text

Vi command-editing mode provides various text deletion functions that are executed in Control Mode by these keys:

Keys:	Function:
DL	Delete current character (shortcut **X**)
DH	Delete one character back (shortcut **Shift + X**)
DW	Delete word forward
DB	Delete word back
DD	Delete the entire line
D0	Delete to the start of the line
D$	Delete to the end of the line (shortcut **Shift + D**)
U	Undo previous deletions

Hot tip

If you want to include all characters when deleting words, rather than just the alphanumeric and underscore characters, use **D Shift** + **W** and **D Shift** + **B** sequences.

To exit Control Mode immediately after making a deletion, just substitute C for D in each case:

1. Enter a **set -o vi** command to use Vi command editing then enter a **cat fruit.txt | sort** command for edit

2. Next, hit **Esc** to enter Control Mode

mike@win-pc: ~
mike@win-pc:~$ set -o vi
mike@win-pc:~$ cat fruit.txt | sort

3. Now, press **2 B** to move the cursor onto the pipe character ready to remove the pipeline

mike@win-pc: ~
mike@win-pc:~$ cat fruit.txt | sort

4. Press **C $** to complete the edit and return to Input Mode

mike@win-pc: ~
mike@win-pc:~$ cat fruit.txt

Hot tip

You can prefix any deletion function with a repeat number – for example, **Esc 2DB** to delete two words back. Also note that the . period (full stop) key repeats the last text modification.

Repeating History

Vi command editing

Vi command-editing mode provides several functions from Control Mode to search your command history. These allow you to recall a previous command and are provided by these keys:

Keys:	Function:
K	Scroll back one line (shortcut -)
J	Scroll forward one line (shortcut +)
/string	Search back for the specified string
?string	Search forward for the specified string
n	Repeat a search in the same direction
N	Repeat a search in the opposite direction

Typically, a command may be recalled for repeat execution or for correction after entering a command with errors. In Control Mode the R key can be used to easily insert a replacement character at the cursor then exit to Input Mode:

You can alternatively use the ↑ and ↓ arrow keys to scroll back and forward through the command history.

1. Enter **echo 1 2 3 | sed 'a/[0-9]*/(&)/g'** to see the pipeline execution fail, then hit **Esc** to enter Control Mode

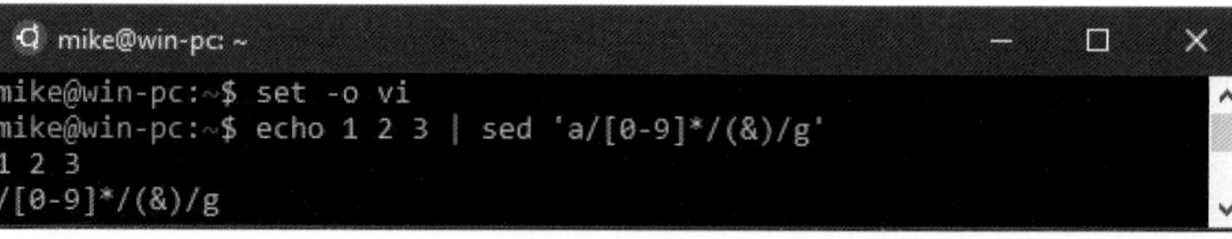

```
mike@win-pc:~$ set -o vi
mike@win-pc:~$ echo 1 2 3 | sed 'a/[0-9]*/(&)/g'
1 2 3
/[0-9]*/(&)/g
```

2. Press **Ctrl** + **L** to clear the screen, then press **K** to recall the command and **7 W** to put the cursor on the letter "a"

```
mike@win-pc:~$ echo 1 2 3 | sed 'a/[0-9]*/(&)/g'
```

3. Now, press **R S** to replace the letter "a" with a letter "s", then hit **Return** to see the command execute correctly

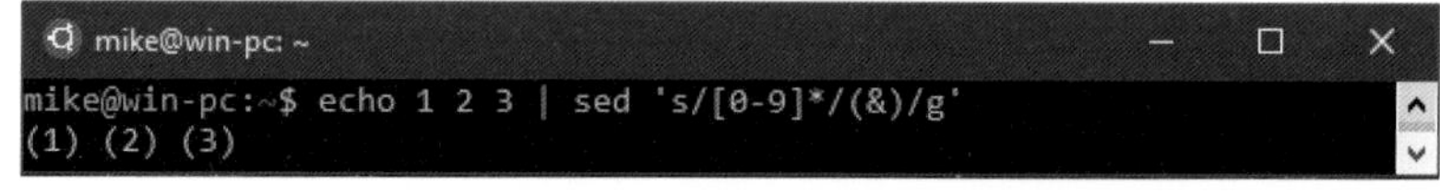

```
mike@win-pc:~$ echo 1 2 3 | sed 's/[0-9]*/(&)/g'
(1) (2) (3)
```

Locating characters

Vi command-editing mode provides various character location functions that are executed in Control Mode by these keys:

Keys:	Function:
F *char*	Move right onto the specified character
Shift + F *char*	Move left onto the specified character
T *char*	Move right up to the specified character
Shift + T *char*	Move left up to the specified character
;	Repeat last search in the same direction
,	Repeat last search in the opposite direction

Hot tip

You can prefix any character location function with a repeat number. For example, press **Esc 2FS** to move onto the second "s" character to the right.

Vi command-editing mode also lets you to perform completion of a string typed at the prompt by entering Control Mode and typing a \ backslash character, or a list of possibilities by typing an * asterisk character. Both functions then exit back to Input Mode:

1. At a prompt in your home directory, type **ls De** then hit **Esc ** to see the "Desktop" directory name get completed

mike@win-pc: ~
mike@win-pc:~$ ls Desktop/

Hot tip

You can hit **Return** to execute a command line at any time – in Control Mode or in Input Mode.

2. Press **Esc CC** to clear the command line then type **ls Do** and hit **Esc ** to see no completion take place

3. Now, hit **Esc *** to see a list of possibilities

mike@win-pc: ~
mike@win-pc:~$ ls Documents Downloads

4. Finally, hit **Esc DB** to leave only the "Documents" option

mike@win-pc: ~
mike@win-pc:~$ ls Documents

Fixing Commands

Bash command editing

Old commands issued at a Bash prompt are recorded after a session in a hidden text file called **.bash_history** within your home directory. This is in part where Emacs and Vi command editing finds your past command history. Although the history file can be displayed like any other, there is shell built-in **history** command that can be used instead to also include most recent commands. The **history** command will by default display all previous commands issued but can accept a numerical argument to limit how far back in history to display. Helpfully, the commands are numbered when displayed by the **history** command and that number can be used to recall the command for editing in the default system text editor if desired.

You can enter **cat .bash_history** to see the contents of the command history file.

The shell built-in **fc** (fix command) can accept the command history number as its argument and will open that command in the default system text editor. Specifying its **-l** option will display the last 16 commands in the history list for selection. Additionally, two numbers can be specified after the **-l** option to display a range of numbered commands. Alternatively, you can specify the start of a command as its argument and it will open the most recent command with that beginning. When no arguments are specified to the **fc** command it will simply open the most recent command in the editor.

It is important to recognize that after editing, the **fc** command will automatically execute the edited command:

Enter **fc -l 1 10** to see the first 10 commands in your command history – notice that command number 7 contains an error that can be edited

You can delete the Bash history using the command **cat /dev/null > .bash_history**.

```
mike@win-pc: ~
mike@win-pc:~$ fc -l 1 10
1        cat /dev/null > .bash_history
2        ps $$
3        bash --version
4        whoami
5        hostname
6        exit
7        echo 1 2 3 | sed 'a/[0-9]*/(&)/g'
8        grep 'sword' ballad.txt
9        pwd
10       ls
mike@win-pc:~$ _
```

2. Next, issue an **fc 7** command to open command number 7 in the system default text editor – Nano in this case, but your system may differ

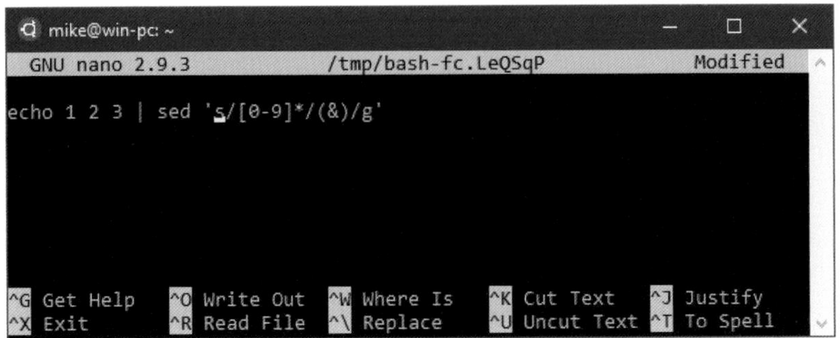

3. Now, edit the file to replace the errant "a" with an "s"

4. Press **Ctrl** + **O** to save the change then **Ctrl** + **X** to exit the Nano text editor – see the edited command get executed in the Terminal

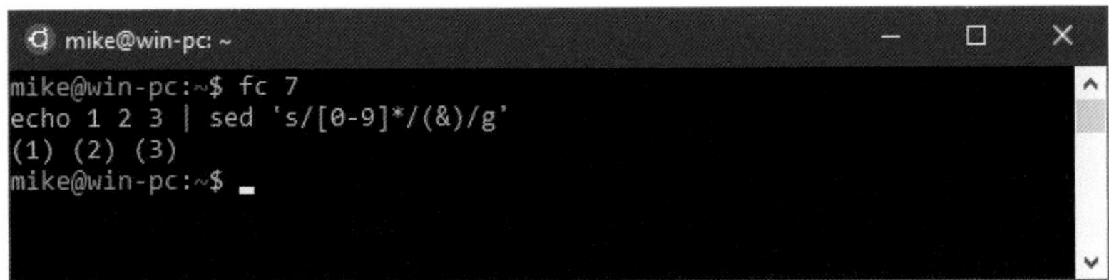

5. Press **Ctrl** + **L** to clear the screen using a shortcut

6. Finally, issue a **history 3** command to list the three most recent commands – see the edited command has its own new number but the shortcut clear action is not listed

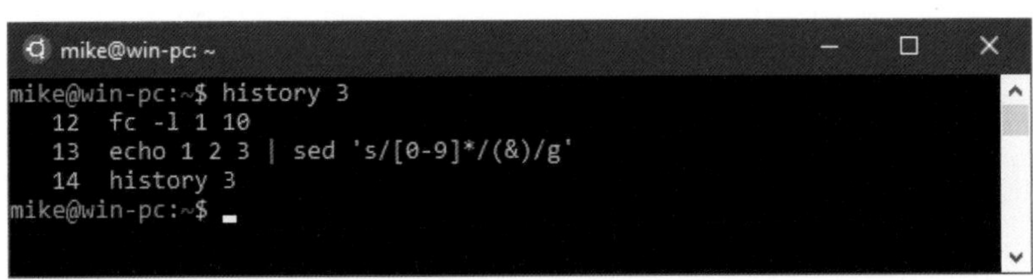

If you prefer to have **fc** use a different text editor its path can be specified to an **-e** option – for example, to use Vi with **fc -e /usr/bin/vi 7**.

If the command you wish to edit removes files remember that it will be executed by the **fc** command after you have finished editing.

The command **fc echo** could be used to recall the command in this example – as it is now the most recent **echo** command in the history.

Expanding History

Bash command editing (continued)

Commands in Bash history can be recalled and edited using its intrinsic history expansion facility. This allows a command in history to be identified by an "event designator". Specific words can be identified in a command by appending a "word designator" and can be adapted by appending one or more "modifiers":

Event:	Designator Description:
!!	Last command
!*n*	Command number ***n***
!-*n*	Current command number minus ***n***
!*string*	Most recent command beginning with ***string***
!?*string*	Most recent command containing ***string***
^*str1*^*str2*	Last command replacing ***str1*** with ***str2***

You can use an **fc -l** command to get a list of past commands and their command number.

Word:	Designator Description:
:0	The first word in the line
:*n*	The *n*th word in the line, counting from zero
:^	The second word in the line
:$	The last word in the line
:%	Most recent **!?*string*** search result word
:*	All words except the first word

The word count on a line begins at zero, not one – the first word is zero; the second word is one; and so on.

Modifier:	Description:
:h	Remove trailing part of path address
:r	Remove trailing file extension
:e	Remove all except trailing file extension
:t	Remove leading part of path address
:p	Display command but do not execute
:q	Enclose in quote marks
:x	Break words at spaces and enclose in quotes
:s/*old*/*new*/	Substitute ***old*** for ***new***

...cont'd

History expansion is useful to quickly repeat the last command; to run commands with different arguments; and to extract words:

1. Enter **!!** then hit **Return** to execute the last command – see a **grep** command return a search result

```
mike@win-pc:~$ !!
grep 'sword' ballad.txt
          The brave man with a sword!
        For, right within, the sword of Sin
          The brave man with a sword!
mike@win-pc:~$
```

2. Next, press **Ctrl** + **L** to clear the screen then issue a **^sword^flame** command – to run the last command once more but now searching for a different word

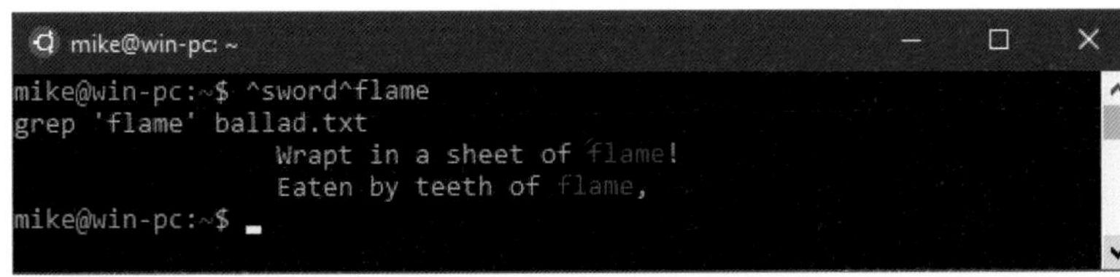
mike@win-pc: ~
mike@win-pc:~$ ^sword^flame
grep 'flame' ballad.txt
Wrapt in a sheet of flame!
Eaten by teeth of flame,
mike@win-pc:~$

Hot tip

The substitution made here by **^sword^flame** could also be made with **!!:s/sword/flame/**.

3. Now, press **Ctrl** + **L** to clear the screen then issue a **!!:$:p** command – to select the last word in the command and simply print it as standard output

mike@win-pc: ~
mike@win-pc:~$!!:$:p
ballad.txt
mike@win-pc:~$

Beware

Multiple modifiers cannot be combined – they must be separated by a **:** colon character.

4. Finally, press **Ctrl** + **L** to clear the screen then issue a **!!:$:p:r:q** command – to select the last word in the command, print it as standard output, remove the file extension, and add quote marks

```
mike@win-pc:~$ !!:$:p:r:q
'ballad'
mike@win-pc:~$
```

Summary

- The command line can be edited using the ← and → arrow keys and the ⌫ Backspace key.
- A Bash Terminal has two command-editing modes named Emacs and Vi.
- Typically, Bash will start in Emacs command-editing mode but can be entered at any time using a **set -o emacs** command.
- Emacs functions are executed using a **Ctrl** key plus letter key combination or an **Esc** key and letter key sequence.
- Emacs provides functions to edit individual characters, individual words, or the entire command line.
- Emacs provides functions to recall commands by scrolling through the command history or by intelligent search.
- Emacs can perform textual completion of a string at the prompt and provides useful utility functions.
- Vi command-editing mode can be entered at any time using a **set -o vi** command.
- Vi has an Input Mode in which to type command lines, and a Control Mode in which to edit command lines.
- Vi's Control Mode is entered by pressing the **Esc** key and has functions to edit characters, words, or the entire line.
- Vi distinguishes between words containing only alphanumeric characters or underscore, and those containing others.
- Vi's Control Mode has several different exit functions that allow a return to Input Mode at a preferred line position.
- Vi provides functions to recall commands by scrolling or searching and can perform textual completion.
- The Bash **history** command displays a numbered list of command history.
- The Bash **fc** command passes a specified command to the text editor for editing then executes the command on completion.
- History expansion recalls previous commands specifying an event designator, and optionally word designator and modifier.

5 Customizing Environment

This chapter demonstrates how to implement some personal system preferences.

Switching Users

A regular user can call upon most shell commands but some are only available to the privileged root "superuser". These restricted commands typically perform system administration functions to which regular users should not be allowed access in a multi-user environment. For instance, the superuser can use the **reboot** command to immediately restart the system – obviously, it would be undesirable to allow regular users access to this command in a multi-user environment.

The **sudo** command can allow a command to be executed as another user or as the root superuser.

On a typical Linux (Unix-based) system, the user created during installation is given access to the **sudo** command that allows commands to be executed as if they were the superuser. When **sudo** requests a password it requires the user password – not the password of the root superuser:

1. At a shell prompt, enter the command **reboot** to attempt to restart your system

2. If the shell informs you that permission is denied for the **reboot** command, enter the command **sudo reboot**

3. Enter your user password, created during installation, then hit **Return** to immediately restart your system

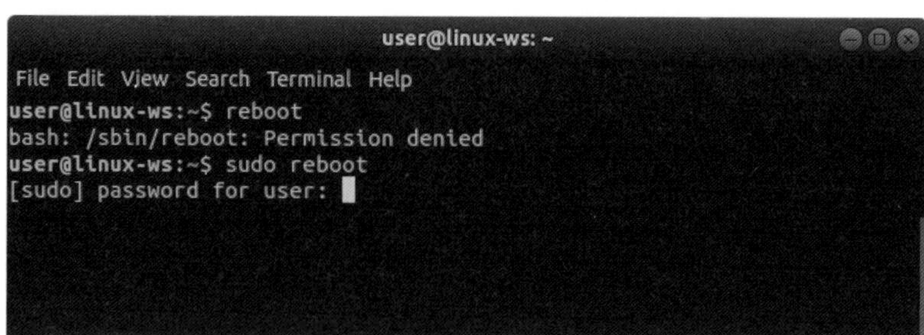
user@linux-ws: ~
File Edit View Search Terminal Help
user@linux-ws:~$ reboot
bash: /sbin/reboot: Permission denied
user@linux-ws:~$ sudo reboot
[sudo] password for user:

This screenshot illustrates a multi-user workstation. Many Linux systems are configured this way but some, such as Linux Mint, are configured as single-user systems that do allow the regular user to execute the **reboot** command. The Windows Subsystem for Linux (WSL) does not allow the Linux user to reboot the host Windows system.

Where the root superuser account is locked by default it can be enabled by providing a password for root with the **passwd** command:

4. Issue the command **sudo passwd root** then enter a password of your choice for the root superuser

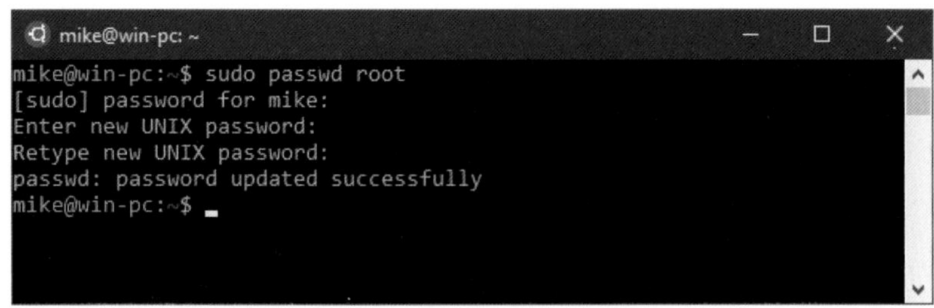

The shell displays no characters for password entries.

Now that the root superuser account is enabled you can log in as root using the **su** command with its - dash option. When a regular user first logs into the shell the working directory is by default that user's home directory. When the superuser logs in with the **su -** command the working directory is the **/root** directory.

The **pwd** command prints the current working directory and the **whoami** command reveals the name of the current user:

5. Enter the **pwd** command to show the current working directory, then enter the **whoami** command to see the name of the current user

6. Enter a **su -** command and log in as the superuser, then enter a **pwd** command to see the current directory now and **whoami** command to see the current user now

7. Log out from the root superuser account by entering the **exit** command – to resume regular user status back in the regular user's home directory

From a root command prompt you can access any file or program on the system – with the potential to wreak havoc! Only log in as root when it is absolutely essential.

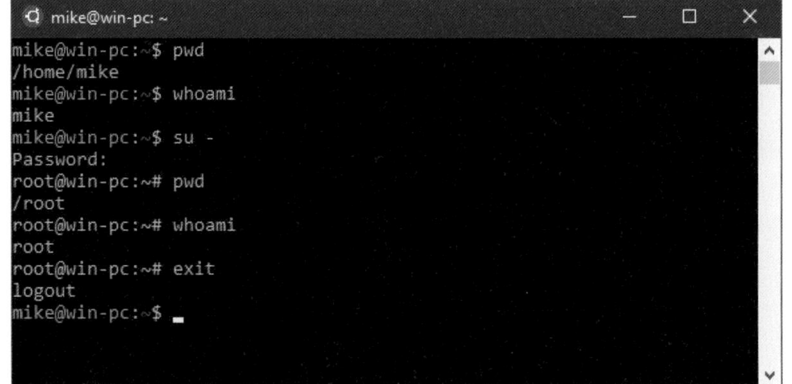

Setting Permissions

On multi-user Linux workstations the root superuser can add a new user by specifying the new user name to a **useradd** command, then allocate that user a password with the **passwd** command. Similarly, a user can be removed by root with a **userdel** command.

Each user is a member of a "group" whose access permissions can be simultaneously modified by the root superuser – for example, to grant the whole group access to some previously inaccessible file. A **groups** command reports to which groups a user belongs.

The root superuser can add a new group by specifying the new group name to a **groupadd** command. Similarly, a group can be removed by root using a **groupdel** command. Root can specify a group and user name to a **usermod -G** command to add that user to that group:

Each group has a unique group ID – you can see the list of all groups and associated IDs using **cat /etc/group | more**.

1. Enter a **groups** command to discover group membership, then enter a **su** command to become the root superuser
2. Issue a **groupadd umbrella** command, to create an "umbrella" group, then **useradd alice** to create a user "alice"
3. Next, enter a **groups alice** command to discover group membership is just "alice" by default in this case
4. Now, issue a **usermod -G umbrella alice** command to make the new user a member of the new "umbrella" group
5. Finally, issue another **groups alice** command to confirm the updated group membership

A group can be renamed using a **groupmod -n** command – for example, **groupmod -n exec alice**.

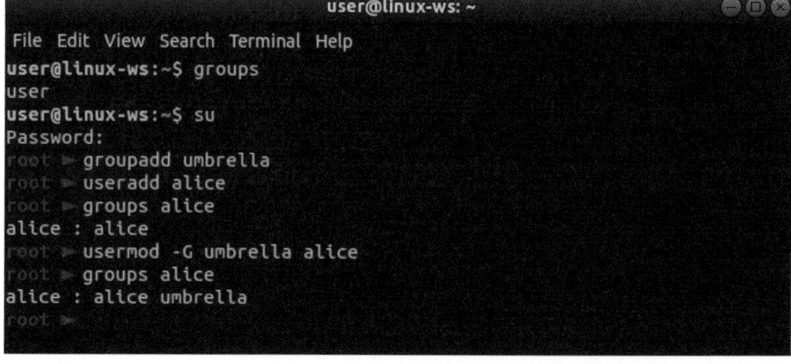

user@linux-ws: ~
File Edit View Search Terminal Help
user@linux-ws:~$ groups
user
user@linux-ws:~$ su
Password:
root ► groupadd umbrella
root ► useradd alice
root ► groups alice
alice : alice
root ► usermod -G umbrella alice
root ► groups alice
alice : alice umbrella
root ►

Each file and directory on a Linux system has access permissions. These can be seen by an **ls -l** long listing command as a string of 10 characters beginning with a **d** (directory) or a - (file). This is followed by sequential **r** (Read), **w** (Write), and **x** (Execute) permissions for the Owner, Group, and Others. Each set of permissions can also be described numerically where Read is 4, Write is 2 and Execute is 1. For instance, a value of 7 describes full permissions to Read, Write and Execute (4 + 2 + 1); 6 describes permissions to Read, Write (4 + 2); and so forth. File permissions can be changed by specifying a numerical value to a **chmod** command, ownership can be changed with a **chown** command, and group changed with a **chgrp** command:

If you are not the Owner of a file you will need to assume root superuser status to change its permissions.

6. Enter an **ls -l** command to see permissions of content in the current directory – in this case see two directories and one file with Read and Write permissions for the Owner

7. Issue a **chown mike script.sh** command to change ownership of the file "script.sh" to user "mike"

8. Next, issue a **chgrp umbrella script.sh** command to change group membership of that file to group "umbrella"

9. Now, issue a **chmod 755 script.sh** command to allow all users to Read and Execute but only the Owner to Write

10. Issue another **ls -l** command to confirm the changes

Do not fall into the habit of setting permissions to 777 – try to maintain useful restrictions.

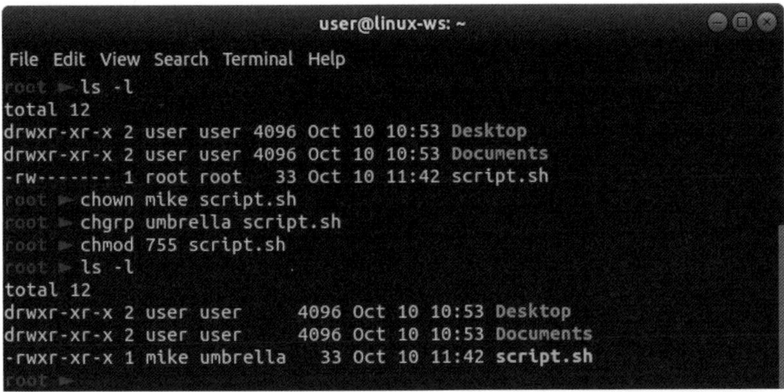

user@linux-ws: ~
File Edit View Search Terminal Help
root ► ls -l
total 12
drwxr-xr-x 2 user user 4096 Oct 10 10:53 Desktop
drwxr-xr-x 2 user user 4096 Oct 10 10:53 Documents
-rw------- 1 root root 33 Oct 10 11:42 script.sh
root ► chown mike script.sh
root ► chgrp umbrella script.sh
root ► chmod 755 script.sh
root ► ls -l
total 12
drwxr-xr-x 2 user user 4096 Oct 10 10:53 Desktop
drwxr-xr-x 2 user user 4096 Oct 10 10:53 Documents
-rwxr-xr-x 1 mike umbrella 33 Oct 10 11:42 script.sh
root ►

Creating Aliases

Convenient aliases can be created for lengthy commands that you use frequently, or that you want to behave in a particular way, simply by specifying **alias *name*='*command*'**. Then, when you enter the alias name at a prompt, the Bash shell will execute the assigned command. For example, you might want to create an alias named "now" to display the current time in 24-hour format:

There must be no space around the = operator in the alias assignment.

1. Enter a **date** command to see a long string output containing the current date and time
2. Issue an **alias now='date +%H:%M'** command to create an alias that extracts the hour and minute date components
3. Now, just issue a **now** command to see the current time

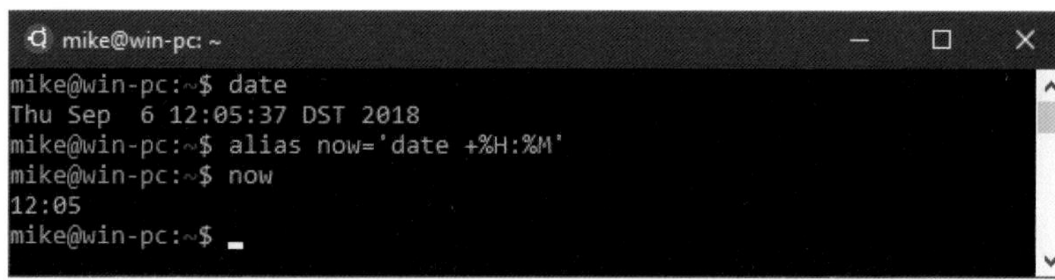

The command must be enclosed within quotes in the alias assignment if it contains spaces. You can specify the alias to be **ls --color=always** to revert to color listing.

If you never want the **ls** command to display the current directory contents in color it can be specified as an alias too:

4. Enter an **ls** command to see the listing in color
5. Issue an **alias ls='ls --color=never'** command to create an alias that lists the current directory in monochrome
6. Enter an **ls** command to see the listing now without color

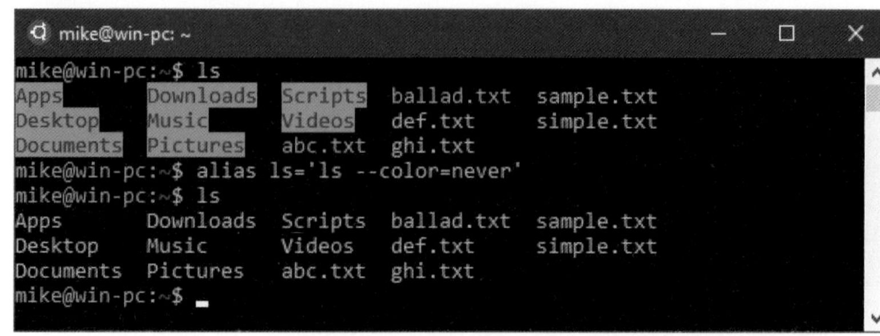

Aliases created in a Terminal will be lost when you exit the session but they can be made permanent by adding them into the **.bashrc** file that is a hidden file within your home directory:

7. In your home directory enter the command **vi .bashrc** to open the **.bashrc** file for editing in the Vi text editor

8. Now, press the **Insert** key and scroll to the end of the file, then add these three alias commands
#ALIASES SECTION
alias now='date +%H:%M'
alias ls='ls --color=never'
alias rm='rm -i'

The **rm** command removes files without warning unless used with an **-i** option to confirm deletion.

9. Next, hit **Esc** and type **:wq** then hit **Return** – to write the changed file and to quit the Vi text editor

10. Then, reopen the Terminal, or enter a **source .bashrc** command, to have it execute the Bash run commands

11. Finally, issue the **now**, **ls**, and **rm** alias commands to see their associated commands get executed

An alias can be removed using the **unalias** command. Other popular aliases include
ll for **'ls -l'** and
.. for **'cd ..'** but you can create any alias you like.

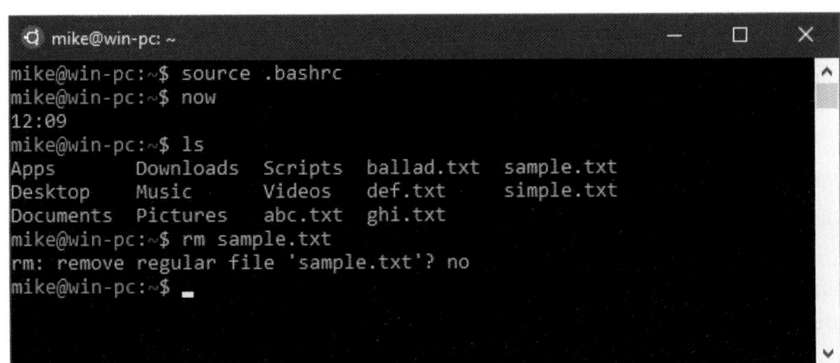

Setting Options

The Bash shell has a number of "options" that can be set on or off to determine whether certain features are available. Some options are turned on by default. The command **set -o** can be used to display a list of options and their current on/off status.

You can enter **help set** to see a description of shell options available to the **set** command.

An option that is turned off can be turned on simply by specifying its name to a **set -o** command. Conversely, an option that is turned on can be turned off by specifying its name to a **set +o** command.

One of the most useful options to turn on is the **noclobber** option that prevents output redirection overwriting an existing file:

1. Enter **echo New Text > file.txt ; cat file.txt** to create a new text file using output redirection and display it
2. Next, enter **echo Updated Text > file.txt ; cat file.txt** to overwrite the file with output redirection and display it
3. Now, issue a **set -o noclobber** command to turn on the noclobber option
4. Then, enter **echo Modified Text > file.txt** to see that the text file can no longer be overwritten by redirected output

A set option will revert to its default on/off status when you exit the Terminal but you can add a **set -o noclobber** command to the **.bashrc** file to always have that option turned on.

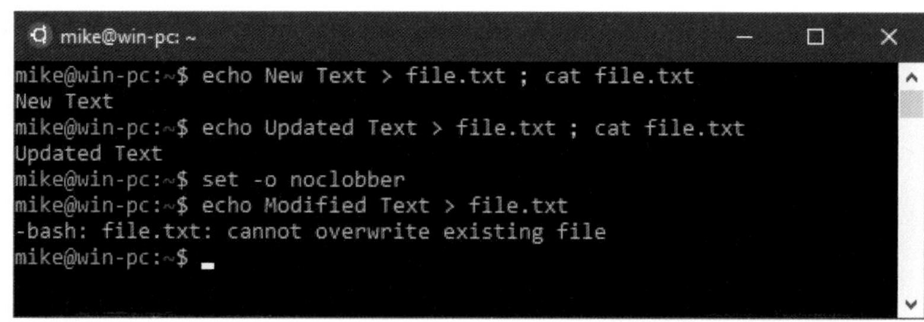

5. Finally, issue a **set +o noclobber** command to turn off the option and see that the text file can be overwritten again

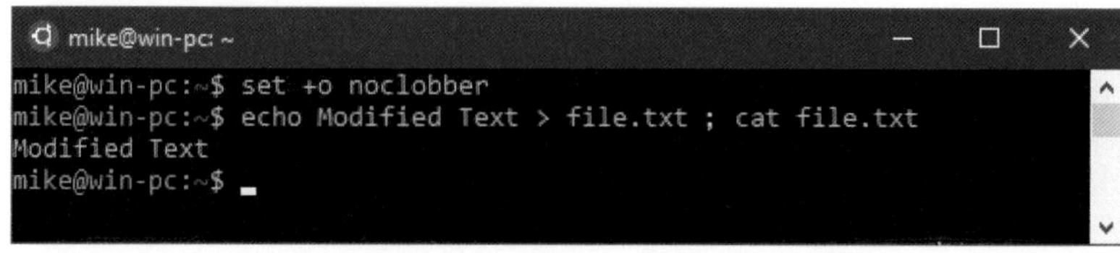

The command **shopt** can be used to display a list of further options and their current on/off status. These options can be set on or off by specifying their name to a **shopt -s** (set) command or a **shopt -u** (unset) command.

One of the most useful of these options to turn on is the **globstar** option that allows recursive listing of directory content using a ** wildcard to include all content of sub-directories:

The **globstar** option is a new feature introduced in Bash version 4.

6. Enter **pwd ; ls** * to list all content of a directory – in this case see it contains two files and two sub-directories

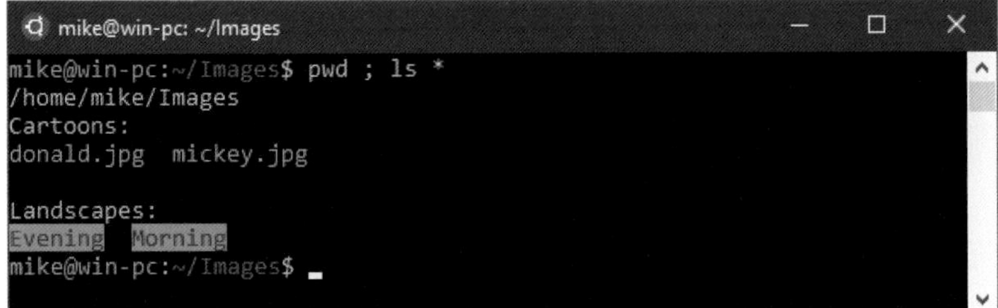

```
mike@win-pc:~/Images$ pwd ; ls *
/home/mike/Images
Cartoons:
donald.jpg  mickey.jpg

Landscapes:
Evening  Morning
mike@win-pc:~/Images$
```

7. Next, issue a **shopt -s globstar** command to turn on the globstar option

8. Now, enter **pwd ; ls** ** to list all content of a directory and also see all content of its sub-directories

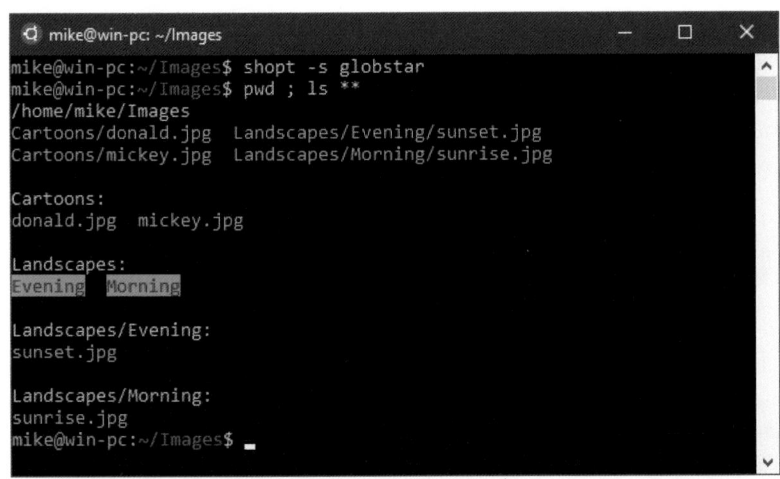

```
mike@win-pc:~/Images$ shopt -s globstar
mike@win-pc:~/Images$ pwd ; ls **
/home/mike/Images
Cartoons/donald.jpg  Landscapes/Evening/sunset.jpg
Cartoons/mickey.jpg  Landscapes/Morning/sunrise.jpg

Cartoons:
donald.jpg  mickey.jpg

Landscapes:
Evening  Morning

Landscapes/Evening:
sunset.jpg

Landscapes/Morning:
sunrise.jpg
mike@win-pc:~/Images$
```

You can add a command **shopt -s globstar** to the **.bashrc** file to always have that option on.

Modifying Variables

In addition to the Bash shell variables that have an on/off state that can be set, there are other shell variables that store a value. These can be modified by assigning a different value to customize how the shell performs. For example, the **EDITOR** shell variable stores the name of the default text editor. You can discover what it is using an **echo $EDITOR** command. Assigning the name of another text editor to the **EDITOR** shell variable will cause that text editor to become the default until you exit the Terminal.

The default editor will also be used by the **fc** command – unless you assign an alternative to an **FCEDIT** shell variable.

Some other shell variables that store values relate to the command history. The **HISTSIZE** variable stores an integer that controls how many past commands to display when you issue a **history** command. By default this is often 500, but can be reduced by assigning a smaller value to the **HISTSIZE** variable:

Enter **HISTSIZE=5** to restrict the number of past commands to be displayed, then issue a **history** command to see just the five most recent commands listed

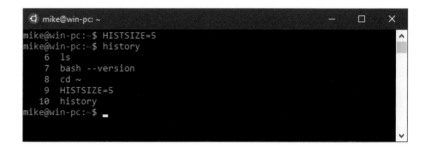

The **HISTFILESIZE** variable stores an integer that controls how many past commands to save in the history file that gets read by the **history** command. By default this is often 500, but can be reduced by assigning a smaller value to the **HISTFILESIZE** variable. The file will then get truncated when you exit the Terminal:

You can add a command **HISTSIZE=5** to the **.bashrc** file to always have that size value.

Enter **HISTFILESIZE=5** to restrict the number of past commands to be saved, then issue an **exit** command to close the Terminal

3 Open a new Terminal then issue another **history** command to see five saved commands plus this latest one

```
mike@win-pc: ~
mike@win-pc:~$ history
    1  cd ~
    2  HISTSIZE=5
    3  history
    4  HISTFILESIZE=5
    5  exit
    6  history
mike@win-pc:~$
```

Command numbering continues for new commands issued at the prompt where commands numbered in the history file end.

The list in the command history file may contain duplicates, like those in the list above, but these can be erased by assigning a value of **erasedups** to a **HISTCONTROL** shell variable:

Enter **HISTCONTROL=erasedups** to remove duplicates from the command history, then issue a **history** command to see five most recent unique commands plus this latest one

```
mike@win-pc: ~
mike@win-pc:~$ HISTCONTROL=erasedups
mike@win-pc:~$ history
    1  cd ~
    2  HISTSIZE=5
    3  HISTFILESIZE=5
    4  exit
    5  HISTCONTROL=erasedups
    6  history
mike@win-pc:~$
```

The **echo $HISTCMD** command will be numbered 7 here – so 8 is the next available.

The next available integer available for command numbering is stored inside a **HISTCMD** shell variable:

Finally, enter **echo $HISTCMD** to discover what number will be given to the next command you issue

Changing Prompts

The Bash command line actually provides four prompt strings whose format is stored in shell variables **PS1**, **PS2**, **PS3**, and **PS4**. The format of prompt strings can be customized to include your preferred information using the commands listed below:

The default PS3 selection prompt string **#?** appears in the programming example on page 142.

Command:	Description:
\A	Current time in 24-hour HH:MM format
\d	Current date as weekday, month, day number
\e	ASCII escape character (033)
\h	Host name
\n	Newline character
\s	Shell name
\T	Current time in 12-hour HH:MM format
\V	Shell version number
\w	Current working directory
\#	Current session command number
\!	Current history command number
n**n**n	Character octal code number
****	Print backslash
\\[	Start sequence of non-printing characters
\\]	End sequence of non-printing characters

The primary prompt string **PS1**, where you enter most commands, can be customized to include a sequence of non-printing characters defining a color. It can also include the command **\u** to display the user name or "root" when assuming superuser status. Many users also like to include the **\w** command to display the current working directory and the **\A** command to display the current time – but it is a matter of personal preference.

The default PS4 debugging prompt string **+** appears in the programming example on page 165.

The **PS2** prompt string is the continuation prompt that appears when entering multi-line commands. This is a > right angle bracket by default but may also be customized. For more decorative prompts you can choose special characters from the font used by your Terminal profile and insert their octal code:

1. Browse the character map for special characters and note their octal character code number – in this case selecting a pointer shape with an octal code of **\342\226\272**

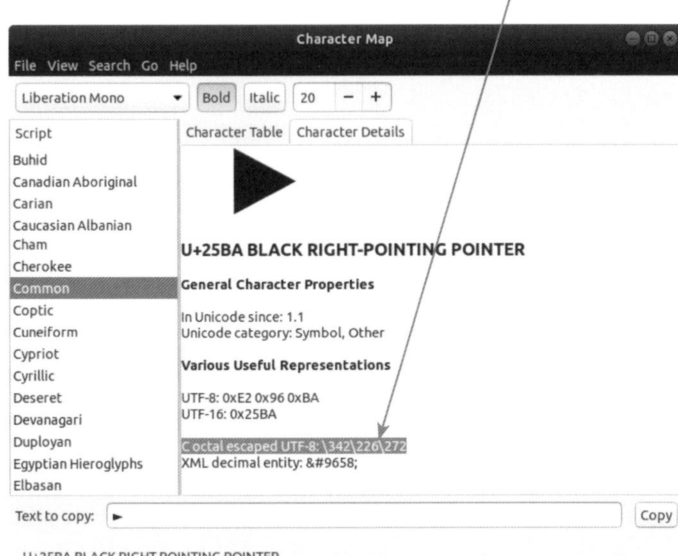

The examples shown here illustrate Bash on Ubuntu Linux – fonts on other systems may be different.

2. Open the **.bashrc** file in a text editor and add these prompt string commands at the end of the file
PS1="\[\e[01;31m\]\u \342\226\272 \e[0m"
PS2="\[\e[01;31m\]\342\226\272 \e[0m"

In this example the non-printing character sequence **\[\e[01;31m\]** colors the user name and special character red, and the non-printing character sequence **\e[0m** prints commands and output in white.

3. Save the file then open a Terminal and enter multi-line commands to see the **PS1** and **PS2** prompt characters

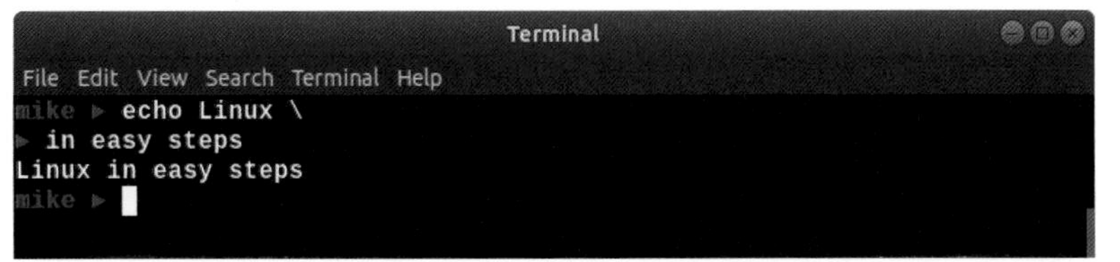

Adjusting Paths

Except for the shell built-in commands all other commands are executable files located somewhere on the Linux filesystem. Entering a non-built-in command obliges the shell to seek the appropriately named file for execution. A : colon-separated search list of directories where it will look is stored in a **PATH** variable. It is useful to customize a Linux system by extending the list of directories in which the shell seeks commands to include other directories where you can place or create other executable files:

Beware

Always append further directories to the end of the existing **PATH** list – the search is made sequentially so it is better to begin with the default locations.

1. Enter **pwd ; ls** commands to see directory and contents then issue an **echo $PATH** command to see the search list
2. Next, enter **ls Apps** to see the contents of an "Apps" sub-directory and see an executable "cprogram" file (in green)

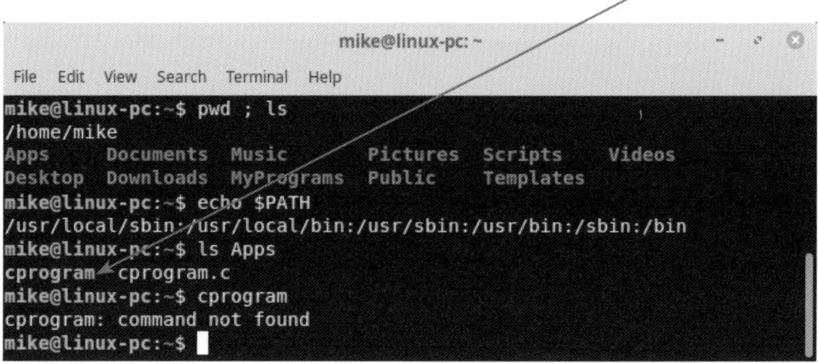

3. Enter **cprogram** to see the shell search fail
4. Enter **PATH=$PATH":/home/mike/Apps"** to add the sub-directory to the search list then **echo $PATH** to confirm
5. Now, enter **cprogram** then hit **Return** to run the executable and see the shell search does now succeed

You can discover how to program in the C language with the companion book **C Programming in easy steps**.

To make a sub-directory readily available whenever you open a Terminal, the extension to the **PATH** search list can be added to the **.bashrc** file in your home directory:

6. Enter **nano .bashrc** to open that file in a text editor, then add **PATH=$PATH":~/Scripts"** to add a sub-directory

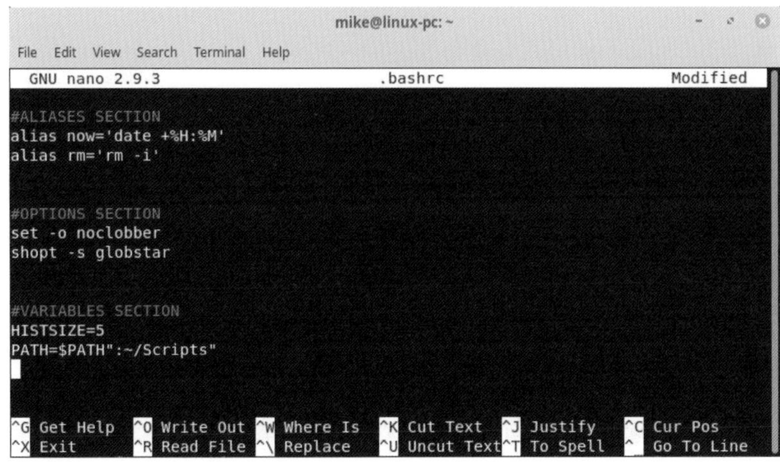

The **.bashrc** file here lists customizations made in this chapter under **#** commented line section headings.

7. Save the file then reopen the Terminal and issue an **echo $PATH** command to confirm the search list

8. Next, enter **ls Scripts** to see the contents of a "Scripts" sub-directory and see an executable "bashscript" file (in green)

9. Enter **bashscript** then hit **Return** to run the executable

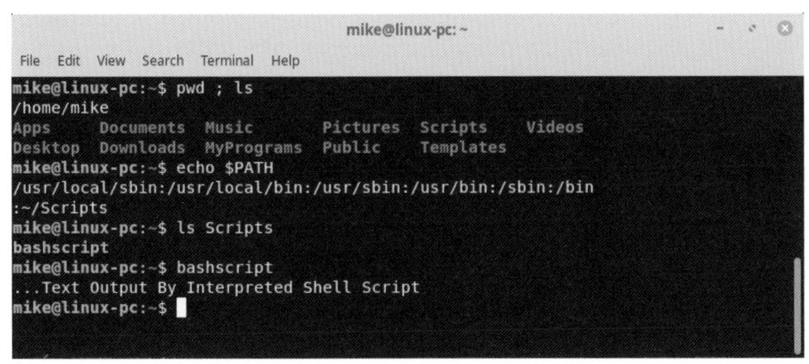

The term "program" sometimes refers to files that have been compiled into machine bytecode for execution, whereas Bash "script" programs can simply remain in text form for execution.

Summary

- System administration functions can be performed by using the **sudo** or **su** commands to assume superuser status.
- Regular user status can be resumed by the **exit** command and the name of the user who began the session with **logname**.
- The superuser can add and delete users with the **useradd** and **userdel** commands, and allocate passwords with **passwd**.
- The superuser can add and delete groups with **groupadd** and **groupdel**, and add a user to a group with **usermod -G**.
- File permissions specify the ability to read, write, and execute a file by its owner, by its group, and by others.
- File permissions can be modified by the superuser and owner by specifying a numerical read, write, execute value to **chmod**.
- File ownership can be changed using the **chown** command and group membership changed using the **chgrp** command.
- An **alias** command provides a name for a specified command.
- Some shell options, such as **noclobber**, have on/off status that can be switched on with **set -o** or switched off with **set +o**.
- Some shell options, such as **globstar**, have on/off status that can be switched on with **shopt -s** or switched off with **shopt -u**.
- Some shell options, such as **HISTSIZE** and **HISTFILESIZE**, store values that can be modified to customize shell performance.
- Prompt strings can be customized to provide a variety of information by modifying the value of their shell variables.
- Adding a directory to the list stored in the **PATH** variable allows the shell to execute programs there from any location.
- Each Terminal session begins by executing commands in the **.bashrc** file to implement preferences for aliases; shell options; prompt string color and format; and shell variables.

6 Controlling Behavior

This chapter demonstrates how to control various behaviors of the Bash shell.

Disabling Defaults

Beware

There is a shell built-in command named **test** that would by default get executed rather than a script of that name.

When executing commands the shell will, by default, first check to see if an alias exists with the specified command name. If it finds no alias the shell will next check to see if a built-in command exists with the specified command name. If it finds no built-in the shell will finally check to see if a program or script exists along the **PATH** list with the specified command name. This means that an alias named the same as a built-in command will, by default, be executed instead of the built-in command:

Enter **alias history='echo ...Text From An Alias'** then issue a **history** command to see only the alias get executed

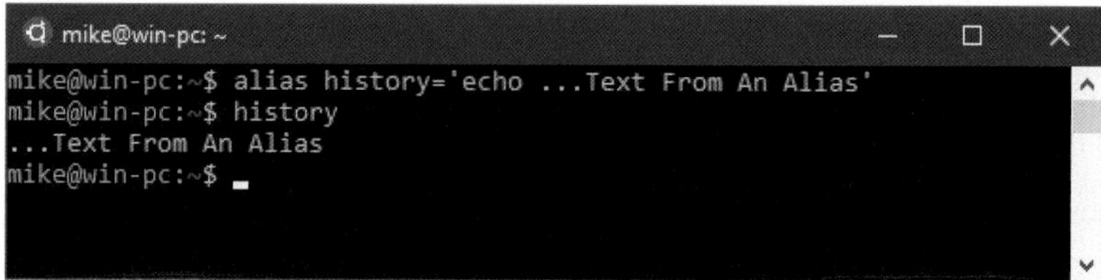
mike@win-pc: ~
mike@win-pc:~$ alias history='echo ...Text From An Alias'
mike@win-pc:~$ history
...Text From An Alias
mike@win-pc:~$

Where an alias exists with the same name as a built-in command you can explicitly execute the built-in with a **command** command:

Issue a **command history** command to ignore the "history" alias and to execute the built-in **history** command instead

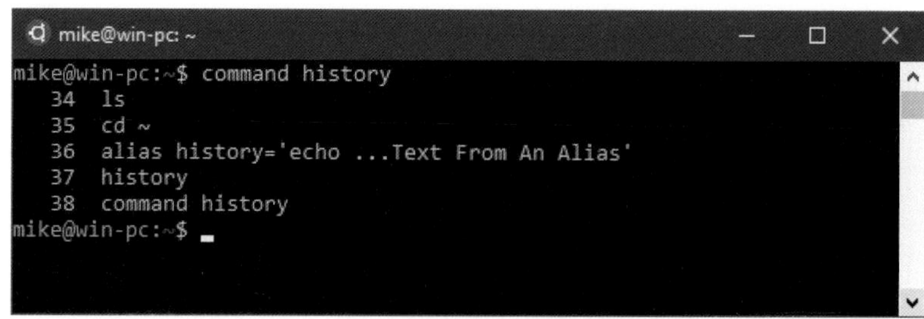
mike@win-pc: ~
mike@win-pc:~$ command history
34 ls
35 cd ~
36 alias history='echo ...Text From An Alias'
37 history
38 command history
mike@win-pc:~$

Hot tip

The **command** command ignores only aliases but the **builtin** command ignores both aliases and scripts along the path.

The shell built-in commands are all enabled by default but can be individually disabled by specifying a command name to an **enable -n** command. A disabled command can be re-enabled by specifying its name to the **enable** command without an option. Issuing an **enable -n** command without a command name argument usefully displays a list of all disabled commands.

Where a script exists along the **PATH** with the same name as a built-in command you can execute that script by first disabling the built-in command:

3. Enter **enable -n history** to disable the built-in **history** command then enter **command history** to ignore the like-named alias and see a like-named script get executed

```
mike@win-pc: ~
mike@win-pc:~$ enable -n history
mike@win-pc:~$ command history
...Text Output By An Interpreted Shell Script
mike@win-pc:~$
```

This assumes a script named "history" has been placed in the "Scripts" directory that gets added to **PATH** by the example on page 95.

Where a built-in command has been disabled you can explicitly execute the built-in with a **builtin** command:

4. Issue an **enable -n** command to list all disabled commands and confirm that the **history** command is disabled

5. Now, enter **builtin history** to explicitly execute the built-in **history** command, but see the attempt fail

```
mike@win-pc: ~
mike@win-pc:~$ enable -n
enable -n history
mike@win-pc:~$ builtin history
-bash: builtin: history: not a shell builtin
mike@win-pc:~$ enable history
mike@win-pc:~$ builtin history
  101  clear
  102  enable -n
  103  builtin history
  104  enable history
  105  builtin history
mike@win-pc:~$
```

Add an **enable -n** command to the **.bashrc** file if you want to automatically disable a command for each Terminal session.

6. Issue an **enable history** command to re-enable the disabled command

7. Now, enter **builtin history** to explicitly execute the built-in **history** command, and see the attempt succeed

Formatting Output

A more powerful alternative to the **echo** command is provided by the **printf** command that allows you to specify how input should be formatted for output. A string supplied to a **printf** command is sent to standard output without an added newline character but one can be added to the end of the string as a **\n** escape sequence – for example, with a command of **printf "Bash in easy steps \n"**.

String arguments that contain spaces must be enclosed within quotes or each word will be output individually.

Additionally, a string supplied to a **printf** command may contain one or more format specifiers. Subsequent arguments following the string will be substituted and formatted in the output – for example, with a command of **printf "%s \n" "Bash in easy steps"**. Other possible format specifiers are listed in the table below:

Specifier:	Format Output:	Example:
%c	Character	C
%s	String	Unix
%d	Decimal integer	-10
%f	Floating-point number	7.50
%u	Unsigned decimal integer	10
%x	Unsigned hexadecimal with a-f	0x5b
%X	Unsigned hexadecimal with A-F	0x5B
%o	Unsigned octal number	0200

You can have a field width padded with leading zeroes by including a **0** zero in the field width value – for example, **"%010s \n"**.

A format specifier may also include a numerical field width value immediately after the **%** character. A positive value will add spaces before the output where it is less than the field size (right justify); a negative value will add spaces after the output where it is less than field size (left justify) – for example, **"%10s \n"** or **"%-10s \n"**. Output doesn't get truncated when it is greater than the field size.

For floating-point numbers a format specifier may additionally include a precision value immediately after the **%** character. This is a period (full stop) . followed by a numerical value specifying how many digits should appear after the decimal point. For example, **"%.2f \n"** formats to two decimal places. Output is rounded for the final digit if necessary. Where a field size is included the precision value must immediately follow that. For example, **"%10.2f \n"** formats to two decimal places in a 10 width field.

1. Enter **printf "Float: %f \n" 7.5** to output a floating-point and see it output with six decimal places

2. Next, edit the command to include a **.2** precision specifier and see the output with two decimal places

```
mike@win-pc: ~
mike@win-pc:~$ printf "Float: %f \n" 7.5
Float: 7.500000
mike@win-pc:~$ printf "Float: %.2f \n" 7.5
Float: 7.50
mike@win-pc:~$
```

You can have numbers output with + or - signs by including a **+** character at the start of the specifier – for example, **"%+.2f \n"**.

3. Enter **printf "|%30s| \n" "Right Justified"** to output a string with spaces added in front

4. Next, edit the command by changing the field width to **-30** and see the output string with spaces added behind

```
mike@win-pc: ~
mike@win-pc:~$ printf "|%30s| \n" "Right Justified"
|               Right Justified|
mike@win-pc:~$ printf "|%-30s| \n" "Left Justified"
|Left Justified                |
mike@win-pc:~$
```


The **printf** command is useful to convert numbers to base 8 (octal), base 10 (decimal), or base 16 (hexadecimal) equivalents. For example, to convert hexadecimal code values to an escaped octal sequence to include a special character in a prompt string:

The output octal sequence is the same one that is used to include the pointer character in the prompt string on page 93.

5. Type **printf "\\%o"** to output a backslash and octal number then type three hexadecimal arguments **0xE2 0x96 0xBA**

6. Now, type **; printf "\n"** to add a final newline then hit **Return** to perform the conversion

```
mike@win-pc: ~
mike@win-pc:~$ printf "\\%o" 0xE2 0x96 0xBA ; printf "\n"
\342\226\272
mike@win-pc:~$
```

Reading Input

Input can be gathered from the command line or from a file by the **read** command. Used alone, this will pause awaiting input that is by default assigned to a **REPLY** shell variable. Optionally, a prompt message can be displayed by specifying the message string after an **-p** option to the **read** command. Input that is longer than the Terminal screen width can be read using a \ backslash continuation character but this can be overridden by specifying a **-r** argument to the **read** command to preserve escape sequences:

The **read** and **echo** commands provide the shell's basic I/O input/output facilities.

1. Issue a **read** command then hit **Return** and enter some text input – hit **Return** again to finish

2. Next, enter **echo $REPLY** to see the stored input text

```
mike@win-pc: ~
mike@win-pc:~$ read
Bash in easy steps
mike@win-pc:~$ echo $REPLY
Bash in easy steps
mike@win-pc:~$
```

The **read -p** command is mostly useful from a shell script to prompt the user for input to be stored in a variable.

3. Now, issue a **read -p** command with a prompt message then hit **Return** and enter some text input

```
mike@win-pc: ~
mike@win-pc:~$ read -p 'Choose A Directory: '
Choose A Directory: /home/mike/Pictures
mike@win-pc:~$ echo $REPLY
/home/mike/Pictures
mike@win-pc:~$
```

4. Then, issue a **read -r** command then hit **Return** and enter some text input containing escape sequences to preserve

mike@win-pc: ~
mike@win-pc:~$ read -r
One\nTwo\nThree
mike@win-pc:~$ echo -e $REPLY
One
Two
Three
mike@win-pc:~$

...cont'd

Input can be stored in a variable name of your choice by specifying a variable name to the **read** command. Multiple variable names can also be specified and the input will be split around delimiting space characters:

5. Issue a **read flavor version** command then hit **Return** and enter two items of text to be stored in named variables

6. Next, enter **echo $flavor** and **echo $version** to see the stored input text

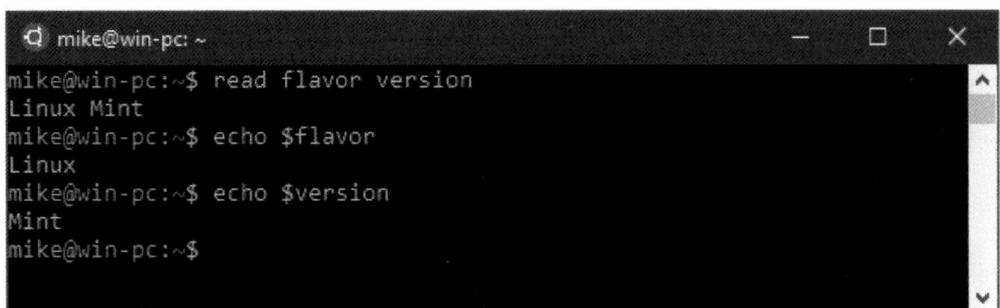
mike@win-pc: ~
mike@win-pc:~$ read flavor version
Linux Mint
mike@win-pc:~$ echo $flavor
Linux
mike@win-pc:~$ echo $version
Mint
mike@win-pc:~$

Don't forget

Where the number of text items exceeds the number of named variables the excess text items all get stored in the final named variable.

A text file can be input to a **read** command by using the **<** input redirection operator to specify the file name. The text will by default be assigned to the **REPLY** shell variable or you may specify a variable name of your choice to the **read** command. Multiple variable names can be specified and the input will be split around delimiting space characters, or you may specify an alternative delimiting character after an **-d** option to the **read** command:

7. Issue a **read < csv.txt** command to input text from a file

8. Finally, issue a **read -d , num < csv.txt** command to input text from a file split around a comma delimiter character into a named variable

```
mike@win-pc: ~
mike@win-pc:~$ read < csv.txt
mike@win-pc:~$ echo $REPLY
One,Two,Three,Four,Five
mike@win-pc:~$ read -d , num < csv.txt
mike@win-pc:~$ echo $num
One
mike@win-pc:~$
```

Hot tip

The **read** command also supports a **-n** argument that can be used to specify how many characters to read input.

Substituting Commands

The technique of "command substitution" allows the output from a command to be used as input to another command, rather than sent to standard output, by enclosing the command whose output is to be redirected within the parentheses of a **$()** statement. For example, **echo $(pwd)** prints the current directory and is equivalent to the shell environment variable **$PWD**.

Beware

The archaic form of command substitution enclosed the command within ` ` backtick characters – but this should not be used now to avoid nesting issues.

Expansion of the inner command is performed first to substitute the standard output of the command but with any trailing newlines deleted. Embedded newlines are not deleted although they may be removed during word splitting. Embedded newlines can, however, be preserved by enclosing a command substitution within double quotes so that word splitting is not performed:

1. Enter **echo -e "One\nTwo\nThree\n" > nums.txt** to create a text file containing embedded and trailing newlines

2. Next, issue a **cat nums.txt** command to display the file contents on standard output and see the newlines appear

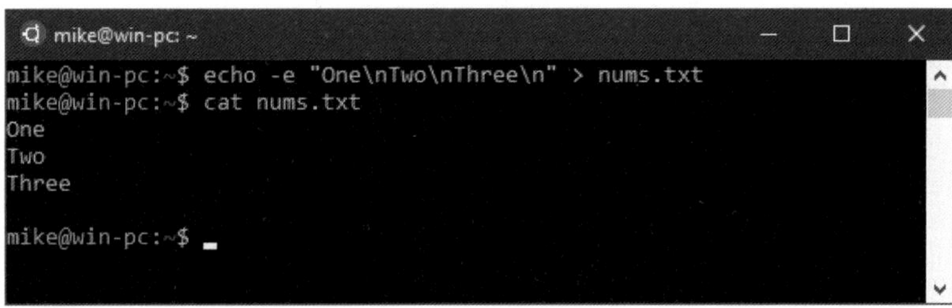
mike@win-pc: ~
mike@win-pc:~$ echo -e "One\nTwo\nThree\n" > nums.txt
mike@win-pc:~$ cat nums.txt
One
Two
Three
mike@win-pc:~$

3. Now, issue an **echo $(cat nums.txt)** command to substitute the file contents and see all newlines removed in output

Hot tip

The command substitution **$(cat *file*)** can be replaced by the equivalent but faster statement **$(< *file*)**.

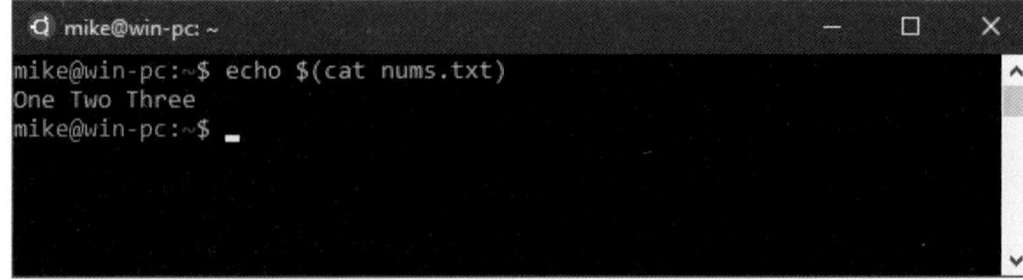
mike@win-pc: ~
mike@win-pc:~$ echo $(cat nums.txt)
One Two Three
mike@win-pc:~$

4. Then, issue an **echo -e "$(cat nums.txt)"** command to substitute file contents and see a trailing newline removed

```
mike@win-pc: ~
mike@win-pc:~$ echo -e "$(cat nums.txt)"
One
Two
Three
mike@win-pc:~$
```

You must use double-quote characters to allow substitution, not single-quote characters.

A string containing a command substitution can be assigned to a named variable to store its value after substitution has been made. It should be noted that each command substitution is actually performed in a "subshell" that has its own parcel of memory in which to hold values. This means that any changes to variables or the current directory inside the command substitution affect only the rest of that substitution and not the parent shell:

5. Enter a **var="Time is $(date +%H:%M)"** command to store a string containing the current time in a variable

```
mike@win-pc: ~
mike@win-pc:~$ var="Time is $(date +%H:%M)"
mike@win-pc:~$ echo $var
Time is 07:30
mike@win-pc:~$
```

6. Now, enter **var=$(cd Documents ; pwd)** to store the path of a sub-directory in a variable from within a subshell

7. Finally, issue a **pwd** command to confirm that the current working directory is unchanged

Command substitutions can be nested – to supply substituted output to successive outer commands.

```
mike@win-pc: ~
mike@win-pc:~$ var=$(cd Documents ; pwd)
mike@win-pc:~$ echo $var
/home/mike/Documents
mike@win-pc:~$ pwd
/home/mike
mike@win-pc:~$
```

Managing Jobs

The **xeyes** program is a simple fun application that follows the cursor around the Desktop and the **xcalc** program is a handy graphical calculator application. Both are part of an "x11-apps" package that might be installed using the command **sudo apt install x11-apps** if it's not already available on a Linux system, but the x11-apps cannot run in the WSL environment.

Linux is a multi-tasking operating system that can execute multiple tasks (jobs) alongside each other as individual processes that run almost simultaneously. For example, the user can run a web browser alongside a text editor and a Terminal window. Most graphical Linux programs can be run from a command prompt in a Terminal window using the program name:

Type **xeyes** then hit **Return** to run the "xeyes" program – notice that the command prompt does not reappear

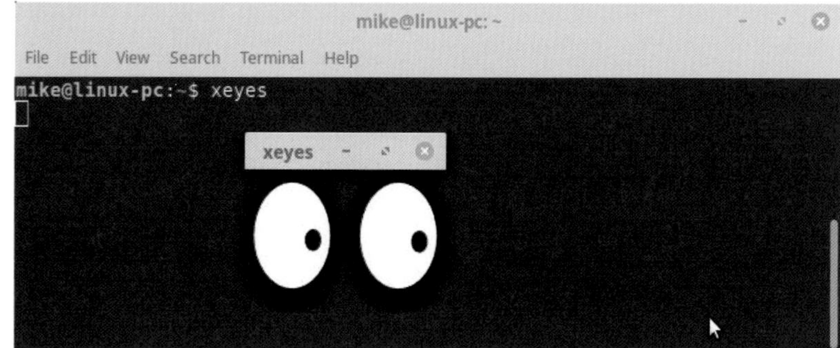

The program is running in the current process but can instead be run as a background job by appending an **&** ampersand after the program name in the launch command:

Close the program window to see the prompt return, then enter **xeyes &** to launch the program as a background job

Here this program is job number 1 and process number 1872. You can see a list of all processes using the **ps** command.

The command prints out the job number [in square brackets] and the process number, then the command prompt reappears. A list of all jobs can be seen at any time using a **jobs** command.

3. Enter **xcalc &** to launch a second background program job then issue a **jobs** command to see a list of all jobs

A background job can be brought to the foreground with a **fg** command followed by a **%** character and the job number. Once in the foreground a job can be stopped by pressing **Ctrl** + **C** keys or suspended by pressing **Ctrl** + **Z** keys. A suspended job can be resumed by sending it to the background with a **bg** command followed by a **%** character and the job number:

4. Next, enter **fg %1** to see the running "xeyes" program name displayed – then press **Ctrl** + **C** to stop this job

5. Now, enter **fg %2** to see the running "xcalc" program name displayed – then press **Ctrl** + **Z** to suspend this job

6. Issue a **bg %2** command to return the suspended job to the background and resume its execution

7. Finally, issue another **jobs** command to confirm that the "xcalc" program is running once more

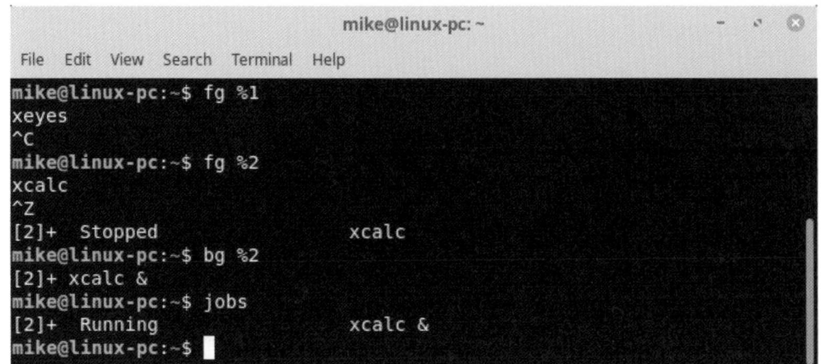

Jobs can be any long-running commands, scripts, or programs.

The symbols after the job number indicate the current job (+) and the previous job (-).

Killing Processes

The ability to control jobs, described in the previous example, applies only to processes started by yourself from the current Terminal – in other words, only those processes that you "own".

All processes started from the current Terminal can also be listed using the **ps** command. Additionally this can accept an **-a** (all) option to list all processes including those from other Terminals – including those processes that you do not "own".

Hot tip

A process can be disowned by specifying its **%** job number or its process number to a **disown** command.

Usefully, the **ps** command lists the process number, Terminal number, time used, and command name of running processes. Individual processes can be terminated by specifying their process number to a **kill** command:

1. Launch a Terminal and enter **xeyes &** to launch a program in the background
2. Next, issue a **ps** command to see this Terminal's running processes are the **bash** shell, **xeyes** and **ps** programs

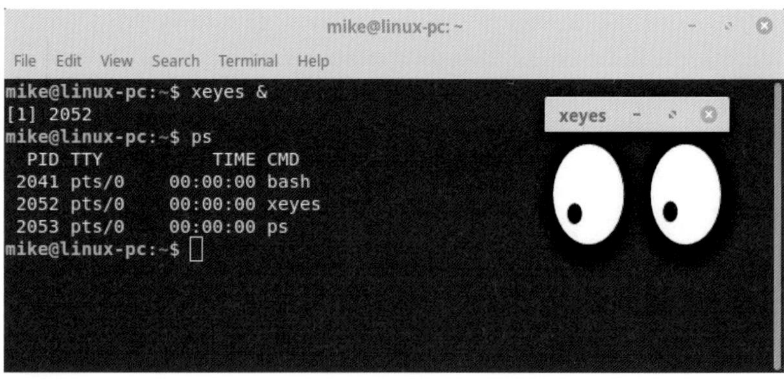
mike@linux-pc: ~
File Edit View Search Terminal Help
mike@linux-pc:~$ xeyes &
[1] 2052
mike@linux-pc:~$ ps
PID TTY TIME CMD
2041 pts/0 00:00:00 bash
2052 pts/0 00:00:00 xeyes
2053 pts/0 00:00:00 ps
mike@linux-pc:~$
xeyes

Beware

Listed time is processor time – it is zero here as negligible time is used.

3. Now, launch another Terminal and enter **xcalc &** to launch another program in the background
4. Then, issue a **ps** command to see that Terminal's running processes are the **bash** shell, **xcalc** and **ps** programs

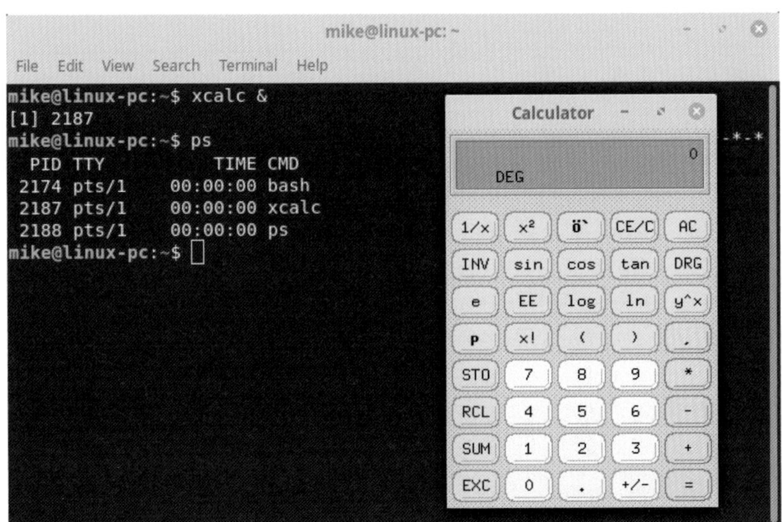

Notice that each **ps** process has a unique number here as it gets allocated each time that program runs.

5. Issue a **ps -a** command in the first Terminal to see the running processes are the **xeyes**, **xcalc** and **ps** programs

6. Issue a **kill 2187** command in the first Terminal to terminate the **xcalc** program

7. Finally, issue another **ps -a** command to see only the **xeyes** and **ps** programs remain as running processes

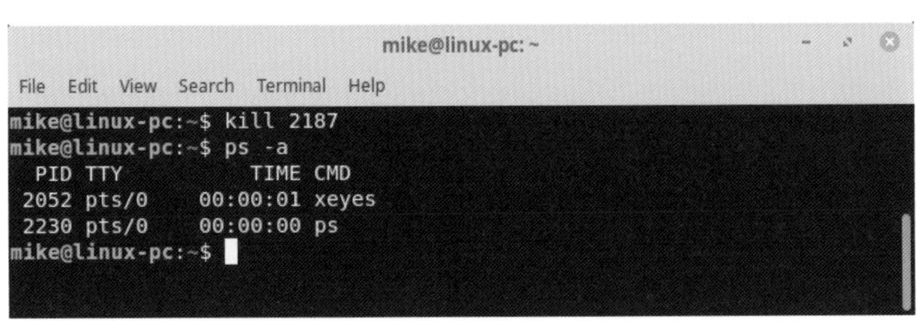

The **ps -a** command lists all processes except the session leader (**bash**) and processes not associated with any Terminal.

Communicating Routines

Hot tip

Older Unix-based systems use the **mknod** program to create named pipes.

The ability to send the output from one command as input to another via a pipeline is undoubtedly one of the most useful features of Bash. It allows separate processes to communicate with each other so they can be combined in complex ways. For example, the pipeline **ls | grep D** runs a routine with the **ls** program to generate a list of all contents in the current directory, then runs a routine with the **grep** program that reads the generated list and prints only those lines containing the letter "D". These routines use an "unnamed pipe" that exists only inside the kernel and cannot be accessed by the **bash** shell process that created it.

mike@win-pc: ~
mike@win-pc:~$ ls | grep D
Desktop
Documents
Downloads
mike@win-pc:~$

Another sort of pipe is a "named pipe". This is also known as a "FIFO" (First In, First Out), as the order of bytes going into the pipe is the same coming out. A named pipe is created simply by specifying a name of your choice to the **mkfifo** command. The named pipe is created in the current directory and its properties can be examined using the **ls -l** command, like all other content. Named pipes have a "p" in the listed leftmost column to indicate they are a pipe, and permissions control who can read or write to the pipe, just like a regular file.

Beware

Where a blocked pipe has no receiver the process will "hang" but can be terminated by pressing **Ctrl** + **C** keys.

Output can be sent to a named pipe using the **>** output redirection operator and can be received from a named pipe using the **<** input redirection operator. When output gets sent to a named pipe the kernel suspends that process until a second process connects to that pipe for reception. The first process is said to be "blocked" until the connection has been made and both processes terminate:

1. Enter **mkfifo mypipe** to create a pipe named "mypipe"
2. Now, issue an **ls -l mypipe** command to examine the properties of the named pipe you have created

```
mike@win-pc:~$ mkfifo mypipe
mike@win-pc:~$ ls -l mypipe
prw-rw-rw- 1 mike mike 0 Sep 27 08:30 mypipe
mike@win-pc:~$
```

3. Next, enter **ls > mypipe** to run a routine that sends a list of current directory contents to the named pipe – see the process get suspended in the Terminal

mike@win-pc: ~
mike@win-pc:~$ ls > mypipe

Don't forget

This example can also be performed by issuing **grep D < mypipe** first so it will be suspended until **ls > mypipe** is issued in the other Terminal.

4. Launch a second Terminal then issue a **ps -a** command to list running processes and see the suspended **bash** process on the first Terminal

5. Now, enter **grep D < mypipe** to run a routine that receives input from the named pipe and prints only those lines containing the letter "D"

6. Finally, issue another **ps -a** command to list running processes and see the **bash** process on the first Terminal has now terminated

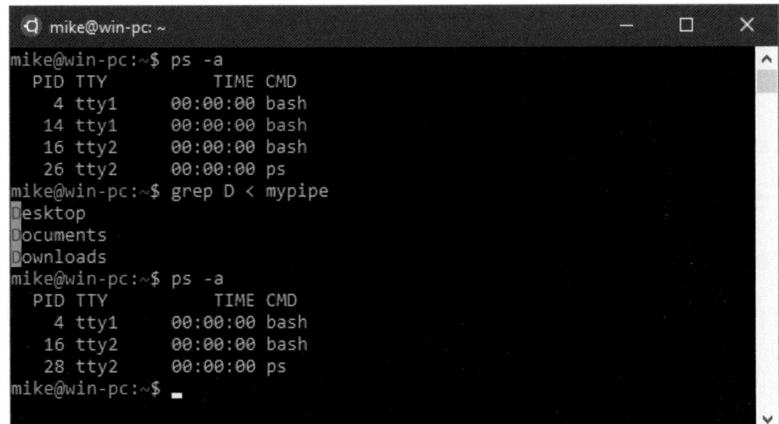
mike@win-pc: ~
mike@win-pc:~$ ps -a
PID TTY TIME CMD
4 tty1 00:00:00 bash
14 tty1 00:00:00 bash
16 tty2 00:00:00 bash
26 tty2 00:00:00 ps
mike@win-pc:~$ grep D < mypipe
Desktop
Documents
Downloads
mike@win-pc:~$ ps -a
PID TTY TIME CMD
4 tty1 00:00:00 bash
16 tty2 00:00:00 bash
28 tty2 00:00:00 ps
mike@win-pc:~$

NEW

Bash version 4 introduced the **coproc** keyword that can also be used to provide communicating routines.

Relating Shells

When you launch a Terminal a new **bash** shell process gets started that is given its own unique process ID number. Another shell process ("subshell") can be started by issuing a command surrounded by parentheses from within the first shell. This will be given its own unique process ID number. The shell's **bash** process ID that is listed when you issue a **ps** command is actually stored in a **BASHPID** shell variable – so can also be found by issuing an **echo $BASHPID** command:

Beware

There is also a shell variable **$$** that contains the process ID of the parent shell or that of the script when it is used in a shell script – so the command **(echo $$)** will return the process ID of the parent shell.

1. Launch a Terminal and issue a **ps** command to see the shell's **bash** process ID number
2. Next, enter an **echo $BASHPID** command to confirm the shell's **bash** process ID number – in this case it's 4
3. Now, enter an **(echo $BASHPID)** command to start a subshell and see its **bash** process ID number – here it's 31

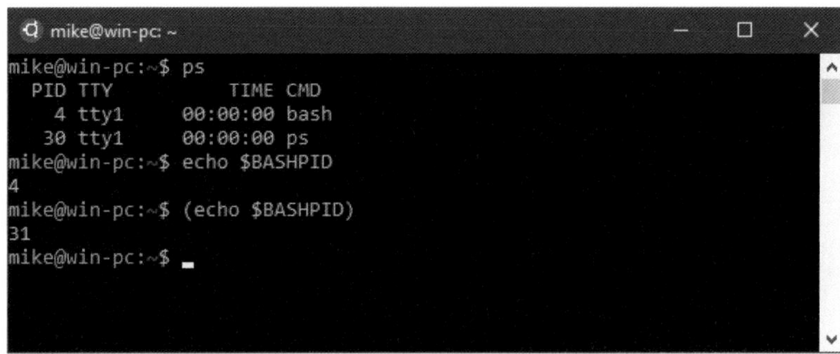
mike@win-pc: ~
mike@win-pc:~$ ps
PID TTY TIME CMD
4 tty1 00:00:00 bash
30 tty1 00:00:00 ps
mike@win-pc:~$ echo $BASHPID
4
mike@win-pc:~$ (echo $BASHPID)
31
mike@win-pc:~$

These two shell processes have a hierarchical parent-child relationship in which the child subshell inherits the following features from its parent shell:

- Current working directory (**pwd**).
- Standard Input/Output (**stdin, stdout, stderr**).
- Environment variables (**printenv**).

Note that the subshell does not automatically inherit variables created in the parent shell – so like-named variables of different values can happily exist in each shell process.

Hot tip

The visibility and accessibility of variables within a particular environment is known as variable "scope".

Shell scripts always run in subshells of the parent shell in which they are called, which allows multiple scripts to be run simultaneously. They may also be run in the background by appending an **&** ampersand after the script name in the command. A **wait** command can usefully be entered in a parent shell to ensure background scripts finish before continuing on:

This script outputs a message including its **$BASHPID** value when it starts and ends, silently counting 60 seconds between each message.

4. Launch a Terminal and enter **./count60.sh &** to run a script named "count60.sh" in the background – see it display its unique **bash** process ID (295) and start time

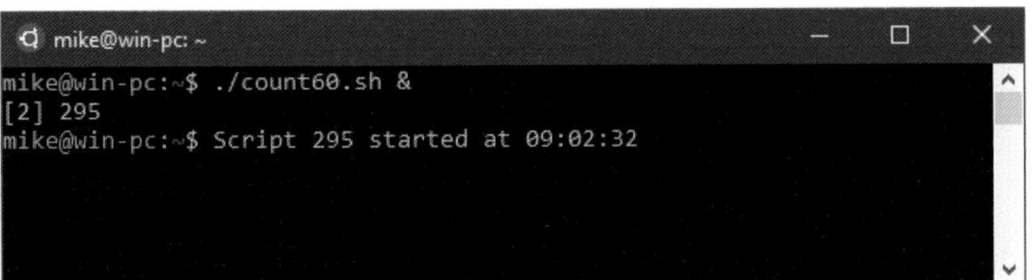

mike@win-pc: ~
mike@win-pc:~$ ./count60.sh &
[2] 295
mike@win-pc:~$ Script 295 started at 09:02:32

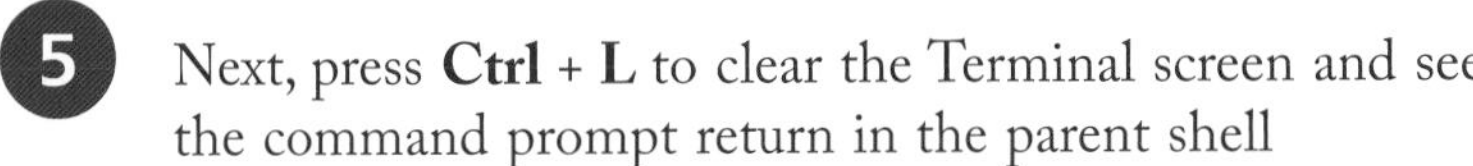

5. Next, press **Ctrl** + **L** to clear the Terminal screen and see the command prompt return in the parent shell

6. Now, issue an **echo $BASHPID** command to confirm that the parent shell has a different **bash** process ID (4) to that of the subshell in which the script is running

7. Enter a **wait** command to ensure the parent shell waits until the script running in the background ends – see it display its unique **bash** process ID (295) and end time

```
mike@win-pc: ~
mike@win-pc:~$ echo $BASHPID
4
mike@win-pc:~$ wait
Script 295 ended at 09:03:35
[2]-  Done                    ./count60
mike@win-pc:~$ _
```

Background scripts may appear to hang without the **wait** command ensuring completion.

Summary

- The order of command execution first seeks an alias of the specified name, then a built-in, then a program on the **PATH**.
- Built-in commands can be disabled using an **enable -n** command or enabled using a plain **enable** command.
- A disabled built-in command can be explicitly executed using the **builtin** command.
- The **printf** command allows input to be formatted for output and may contain one or more format specifiers.
- Floating-point numbers can be formatted for precision by the **printf** command to determine their number of decimal places.
- Input can be gathered from the command line by the **read** command that by default stores the input in a **REPLY** variable.
- Values stored in a variable can be accessed by prefixing a **$** character before the variable name.
- Input can be gathered from a text file by the **read** command using the **<** input redirection operator.
- Command substitution has the syntax **$()** and allows output from one command to be used as input to another command.
- Jobs can be run in the background by adding an **&** ampersand after their name in the run command.
- The **jobs** command shows all jobs that may be moved between foreground and background with the **fg** and **bg** commands.
- Foreground jobs can be stopped by pressing the **Ctrl** + **C** keys or suspended by pressing the **Ctrl** + **Z** keys.
- The **ps** command shows processes started from the current Terminal that can be terminated by a **kill** command.
- A named pipe can be created by the **mkfifo** program to allow routines to communicate with each other.
- Commands can be made to run in a subshell by enclosing the command within **( )** parentheses.
- Shell scripts always run in a subshell of the parent shell in which they are called and have their own unique **BASHPID**.

7 Performing Operations

This chapter demonstrates shell operators that perform arithmetic, manipulation, and comparison.

Storing Values

A "variable" is simply a container in which a data value can be stored inside the computer's memory. A variable is created in the Bash shell by assigning a data value to a variable name of your choice, using the = assignment operator. The stored data value can then be referenced using that variable's name prefixed by a **$** character. The stored value can be changed by making a further assignment and its new value referenced with a **$** prefix as before:

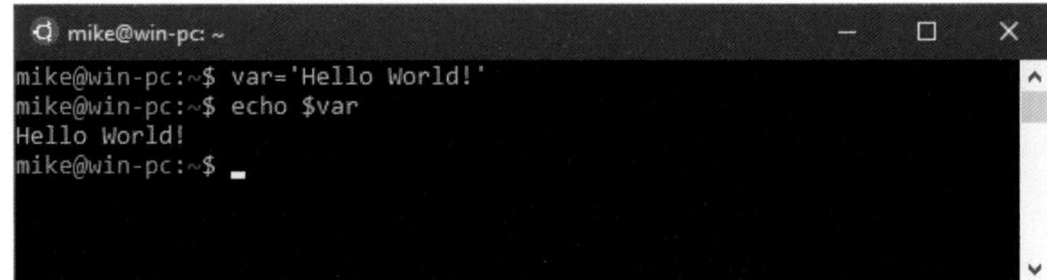
mike@win-pc: ~
mike@win-pc:~$ var='Hello World!'
mike@win-pc:~$ echo $var
Hello World!
mike@win-pc:~$

Beware

There must be no spaces around the = assignment operator – so use **var=data** rather than **var = data**.

Storing data in variables is mostly useful in shell scripts rather than on the command line. Shell scripts are just plain text files that begin with a "shebang" line that defines that file as a shell script and indicates the path to the shell interpreter, like this:

#!/bin/bash

All ensuing lines in a script can then contain commands and assignments just like those you can enter at the command prompt:

```
mike@win-pc: ~
#!/bin/bash

var='Hello World!'
echo $var
~
~
"hello.sh" [New] 4L, 42C written                4,9            All
```

Don't forget

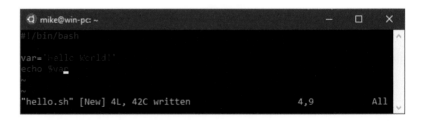

If you try to execute a script that does not have executable permission Bash will simply produce a "Permission denied" error message.

After saving the script it must be made executable before it can run by setting its file permissions with a **chmod +x** command. This is equivalent to permissions of 711 allowing only the owner to read and write the script, but allowing anyone to execute it.

Unless the current directory containing the shell script is included in the **PATH** variable list it can only be executed by prefixing its filename by ./ on the command line. This instructs the shell to execute only in the current directory instead of on the **PATH**:

```
mike@win-pc: ~
mike@win-pc:~$ chmod +x hello.sh
mike@win-pc:~$ ./hello.sh
Hello World!
mike@win-pc:~$
```

The **.sh** file extension is not essential, as the shebang line describes the file as being a script, but it makes it easily recognizable with **ls *.sh**.

Input can be stored in a variable using the **read** command just as it is used on the command line. Additionally, Bash provides a number of special built-in variables called "positional parameters". These automatically store the values of arguments passed to the script from the command line whenever the script is executed. Positional parameters are named **1**, **2**, **3**; etc. so their values can be retrieved using **$1**, **$2**, **$3**; etc. Additionally, positional parameter **$0** retrieves the first part of the command (containing the script name), **$@** retrieves a space-separated list of all passed values, and **$#** retrieves an integer that is the total number of passed values:

1. Open any plain text editor and precisely type this script

```
#!/bin/bash
echo -n 'Please enter your name: '
read var
echo "Welcome to $@ , $var"
```

param.sh

2. Next, save the script as "param.sh" then issue the command **chmod +x param.sh** to make the file executable

3. Now, enter **./param.sh Bash in easy steps** to execute the script with four passed word values

4. Finally, enter your name when asked then hit **Return** to see the stored variable values displayed in a message

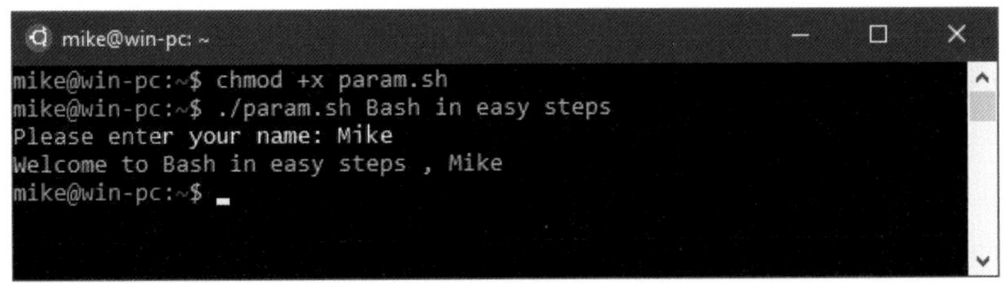

Use the **-n** option with **echo** when requesting input so it does not add a newline automatically.

Filling Arrays

An "array variable" can store multiple items of data, unlike a regular variable that can only store a single item of data. The items of data are stored sequentially in array "elements" that are numbered in an index starting at zero. So, the first array value is stored in array element zero; the second array value is stored in array element one; and so on.

An array is given a name of your choice, just like a regular variable, and each array element can be addressed by the variable name followed by its element index number in square brackets. For example, the address of the first element of array "arr" is **arr[0]**.

In Bash scripting an array can be created by assigning a space-separated list of values within parentheses to the given name. Listing three strings for assignment to an array looks like this:

```
arr=('First String' 'Second String' 'Third String')
```

The quote marks around the strings are only needed where the string contains spaces – to avoid the space being regarded as a separator.

This will automatically assign each successive string in the list to each successive element in the index. Alternatively, the same array can be created by explicitly assigning each string to a specific element in the array index:

```
arr=([0]='First String' [1]='Second String' [2]='Third String')
```

Or, by making individual string assignments to each element:

```
arr[0]='First String'
arr[1]='Second String'
arr[2]='Third String'
```

The value contained in an array element can be referenced by enclosing the array name and index position inside **{ }** curly bracket braces, then prefixing the whole lot by a **$** character – for example, to reference the first element of array "arr" with **${arr[0]}**.

The syntax to reference array elements may be clearer if you say each component as you type – value of **$**; array **{ }**; named **arr**; element **[0]**.

You can specify the special @ index operator to see a list of all values stored in an array – for example, all elements of array "arr" with **${arr[@]}**. Also, you can find the length of an array with the **#** length operator, such as **${#arr[@]}** , and discover which elements in the array currently store a value with **${!arr[@]}** .

Any regular variable or array variable can be destroyed by specifying its name to an **unset** command, or an individual array element can be emptied by specifying its name and index position.

array.sh

1. Open any plain text editor and begin a Bash script with the shebang line – indicating the path to the interpreter
#!/bin/bash

2. Next, add a line to create and initialize an array variable
arr=(Alpha Bravo Charlie Delta Echo)

3. Now, add these commands to examine the array
echo "Array arr[1]: ${arr[1]}"
echo "Array arr all: ${arr[@]}"
echo "Array arr length: ${#arr[@]}"
echo "Array arr elements filled: ${!arr[@]}"

Array indexes are "zero-based" – the first element is number zero.

4. Save the script as "array.sh", then issue the command **chmod +x array.sh** to make the file executable

5. Then, enter **./array.sh** to execute the script

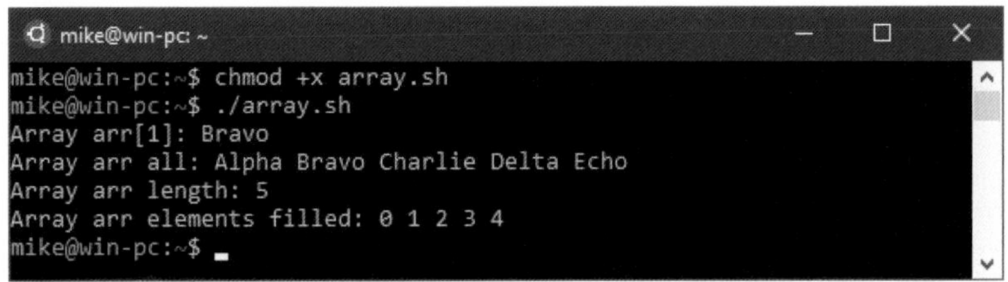

mike@win-pc:~$ ./array.sh
Array arr[1]: Bravo

unset.sh

6. Next, issue a **cp array.sh unset.sh** command at the prompt to make a copy of the script that will be named "unset.sh"

7. Now, open the "unset.sh" script in any plain text editor and insert a line directly below the initializing statement
unset arr[1]

8. Save the edited script then enter **./unset.sh** to execute it

mike@win-pc: ~
mike@win-pc:~$ ./unset.sh
Array arr[1]:
Array arr all: Alpha Charlie Delta Echo
Array arr length: 4
Array arr elements filled: 0 2 3 4
mike@win-pc:~$

No need to change file permissions on the copied script – it is executable already.

Handling Strings

The Bash shell supports a number of string-handling operators that can be used to test for the existence of a specified variable and may provide a default string value if no value exists. These require the variable name to be enclosed within **{ }** braces so the operator can be appended to the name, inside the closing brace:

Operator:	Description:
${*var*:-*string*}	Return ***var*** value, or ***string***
${*var*:=*string*}	Return ***var*** value, or ***string*** – but cannot be used to test positional parameters
${*var*:?*string*}	Return ***var*** value, or ***string***, then exit script
${*var*:+*string*}	Return ***string***, or **null** if absent
${*var*:*pos*:*len*}	Return substring of ***var*** of length ***len*** starting at character position ***pos***

If the string specified in the string operator contains any spaces the string must be enclosed in quote marks.

Each of the string operators listed above tests both that the specified variable exists and that its value is not **null**. If you only wish to test that the variable exists the : colon can be omitted in each operator except the last one, the substring operator.

The string operators are especially useful for the purpose of:

- Ensuring that a variable exists and has been assigned a value.
- Providing a default value when no value has been assigned.
- Generating an error message when a variable is absent.
- Removing part of a supplied variable string value.

There must be no spaces within the string operator – other than those permitted within a quoted string.

Scripts that expect the user to supply an argument can make good use of string operators to test positional parameters. For example, testing the value of **$1** to see if the user has supplied an argument allows a default value to be supplied if the argument is absent, or an error message to be generated if the argument is absent.

The length value in the substring operator may optionally be omitted. In that case, the returned substring will begin at the specified character starting position up to the end of the string.

...cont'd

string.sh

1. Begin a Bash script with the shebang line and display a passed argument value, or a provided default value

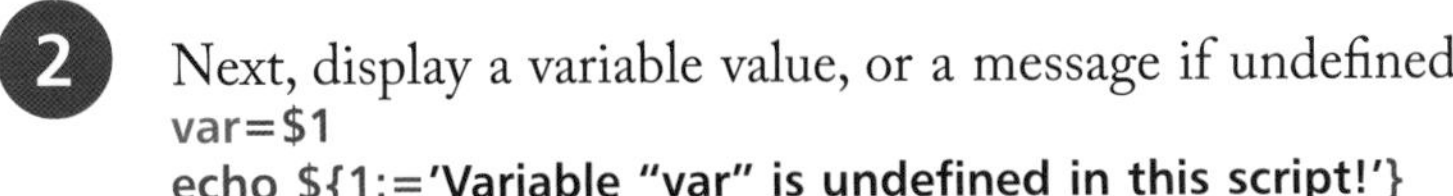

```
#!/bin/bash
echo ${1:-'Default value provided for absent argument!'}
```

2. Next, display a variable value, or a message if undefined

```
var=$1
echo ${1:='Variable "var" is undefined in this script!'}
```

3. Now, display a message and exit if no argument is passed, or a confirmation message if an argument was passed

```
echo ${1:?'No argument passed!'}
echo ${1:+'Argument received!'}
```

4. Then, display a substring of a passed argument

```
echo ${1:0:4}
```

5. Save the script as "string.sh" then issue the command **chmod +x string.sh** to make the file executable

6. Enter **./string.sh** to execute the script with no argument

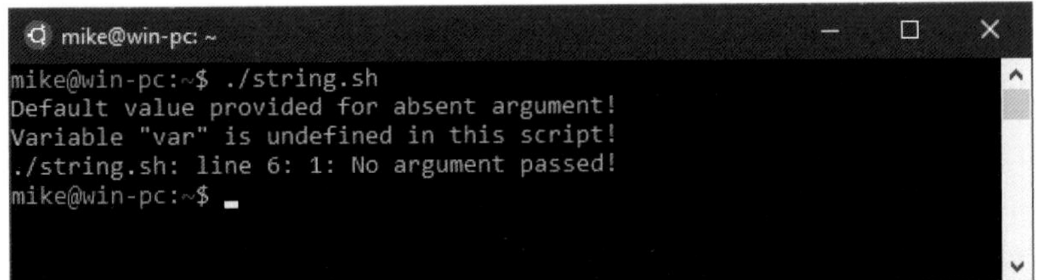

mike@win-pc: ~
mike@win-pc:~$ ./string.sh
Default value provided for absent argument!
Variable "var" is undefined in this script!
./string.sh: line 6: 1: No argument passed!
mike@win-pc:~$

7. Finally, enter **./string.sh 'Bash in easy steps'** to execute the script with a single string argument

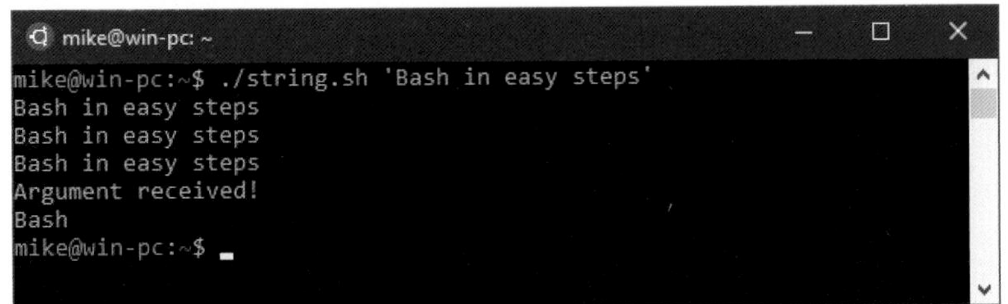

mike@win-pc: ~
mike@win-pc:~$ ./string.sh 'Bash in easy steps'
Bash in easy steps
Bash in easy steps
Bash in easy steps
Argument received!
Bash
mike@win-pc:~$

Double quotes can be used inside a string enclosed in single quotes and vice versa, but inner quotes that are the same type as the outer quotes must be escaped with a \ backslash to avoid premature termination of the string.

Another variable can alternatively be specified as a substitution string – for example, a variable named "msg" with **${1:-msg}**.

Doing Arithmetic

In Bash variables are by default created to store string values, rather than numeric values, so a variable assignment of the arithmetical expression **n=1+2** simply stores a literal string **'1+2'**. There is, however, a **(( ))** arithmetic expression operator that performs arithmetic on expressions within its double parentheses. So, a variable assignment **((n=1+2))** stores the result as string **'3'**. Further arithmetic on this stored value can of course be performed by repeated use of the **(( ))** arithmetic expression operator. Arithmetic expressions are created using any of the arithmetical operators in the table below:

Spaces are permitted inside the double parentheses of the **(( ))** arithmetic expression operator.

Operator:	Operation:	Example:
+	Addition	**a+b**
-	Subtraction	**a-b**
*	Multiplication	**a*b**
/	Division	**a/b**
%	Modulus (remainder)	**a%b**
++	Increment	**a++** or **++a**
--	Decrement	**b--** or **--b**

Note that the **/** division operator only returns an integer result; fractional remainders are ignored – for example, **9/2=4**, not **9/2=4.5**.

The operators for addition, subtraction, multiplication, and division perform as you would expect on two given numbers. The **%** modulus operator divides the first number by the second and returns any remainder. This is useful to determine if a number has an odd or even parity value.

Arithmetical operator precedence has left-to-right order so the expression **((2*3+4))** produces a result of 10 (2x3=6, 6+4=10). Where an expression has multiple operators inner parentheses can be used to group a part of the expression and give it precedence. For example, the expression **((2*(3+4)))** produces a result of 14 because the addition has precedence (3+4=7, 2x7=14).

Bash also has a **declare** command that can specify a variable type upon creation. For example, **declare -i var** creates an integer variable named "var".

The **++** increment and **--** decrement operators alter the given number by one and return the result. These can be placed before or after an operand to different effect; if placed before the operand (prefixed) its value is changed immediately, but if placed after the operand (postfixed) its value is first noted then changed later.

...cont'd

arithmetic.sh

1. Begin a Bash script with the shebang line and initialize three variables with numeric values

```
#!/bin/bash
a=8 b=4 result=0
echo "Assigned: a=$a b=$b"
```

2. Next, assign the result of an addition and display it

```
(( result=a+b ))
echo "Added a+b = $result"
```

3. Now, assign the result of a division and display it

```
(( result=a/b ))
echo "Divided a/b = $result"
```

4. Then, assign a modulus result and display it

```
((result=a%b))
echo "Modulated a%b = $result"
```

5. Assign the value of a variable and postfix increment its value to see it has increased by one when next referenced

```
echo "Currently a = $(( result=a++ ))"
echo "Incremented a = $a"
```

6. Assign the value of a variable and prefix increment its value to see it has increased by one immediately

```
echo "Incremented b = $(( result=++b ))"
```

7. Save the script as "arithmetic.sh" then issue the command **chmod +x arithmetic.sh** to make the file executable

8. Enter **./arithmetic.sh** to execute the script and see results

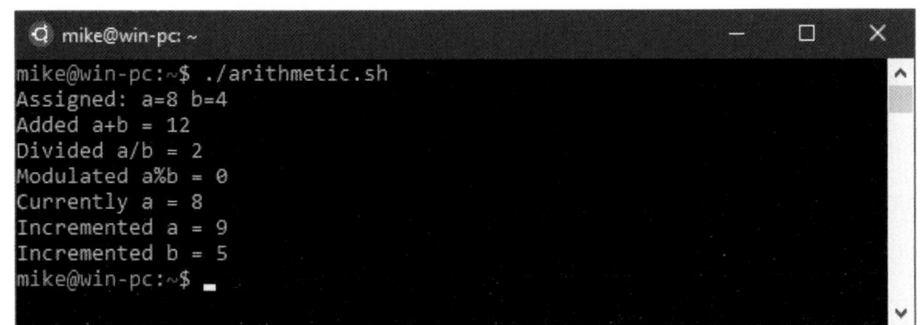

mike@win-pc: ~
mike@win-pc:~$ ./arithmetic.sh
Assigned: a=8 b=4
Added a+b = 12
Divided a/b = 2
Modulated a%b = 0
Currently a = 8
Incremented a = 9
Incremented b = 5
mike@win-pc:~$

There is also a **let** command that lets an assignment be interpreted as an arithmetical expression – for example, **let n=6*3**.

Notice that the result of the arithmetic is substituted in output by prefixing the **(( ))** arithmetic operator with a **$** in steps 5 and 6.

Assigning Values

The operators that are used in Bash shell scripts to assign values are listed in the table below. All except the simple = assign operator are a shorthand form of a longer expression, so each equivalent is given for clarity.

Operator:	Example:	Equivalent:
=	a = b	a = b
+=	a += b	a = (a + b)
-=	a -= b	a = (a - b)
*=	a *= b	a = (a * b)
/=	a /= b	a = (a / b)
%=	a %= b	a = (a % b)

Unlike a simple = assignment, shorthand operators include arithmetic operators so are arithmetical expressions that should be enclosed within the **(( ))** arithmetic operator.

It is important to regard the = operator to mean "assign" rather than "equals" to avoid confusion with the == equality operator.

In the example above, the variable named **a** is assigned the value that is contained in the variable named **b** – so that becomes the new value stored in the **a** variable.

The **+=** operator is useful to add a value onto an existing value that is stored in the **a** variable. In the table example the **+=** operator first adds the value stored in the variable **a** to the value stored in the variable **b**. It then assigns the result to become the new value stored in the **a** variable.

The == equality operator compares operand values and is described on page 126.

All the other operators in the table work in the same way by making the arithmetical operation between the two values first, then assigning the result to the first variable to become its new stored value.

With the **%=** operator, the first operand **a** is divided by the second operand **b** then the remainder of the operation is assigned to the **a** variable.

1. Begin a Bash script with the shebang line and initialize two variables with numeric values

```
#!/bin/bash
a=8 b=4
echo "Assigned: a=$a b=$b"
```

assign.sh

2. Next, assign the result of an addition and display it

```
(( a+=b ))
echo -e "Added and assigned:\t a+=b (8+=4) a=$a"
```

3. Now, assign the result of a subtraction and display it

```
(( a-=b ))
echo -e "Subtracted & assigned:\t a-=b (12-=4) a=$a"
```

The escaped **\t** prints an invisible Tab character and is used here to format the output.

4. Then, assign the result of a multiplication and display it

```
(( a*=b ))
echo -e "Multiplied & assigned:\t a*=b (8*=4) a=$a"
```

5. Now, assign the result of a division and display it

```
(( a/=b ))
echo -e "Divided and assigned:\t a/=b (32/=4) a=$a"
```

6. Then, assign the result of a modulation and display it

```
(( a%=b ))
echo -e "Modulated and assigned:\t a%=b (32%=4) a=$a"
```

7. Save the script as "assign.sh" then issue the command **chmod +x assign.sh** to make the file executable

8. Enter **./assign.sh** to execute the script and see results

The result of a shorthand assignment can be substituted in output by prefixing the arithmetic operator by a **$** – such as **echo $((a+=b))**.

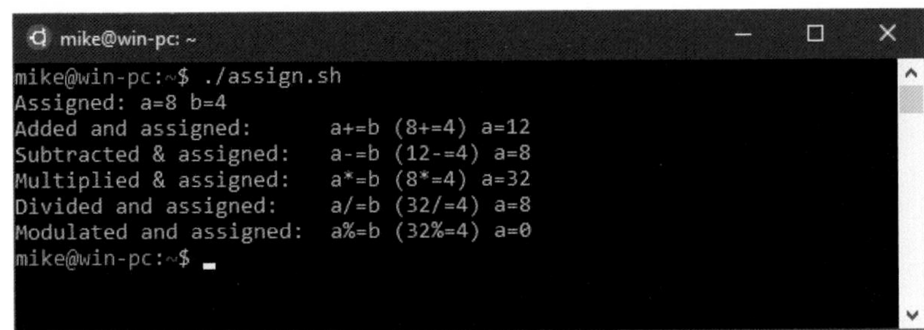

```
mike@win-pc: ~
mike@win-pc:~$ ./assign.sh
Assigned: a=8 b=4
Added and assigned:      a+=b (8+=4) a=12
Subtracted & assigned:   a-=b (12-=4) a=8
Multiplied & assigned:   a*=b (8*=4) a=32
Divided and assigned:    a/=b (32/=4) a=8
Modulated and assigned:  a%=b (32%=4) a=0
mike@win-pc:~$
```

Comparing Values

The relational operators that are commonly used in Bash scripts to compare two values numerically are listed in the table below:

Operator:	Comparative test:
==	Equality
!=	Inequality
>	Greater Than
<	Less Than
>=	Greater Than or Equal
<=	Less Than or Equal

Do not confuse the single-character = assignment operator with the two-character == equality operator.

The == equality operator compares two operands and will return **1** (true) if both are equal in value; otherwise, it will return **0** (false). If both operands are the same number they are equal, or if both are characters their ASCII code value is compared numerically. Conversely, the **!=** inequality operator returns **1** (true) if the two operands are not equal, using the same rules as the == equality operator; otherwise, it returns **0** (false). Equality and inequality operators are useful in testing the state of two variables to perform conditional branching in a script.

The **>** "greater than" operator compares two operands and will return **1** (true) if the first is greater in value than the second, or it will return **0** (false) if it is equal or less in value. The **>** "greater than" operator is frequently used to test the value of a countdown value in a loop.

String comparisons are made differently using the **[[ ]]** conditional test operator demonstrated on page 134.

The **<** "less than" operator makes the same comparison but returns **1** (true) if the first operand is less in value than the second; otherwise, it returns **0** (false).

Adding the = operator after a **>** "greater than" or **<** "less than" operator makes it also return **1** (true) when the two operands are exactly equal in value.

1. Begin a Bash script with the shebang line and initialize two variables with integers and two with characters

```
#!/bin/bash
a=8 b=4 c='A' d='a'
```

compare.sh

2. Next, display equality and inequality comparisons

```
echo -e "Equality\t ($a==$a): $(( a==a ))"
echo -e "Equality\t ($a==$b): $(( a==b ))"
echo -e "Equality\t ($c==$c): $(( c==c ))"
echo -e "Equality\t ($c==$d): $(( c==d ))"
echo -e "Inequality\t ($a!=$b): $(( a!=b ))"
echo -e "Inequality\t ($c!=$d): $(( c!=d ))"
```

Numerically, **1** represents a true result whereas **0** represents a false result.

3. Then, display the result of greater and less comparisons

```
echo -e "Greater Than\t ($a>$b ): $(( a>b ))"
echo -e "Less Than\t ($a<$b ): $(( a<b ))"
```

4. Now, display the result of greater or equal comparisons

```
echo "Greater or Equal ($a>=$b): $(( a>=b ))"
echo "Greater or Equal ($a>=$a): $(( a>=a ))"
```

5. Then, display the result of less or equal comparisons

```
echo -e "Less or Equal\t ($a<=$b): $(( a<=b ))"
echo -e "Less or Equal\t ($a<=$a): $(( a<=a ))"
```

6. Save the script as "compare.sh" then issue the command **chmod +x compare.sh** to make the file executable

7. Enter **./compare.sh** to execute the script and see results

The ASCII code value for uppercase "A" is 65 and for lowercase "a" is 97 – so the **A==a** comparison here returns **0** (false).

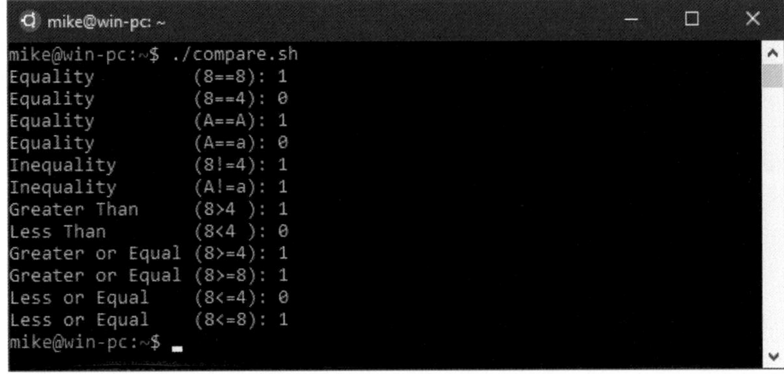

Assessing Logic

The logical operators most commonly used in Bash scripting are listed in the table below:

Operator:	Operation:
&&	Logical AND
||	Logical OR
!	Logical NOT

Notice that the **!** operator appears in the **!=** inequality to literally mean "NOT equal".

The logical operators are used with operands that have the Boolean values of true or false, or an expression that can convert to true or false.

The logical **&&** AND operator will evaluate two operands and return true only if both operands are themselves true. Otherwise, the **&&** AND operator will return false.

This is used in conditional branching, where the direction of a Bash script is determined by testing two conditions. If both conditions are satisfied the program will go in a certain direction; otherwise, it will take a different direction.

Unlike the **&&** AND operator, which requires both operands to be true, the **||** OR operator will evaluate two operands and return true if either one of the operands is itself true. If neither operand is true then the **||** OR operator will return false. This is useful in Bash scripting to perform a certain action if either one of two test conditions has been met.

The term "Boolean" refers to a system of logical thought developed by the English mathematician George Boole (1815-1864).

The third logical **!** NOT operator is a "unary" operator – which is used before a single operand. It returns the inverse value of the given operand, so if the variable **var** is a true value then **!var** would return a false value. The **!** NOT operator is useful in Bash scripting to toggle the value of a variable in successive loop iterations with a statement like **var = !var**. This ensures that on each pass the value is reversed, like flicking a light switch on and off.

In Bash scripting a zero **0** represents the Boolean false value and a number one **1** represents the Boolean true value.

...cont'd

1. Begin a Bash script with the shebang line and initialize two variables with integers representing true and false
```
#!/bin/bash
tru=1 fal=0
```

logic.sh

2. Next, display AND evaluations of the two variables to see whether they return a true (1) or false (0) value
```
echo -e "AND\t ($fal && $fal): $(( fal && fal ))"
echo -e "AND\t ($tru && $fal): $(( tru && fal ))"
echo -e "AND\t ($tru && $tru): $(( tru && tru ))"
```

Notice that these logic evaluations are made numerically so need the **(( ))** arithmetic operator.

3. Now, display OR evaluations of the two variables to see whether they return a true (1) or false (0) value
```
echo -e "OR\t ($fal || $fal): $(( fal || fal ))"
echo -e "OR\t ($tru || $fal): $(( tru || fal ))"
echo -e "OR\t ($tru || $tru): $(( tru || tru ))"
```

4. Then, display the actual variable values and their NOT evaluated inverse equivalents
```
echo -e "NOT\t ($tru  !$tru): $tru $(( !tru ))"
echo -e "NOT\t ($fal !$fal): $fal $(( !fal ))"
```

5. Save the script as "logic.sh" then issue the command **chmod +x logic.sh** to make the file executable

6. Enter **./logic.sh** to execute the script and see that AND evaluations only return true (1) when both operands are themselves true, whereas the OR evaluations return true (1) when either operand is itself true

Notice that **0 && 0** returns **0** (false) – demonstrating the anecdote "two wrongs don't make a right".

Matching Patterns

The Bash pattern-matching operators listed in the table below are useful in shell scripting to remove or replace part of a string value in a specified variable:

Operator:	Description:
${*var*#*pattern*}	Seek ***pattern*** at the start of ***var*** then remove the shortest matching part
${*var*##*pattern*}	Seek ***pattern*** at the start of ***var*** then remove the longest matching part
${*var*%*pattern*}	Seek ***pattern*** at the end of ***var*** then remove the shortest matching part
${*var*%%*pattern*}	Seek ***pattern*** at the end of ***var*** then remove the longest matching part
${*var*/*pattern*/*string*}	Seek first instance of ***pattern*** in ***var*** then replace it with ***string***
${*var*//*pattern*/*string*}	Seek all instances of ***pattern*** in ***var*** then replace each with ***string***

Remember that **#** seeks from the start, just as it precedes a number in #1; and **%** seeks at the end, just as it follows a number in 1%.

The pattern may simply consist of characters to match a substring within the string stored value in the variable – for example, where the string value is a text file name whose file extension could be removed using a **.txt** pattern.

The difference between the pattern-matching operators that remove the longest or shortest match is only apparent when the pattern includes a * wildcard character. For example, where the string value is a path address containing several / slash characters and the given pattern is /*/ then **${*var*#/*/}** will match the first / slash up to the second / slash and remove that shortest part. Conversely, in the same situation **${*var*##/*/}** will match the first / slash up to the final / slash and remove that longest part.

The result is identical for shortest and longest matches unless the pattern contains a * wildcard character.

The pattern-matching operators that perform replacement of matches may optionally specify a pattern that itself begins with a **#** character, to seek a match only at the start of the string value, or with a **%** character to seek a match only at its end. Where no replacement string is specified the match is simply removed.

1. Begin a Bash script with the shebang line and initialize a variable with a string value
```
#!/bin/bash
video='/media/mp4/perry.roar.mp4'
```

pattern.sh

2. Next, display the entire string value, then that string with a substring matching a pattern of characters removed
```
echo $video
echo ${video/perry.}
```

3. Now, display only the shortest and longest parts from the start of the string value delimited by / slash characters
```
echo ${video#/*/}
echo ${video##/*/}
```

If no replacement string is specified the substring matching the pattern is simply removed.

4. Then, display only the shortest and longest parts from the end of the string value delimited by . period (full stop) characters
```
echo ${video%.*}
echo ${video%%.*}
```

5. Now, display replacements of the first, last, and all instances of a substring matching a pattern of characters
```
echo ${video/mp4/vid}
echo ${video/%mp4/vid}
echo ${video//mp4/vid}
```

6. Save the script as "pattern.sh" then issue the command **chmod +x pattern.sh** to make the file executable

Pattern-matching is most often used in scripts to remove a directory prefix or filename suffix from a path address.

7. Enter **./pattern.sh** to execute the script and see the results

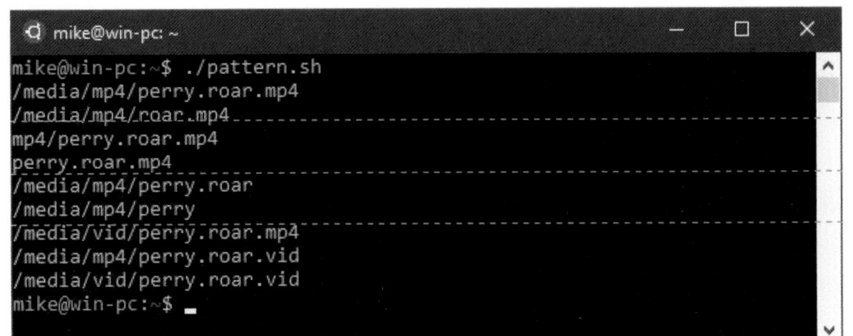

Summary

- Data stored in variable by the = assignment operator can be retrieved by prefixing the variable name with a **$** character.
- Shell scripts are text files that begin with the "shebang" line **#!/bin/bash** and made executable by the **chmod +x** command.
- Arguments are automatically stored in numbered positional parameters so can be referenced with **$1**, **$2**, **$3**; etc.
- Positional parameter **$0** stores the script name, **$@** stores a list of all arguments, and **$#** stores that list's length.
- An array stores multiple data items in a zero-based index of elements in which the first can be referenced with **${*array*[0]}**.
- A list of all element values can be found with **${*array*[@]}** and that array's length can be found with **${#*array*[@]}**.
- String operators, such as **${*variable*:-*string*}**, can test for the existence of a variable and may provide a default value.
- Arithmetic can be performed using the arithmetic operators + - etc. in an expression within the **(( ))** arithmetic operator.
- Increment **++** and decrement -- operators may be postfixed or prefixed to change a numeric variable by a value of one.
- The = assignment operator can be combined with an arithmetic operator for arithmetic assignment shorthand.
- Comparison operators, such as **==** for equality, compare two operands and return a **1** (true) or **0** (false) result.
- The logical **&&** AND operator will only return **1** (true) when both two operands are themselves true.
- The logical **||** OR operator will only return **1** (true) when either of two operands is itself true.
- The logical **!** NOT operator returns the inverse value of its single operand.
- Pattern-matching operators, such as **${*variable*#*pattern*}**, can remove or replace part of a string value in a specified variable.

8 Directing Flow

This chapter demonstrates how to control the flow of programs created with Bash shell scripting.

Examining Conditions

Progress of a Bash shell program is made by making conditional tests to determine which action the program should next perform. These tests can be made using the **if** keyword and **[[ ]]** conditional test operator to enclose a comparison statement. An **if** statement made in this way actually examines the "exit status" of the comparison test. When the test succeeds the exit status is zero, but any other value indicates an error. A block of statements to execute upon success can follow a **then** keyword and the end of the block be denoted with a **fi** keyword, using this syntax:

if [[*conditional test*]]
then
  statements to execute upon success
fi

The operators that can be used to make string comparisons within a **[[ ]]** conditional test are listed in the table below.

Operator:	String comparison:
=	Same
!=	Differs
>	Is Greater
<	Is Less

The string comparison operators are like those used for integer comparison in the **(( ))** arithmetic expression operator. Paradoxically, integer comparisons within conditional tests are made using the operators listed below:

Operator:	Integer comparison:
-eq	Equality
-ne	Inequality
-gt	Greater Than
-lt	Less Than
-ge	Greater Than or Equal
-le	Less Than or Equal

The **[[** and **]]** are shell operators so must have a space on either side. Additionally, **then** and **fi** keywords must be on a new line unless the previous statement is terminated by a semi-colon.

The comparison operators used in arithmetic expressions are listed on page 126 but <= and >= do not apply for string comparison in conditional tests.

...cont'd

1. Begin a shell script by initializing a variable with an empty string then request a value for assignment to it

```
#!/bin/bash
str=''
echo -n 'Enter Your Name: '
read str
```

if.sh

2. Next, display a message containing the user input only if a value was entered

```
if [[ $str != '' ]]
then
  echo "Hello $str"
fi
```

Remember that the (( )) arithmetic operator returns a Boolean true or false value whereas a [[ ]] conditional test examines the exit status for success or failure.

3. Now, initialize a variable with zero then request a value for assignment to it and display a message if received

```
num=0
echo -n 'Enter An Integer: '
read num
if [[ $num -ne 0 ]]
then
  echo "Received $num "
fi
```

4. Finally, display another message only if a value was entered for both variables

```
if [[ $str != '' && $num -ne 0 ]]
then
  echo "Thanks For $num , $str."
fi
```

5. Save the script and make the file executable, then run the program and enter values when requested

Run the script again and omit either requested value to see the appropriate acknowledgement and the final message do not get displayed.

```
mike@win-pc: ~
mike@win-pc:~/a$ chmod +x if.sh
mike@win-pc:~/a$ ./if.sh
Enter Your Name: Mike
Hello Mike!
Enter An Integer: 7
Received 7
Thanks For 7, Mike.
mike@win-pc:~/a$
```

Providing Alternatives

An **else** keyword can be used in conjunction with an **if** statement to create an **if else** statement that provides an alternative action for the program to pursue after making a conditional test. In its simplest form this merely nominates statements to execute when the exit status indicates failure:

```
if [[ conditional test ]]
then
  statements to execute upon success
else
  statements to execute upon failure
fi
```

More powerful **if else** statements can be created to make multiple conditional tests using an **elif** keyword (else if) with this syntax:

```
if [[ conditional test ]]
then
  statements to execute upon this success
elif [[ conditional test ]]
then
  statements to execute upon this success
fi
```

A space character is required on each side of the **[[** and **]]** operators.

The program will make each conditional test in turn until it discovers one that succeeds. It will then execute the statements associated with that test and exit – making no further tests.

It is sometimes desirable to provide a final **else** statement to specify a default action to be performed when all conditional tests fail, using this syntax:

```
if [[ conditional test ]]
then
  statements to execute upon this success
elif [[ conditional test ]]
then
  statements to execute upon this success
elif [[ conditional test ]]
then
  statements to execute upon this success
else
  statements to execute upon all failure
fi
```

Note that the format does matter as the invisible newline characters act as separators between each part of an **if else**, **if elif**, or **if elif else** block.

This program flow construct is known as "conditional branching" as it provides alternative branches for the program to follow according to the result of the various conditional tests.

...cont'd

1. Begin a shell script by requesting a value to initialize a variable with an integer

```
#!/bin/bash
echo -n 'Enter Hours 0-23: '
read hrs
```

else.sh

2. Next, test there exists user input below 24

```
if [[ $hrs = '' || $hrs -gt 23 ]]
  then echo 'Invalid Hours!'
```

3. Now, test whether the input is below 13 and display an appropriate message when that test succeeds

```
elif [[ $hrs -ge 0 && $hrs -lt 12 ]]
  then echo 'Good Morning!'
```

Here the **elif** statements only succeed when the variable value is 0-11 or when it is 12-17.

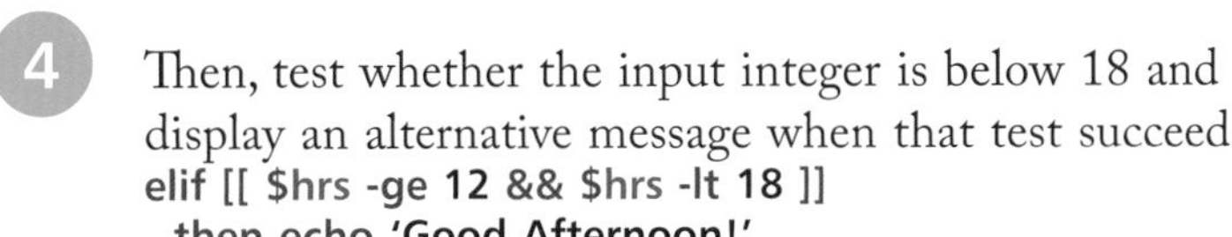

4. Then, test whether the input integer is below 18 and display an alternative message when that test succeeds

```
elif [[ $hrs -ge 12 && $hrs -lt 18 ]]
  then echo 'Good Afternoon!'
```

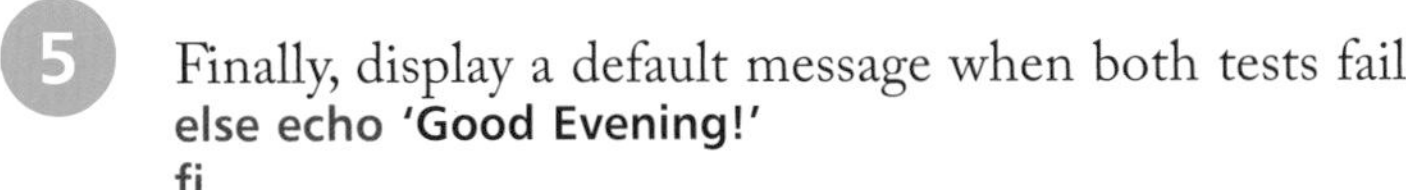

5. Finally, display a default message when both tests fail

```
else echo 'Good Evening!'
fi
```

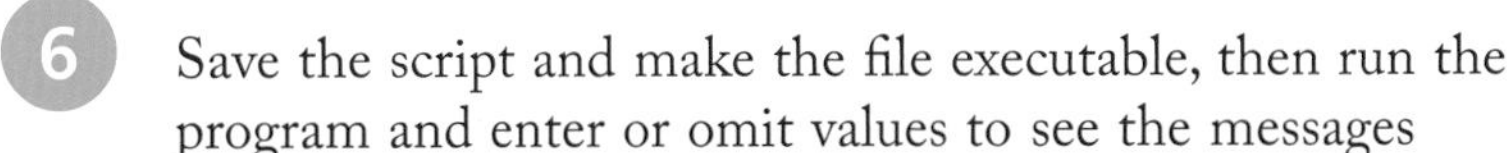

6. Save the script and make the file executable, then run the program and enter or omit values to see the messages

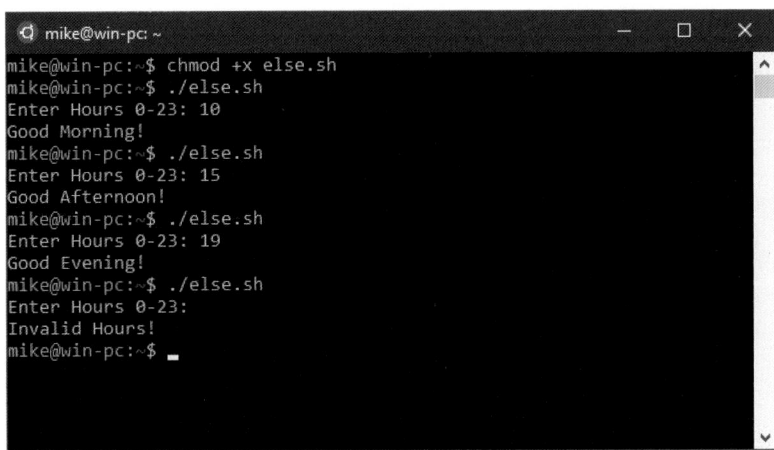

You may also nest **if** blocks to test multiple conditions, like this:

```
if [[ condition ]]
then
  if [[ condition ]]
  then
    statements
  fi
fi
```

Testing Cases

Lengthy **if else** statements, which offer many conditional branches for a program to pursue, can become unwieldy. Where the test expressions repeatedly evaluate the same variable value a more elegant solution is often provided by a **case in** statement.

The syntax of a typical **case in** statement block looks like this:

```
case test-variable in
  pattern-1 ) statements to execute upon this success ;;
  pattern-2 ) statements to execute upon this success ;;
  pattern-3 ) statements to execute upon this success ;;
  * ) statements to execute upon all failure ;;
esac
```

Each standard statement block terminator in a **case in** construct is a ;; double semi-colon – a ; single semi-colon will produce an error.

The **case in** statement works in an unusual way. It takes a specified variable then seeks to match its assigned value from among a number of pattern options. Statements associated with the option whose value matches are then executed.

Optionally, a **case in** statement can include a final option using the * wildcard to specify statements to execute when no **case in** options match the value assigned to the specified variable.

Each option begins with the pattern to match. This is followed by a **)** closing parenthesis and the statements to be executed when the match is made.

It is important to recognize that the statement, or statement block, associated with each **case in** option must be terminated by a ;; double semi-colon. This can optionally be omitted after the final statement block but the entire **case in** construct must end with the **esac** ("case" reversed) keyword.

The **;&** and **;;&** terminator options were added for **case in** constructs in Bash version 4.

Should you wish to also execute statements associated with the next **case in** option when a match is successful, **;&** can be used in place of the ;; double semi-colon terminator.

Alternatively, should you wish to also evaluate the pattern of the next **case in** option when a match is successful, **;;&** can be used in place of the ;; double semi-colon terminator.

case.sh

1. Begin a shell script by requesting a value to initialize a variable with an integer

```
#!/bin/bash
echo -n 'Enter Month 1-12: '
read month
```

2. Next, test whether the input integer is 3 or 4 or 5 and display an appropriate message when that test succeeds

```
case $month in
3 | 4 | 5 )       echo 'Spring!' ;;
```

3. Now, test whether the input integer is 6,7,8 or 9,10,11 or 12,1,2 and display an alternative message upon success

```
6 | 7 | 8 )       echo 'Summer!' ;;
9 | 10 | 11 )     echo 'Autumn!' ;;
12 | 1 | 2 )      echo 'Winter!' ;;
```

4. Finally, display a default message when all tests fail and close the construct

```
* )       echo 'Unrecognized Month' ;;
esac
```

5. Save the script and make the file executable, then run the program and enter values to see appropriate messages

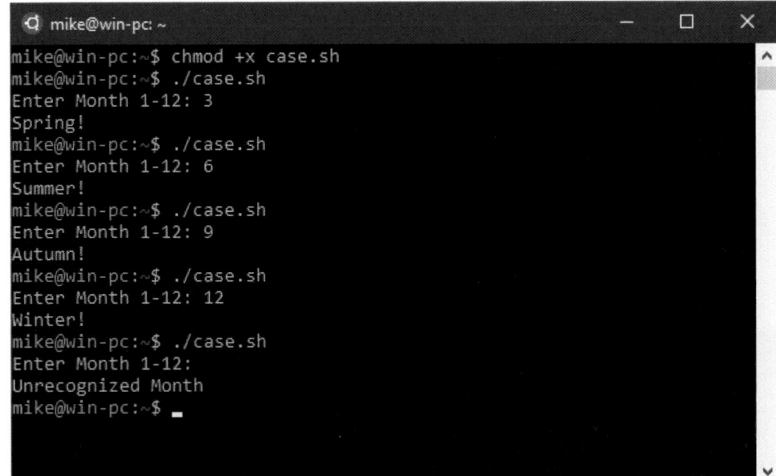

mike@win-pc: ~
mike@win-pc:~$ chmod +x case.sh
mike@win-pc:~$ ./case.sh
Enter Month 1-12: 3
Spring!
mike@win-pc:~$ ./case.sh
Enter Month 1-12: 6
Summer!
mike@win-pc:~$ ./case.sh
Enter Month 1-12: 9
Autumn!
mike@win-pc:~$ ./case.sh
Enter Month 1-12: 12
Winter!
mike@win-pc:~$ ./case.sh
Enter Month 1-12:
Unrecognized Month
mike@win-pc:~$

Notice how the | pipe character is used here as the logical OR operator to provide options.

The pattern in a **case in** construct may also be a string to match against and the string may include * wildcards.

Iterating For

The most useful construct in any programming language provides the ability to loop repeatedly executing one or more statements. With Bash shell scripts, the **for in** keywords can be used to loop through each item in a specified list using this syntax:

for *item* in *list*
do
  statements to execute
done

The range operator such as in **{A..Z}** must have two dots and no spaces.

The item is typically a "counter" variable, traditionally named **i**, and the list might be a range, such as **{1..10}** or **{A..Z}**. Perhaps more usefully, the list can be an array variable in which the loop visits each element on its successive iterations:

iterate.sh

1. Begin a shell script with a loop to output the alphabet

```
#!/bin/bash

for i in {A..Z}
do
  echo $i
done
```

2. Next, initialize an array variable with three string values

```
arr=(Alpha Bravo Charlie)
```

3. Then, add a loop to output the counter value and the value contained in the array element on each iteration

```
for i in ${!arr[@]}
do
  echo -e "\nElement $i: ${arr[$i]}"
done
```

Notice the use of the syntax in **${!arr[@]}** to reference each array element – described on page 118.

4. Save the script and make the file executable, then run the program to see the loop output

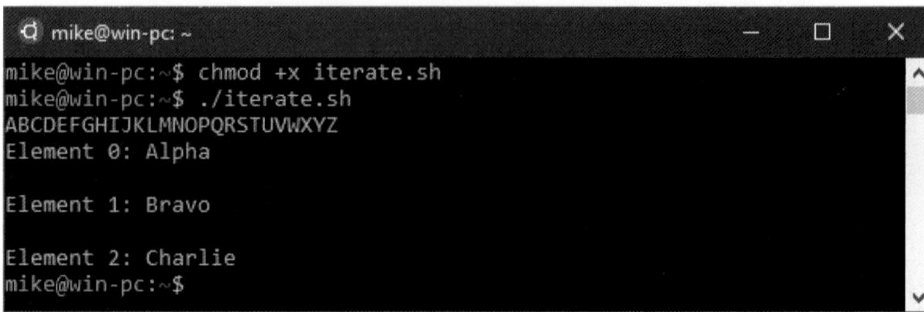

mike@win-pc: ~
mike@win-pc:~$ chmod +x iterate.sh
mike@win-pc:~$ ./iterate.sh
ABCDEFGHIJKLMNOPQRSTUVWXYZ
Element 0: Alpha

Element 1: Bravo

Element 2: Charlie
mike@win-pc:~$

The **for** keyword can also be used in Bash shell scripts to loop for a specified number of times by using the **(( ))** arithmetic operator to initialize a counter variable, test a condition, and increment the counter with this syntax:

```
for (( initializer ; conditional test ; incrementer ))
do
  statements to execute
done
```

The statements will be executed each time the test succeeds but the loop ends on the first occasion the test fails. Loops can also be "nested", one within another, to allow execution of statements of an inner nested loop on each iteration of the outer loop:

The syntax to initialize, test, and increment is similar to that found in programming languages such as C and Java.

1. Begin a shell script with a loop to display the value of its counter variable upon each of two iterations – and include a placeholder comment

```
#!/bin/bash

for (( i=1 ; i < 3; i++ ))
do
  echo "Outer Loop Iteration: $i"
  # Inner Loop To Be Added Here.
done
```

for.sh

2. Next, replace the placeholder comment, nesting an inner loop that also displays its counter value on each iteration

```
  for (( j=1 ; j < 3; j++ ))
  do
    echo -e "\tInner Loop Iteration: $j"
  done
```

3. Save the script and make the file executable, then run the program to see the loop output

```
mike@win-pc: ~
mike@win-pc:~$ chmod +x for.sh
mike@win-pc:~$ ./for.sh
Outer Loop Iteration 1
        Inner Loop Iteration 1
        Inner Loop Iteration 2
Outer Loop Iteration 2
        Inner Loop Iteration 1
        Inner Loop Iteration 2
mike@win-pc:~$
```

Nested loops are used in many programming algorithms, such as the "bubble sort" algorithm.

Selecting Options

The Bash shell provides a **select in** construct that easily generates a menu of options from which the user may select one item. Its syntax is similar to that of the **for in** iterator and looks like this:

```
select item in list
do
  statements to execute
done
```

Hot tip

A **select in** construct is not available in other programming languages.

The generated menu automatically numbers each list item and requests the user input the associated number of their selection:

#!
SH

menu.sh

1. Create a shell script that generates a menu of three letters

```
#!/bin/bash

select i in {A..C}
do
  echo $i
done
```

2. Save the script and make the file executable, then run the program to see the generated menu

3. Enter a menu number to make a selection then see a further request – press **Ctrl** + **C** to return to a prompt

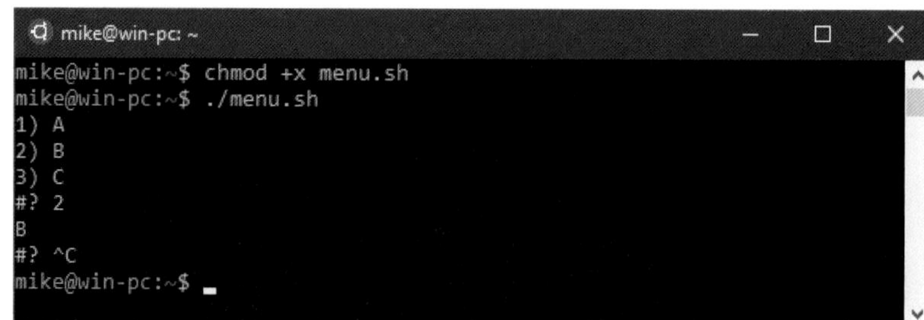
mike@win-pc: ~
mike@win-pc:~$ chmod +x menu.sh
mike@win-pc:~$ ./menu.sh
1) A
2) B
3) C
#? 2
B
#? ^C
mike@win-pc:~$

Beware

Do not expect the user to use **Ctrl** + **C** to exit your programs.

The menu generated by a **select in** construct uses the default **PS3** prompt string of **#?** to indicate the user should select a number and will automatically loop to request further selections. Frequently this may not be desirable, but a more user-friendly string can be assigned to the **PS3** shell variable and the loop action can be suppressed by including a final **break** command in the statement block. It may also be useful to recognize that the number input by the user gets stored in the **REPLY** shell variable:

1. Begin a shell script by initializing an array with three string values

```
#!/bin/bash

arr=(Alpha Bravo Charlie)
```

#!
SH
select.sh

2. Next, assign a user-friendly string to the PS3 shell variable to request user input

```
PS3='Please Choose A Number: '
```

3. Now, add a **select in** construct to generate a menu to list the array values as individual items that the user may select – and include a placeholder comment

```
select name in ${arr[@]}
do
  # Statements To Be Added Here
done
```

Don't forget

You can also add the PS3 assignment to your **.bashrc** file to constantly override the **#?** default – seen on page 142.

4. Then, replace the placeholder comment with a statement to display the number and value selected

```
  echo "$REPLY Chosen For $name"
```

5. Finally, insert a statement to suppress the loop

```
  break
```

6. Save the script and make the file executable, then run the program and enter a number to make a selection

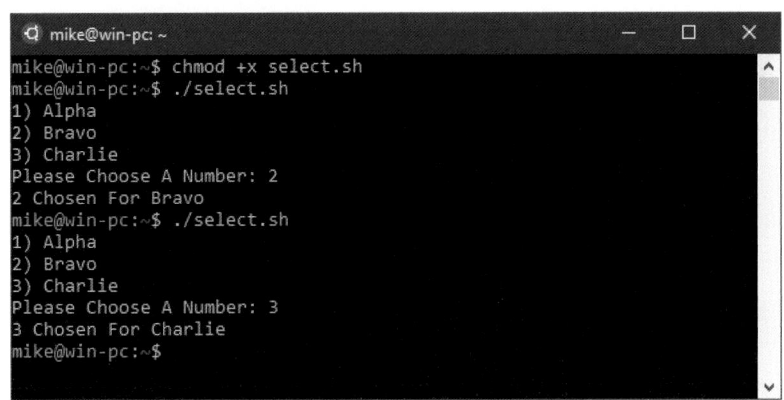
mike@win-pc: ~
mike@win-pc:~$ chmod +x select.sh
mike@win-pc:~$ ./select.sh
1) Alpha
2) Bravo
3) Charlie
Please Choose A Number: 2
2 Chosen For Bravo
mike@win-pc:~$ ./select.sh
1) Alpha
2) Bravo
3) Charlie
Please Choose A Number: 3
3 Chosen For Charlie
mike@win-pc:~$

Hot tip

You could write a script that provides an exit option – so choosing that number would implement the **break** command.

Looping While

A **while** loop is an alternative to the **for** loop that is described on page 141. The **while** loop also requires an initializer, conditional test, and an incrementer, but these are not all neatly listed within an arithmetic operator as they are with a **for** loop. Instead, the initializer must appear before the start of the loop block; the conditional test must appear after the **while** keyword; and an incrementer must be included in the block of statements to be executed on each iteration, with this syntax:

```
initializer
while conditional test is true
do
  statements to execute
  incrementer
done
```

A **while** loop will proceed to make iterations until the conditional test fails, at which point the loop will exit. It is therefore essential that the loop's statement block contains code that will, at some point, change the result of the conditional test evaluation – otherwise, an infinite loop is created that will lock the system:

length.sh

1. Begin a shell script that initializes an array with three string values

```
#!/bin/bash

arr=(Alpha Bravo Charlie)
```

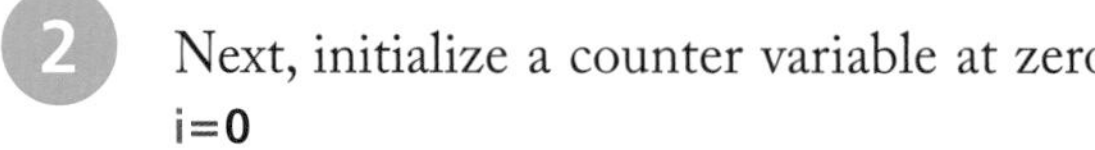

2. Next, initialize a counter variable at zero

```
i=0
```

The array length value is used in this conditional test to end the loop when the final array element has been reached – see pages 118-119.

3. Now, add a loop to output the value contained in the array element and increment the counter on each iteration

```
while (( i < ${#arr[@]} ))
do
  echo ${arr[$i]}
  (( i++ ))
done
```

4. Save the script and make the file executable, then run the program to see the loop output

```
mike@win-pc: ~
mike@win-pc:~$ chmod +x length.sh
mike@win-pc:~$ ./length.sh
Alpha
Bravo
Charlie
mike@win-pc:~$
```

The incrementer must be enclosed within the **(( ))** arithmetic operator.

All **while** loops can be nested to allow execution of statements of an inner nested loop on each iteration of the outer loop:

while.sh

1. Begin a shell script with a loop to display the value of its counter variable upon each of two iterations – and include a placeholder comment

```
#!/bin/bash

i=1
while (( i < 3 ))
do
  echo "Outer Loop Iteration: $i"
  (( i++ ))
  # Inner Loop To Be Added Here.
done
```

If you forget to include an incrementer within the statement block an infinite loop will be created when the program runs – press **Ctrl** + **C** to exit from that.

2. Next, replace the placeholder comment, nesting an inner loop that also displays its counter value on each iteration

```
  j=1
  while (( j < 3 ))
  do
    echo -e "\tInner Loop Iteration: $j"
    (( j++ ))
  done
```

3. Save the script and make the file executable, then run the program to see the loop output

```
mike@win-pc: ~
mike@win-pc:~$ chmod +x while.sh
mike@win-pc:~$ ./while.sh
Outer Loop Iteration 1
        Inner Loop Iteration 1
        Inner Loop Iteration 2
Outer Loop Iteration 2
        Inner Loop Iteration 1
        Inner Loop Iteration 2
mike@win-pc:~$
```

This example exactly recreates the earlier nested **for** loop example – the choice of **for** loop or **while** loop is largely personal preference.

Looping Until

As with a **while** loop an infinite loop will be created if you forget to include an incrementer within the **until** loop statement block – press **Ctrl** + **C** to exit from that.

An **until** loop is yet another alternative to the **for** loop and the **while** loop introduced on the previous pages. Like the **while** loop construct, an **until** loop requires an initializer before the start of the loop block; a conditional test after the **until** keyword; and an incrementer in the block of statements to be executed on each iteration, with this syntax:

```
initializer
until conditional test becomes true
do
  statements to execute
  incrementer
done
```

Unlike the w**hile** loop, which will proceed to make iterations until the conditional test fails, an **until** loop will proceed to make iterations until the conditional test succeeds – at which point the loop will exit. The difference between **while** and **until** loops in Bash is purely one of semantics as **while** seeks a true condition to proceed and **until** seeks a false condition to proceed:

beyond.sh

1. Begin a shell script that initializes an array with three string values

```
#!/bin/bash

arr=(Alpha Bravo Charlie)
```

2. Next, initialize a counter variable at zero

```
i=0
```

The array length value is again used in this conditional test to set a limit beyond which the loop will not proceed.

3. Now, add a loop to output the value contained in the array element and increment the counter on each iteration

```
until (( i == ${#arr[@]} ))
do
  echo ${arr[$i]}
  (( i++ ))
done
```

4. Save the script and make the file executable, then run the program to see the loop output

```
mike@win-pc:~$ chmod +x beyond.sh
mike@win-pc:~$ ./beyond.sh
Alpha
Bravo
Charlie
mike@win-pc:~$
```

Unlike other languages, **until** loops in Bash test at the start of the loop.

All **until** loops can be nested to allow execution of statements of an inner nested loop on each iteration of the outer loop:

until.sh

1. Begin a shell script with a loop to display the value of its counter variable upon each of two iterations – and include a placeholder comment

```
#!/bin/bash

i=1
until (( i > 2 ))
do
  echo "Outer Loop Iteration: $i"
  (( i++ ))
  # Inner Loop To Be Added Here.
done
```

2. Next, replace the placeholder comment, nesting an inner loop that also displays its counter value on each iteration

```
  j=1
  until (( j > 2 ))
  do
    echo -e "\tInner Loop Iteration: $j"
    (( j++ ))
  done
```

3. Save the script and make the file executable, then run the program to see the loop output

This example also recreates the earlier nested **for** loop example – the choice of **for** loop, **while** loop, or **until** loop is personal preference.

```
mike@win-pc:~$ chmod +x until.sh
mike@win-pc:~$ ./until.sh
Outer Loop Iteration: 1
        Inner Loop Iteration: 1
        Inner Loop Iteration: 2
Outer Loop Iteration: 2
        Inner Loop Iteration: 1
        Inner Loop Iteration: 2
mike@win-pc:~$
```

Breaking Out

The **break** command can be used to prematurely terminate a loop when a specified condition is met. The **break** command is situated inside the loop statement block within a test expression. When the test evaluates as true the loop ends immediately and the program proceeds onto the next task. For example, in a nested inner loop it proceeds to the next iteration of the outer loop:

#!
SH

break.sh

1. Create a shell script that displays the incrementer values of an outer and inner loop on each of their iterations – and include a placeholder comment in the nested loop

```
#!/bin/bash

for (( i = 1; i < 4; i++ ))
do

  for (( j = 1; j < 4; j++ ))
  do
    # Test for break to be added here
    echo -e "Outer $i \tInner: $j"
  done
done
```

Hot tip

The **break** keyword is used on page 143 to suppress a **select** loop.

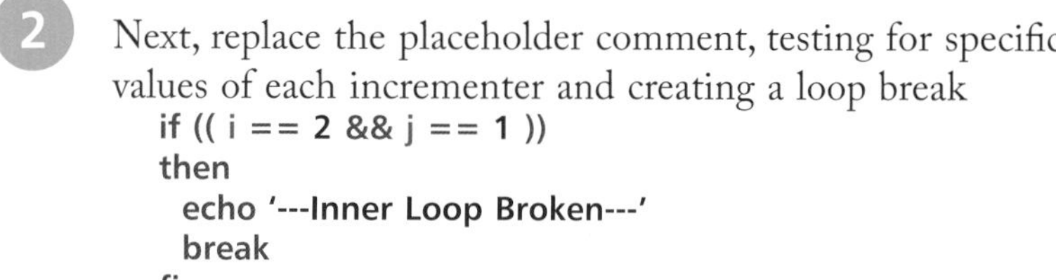

2. Next, replace the placeholder comment, testing for specific values of each incrementer and creating a loop break

```
    if (( i == 2 && j == 1 ))
    then
      echo '---Inner Loop Broken---'
      break
    fi
```

3. Save the script and make the file executable, then run the program to see the inner loop break – skipping the entire second outer loop iteration

Don't forget

A **break** statement ends all iterations of a loop.

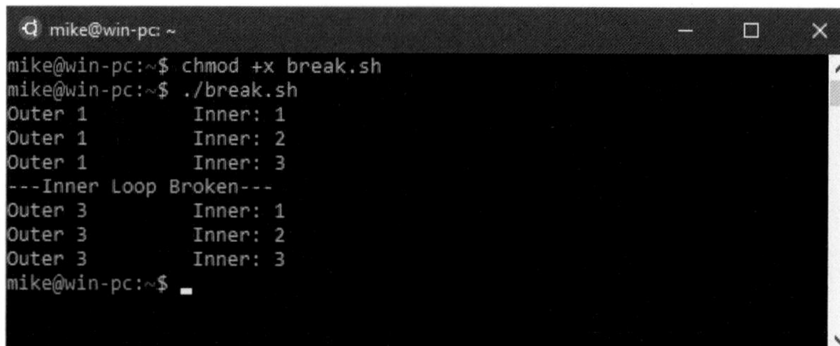

mike@win-pc: ~
mike@win-pc:~$ chmod +x break.sh
mike@win-pc:~$ ./break.sh
Outer 1   Inner: 1
Outer 1   Inner: 2
Outer 1   Inner: 3
---Inner Loop Broken---
Outer 3   Inner: 1
Outer 3   Inner: 2
Outer 3   Inner: 3
mike@win-pc:~$

The **continue** command can be used to skip a single iteration of a loop when a specified condition is met. The **continue** command is situated inside the loop statement block within a test expression. When the test evaluates as true that iteration of the loop ends immediately and the program proceeds to the next iteration:

continue.sh

1. Create a shell script that displays the incrementer values of an outer and inner loop on each of their iterations – and include a placeholder comment in the nested loop

```
#!/bin/bash

for (( i = 1; i < 4; i++ ))
do

  for (( j = 1; j < 4; j++ ))
  do
    # Test for continue to be added here
    echo -e "Outer $i \tInner: $j"
  done
done
```

The **break** and **continue** keywords can be used to control **for**, **while** and **until** loops.

2. Next, replace the placeholder comment, testing for specific values of each incrementer and creating a loop continue

```
    if (( i == 2 && j == 1 ))
    then
      echo '---Inner Loop Continued---'
      continue
    fi
```

3. Save the script and make the file executable, then run the program to see the inner loop continue – skipping only the first inner loop iteration

```
mike@win-pc: ~
mike@win-pc:~$ chmod +x continue.sh
mike@win-pc:~$ ./continue.sh
Outer 1         Inner: 1
Outer 1         Inner: 2
Outer 1         Inner: 3
---Inner Loop Continued---
Outer 2         Inner: 2
Outer 2         Inner: 3
Outer 3         Inner: 1
Outer 3         Inner: 2
Outer 3         Inner: 3
mike@win-pc:~$
```

A **continue** statement ends only the current iteration of a loop.

Summary

- An **if** statement makes a conditional test **then** upon success executes statements in a block terminated by the **fi** keyword.
- String comparisons within a **[[ ]]** conditional test are made with **==**, **!=**, **<** and **>** operators.
- Integer comparisons within a **[[ ]]** conditional test are made with **-eq**, **-ne**, **-gt**, **-lt**, **-ge**, and **-le** operators.
- The **else** and **elif** keywords can be used to provide alternative conditional branching within an **if** statement block.
- A **case in** statement seeks to match a specified variable against patterns in a block terminated by the **esac** keyword.
- Each **case** pattern ends with a **)** closing parenthesis and its statements must be terminated by a **;;** double semi-colon.
- A **for in** statement loops through items in a list executing statements within a **do done** block on each iteration.
- The **for** keyword can loop for a specified number of iterations by stating an initializer, test condition, and incrementer within the **(( ))** arithmetic expression operator.
- A **select in** statement generates a menu of options then executes statements within a **do done** block upon selection.
- The **select** statement performs a loop by default but this can be suppressed using the **break** keyword.
- A **while** loop will iterate while a test condition succeeds but its **do done** block must contain a statement that will at some point make the test fail so the loop will end.
- An **until** loop will iterate while a test condition fails but its **do done** block must contain a statement that will at some point make the test succeed so the loop will end.
- Loops can be prematurely terminated using the **break** keyword to instantly end the loop.
- Loop iterations can be prematurely terminated using the **continue** keyword to instantly end a single iteration.

9 Employing Functions

This chapter demonstrates how to create reusable functions in shell programs.

Creating Scripts

Scripts can usefully be organized into modular sections of code for repeat use by grouping statements within a named "function". That function name can then be used as a command within the script to execute all its statements whenever required. A Bash function must first be defined in a script using this syntax:

function *name*
{
        statements to be executed
}

A definition may use the **function** keyword or use this syntax:

***name* ( )**
{
        statements to be executed
}

There is no practical difference between the choice of syntax but using that with the **function** keyword is perhaps more readable.

As usual, scripts must be made executable with **chmod +x** then executed by prefixing the script name with **./** at the command line. Scripts can alternatively be executed using the **source** command followed by the script name – so the Bash interpreter treats the script contents as if you had typed them at a command prompt.

Once a script has been executed using the **source** command any functions defined there are stored in the shell's memory for the duration of that shell session. This means they can be called by name from a command prompt at any time until the user ends the shell session.

The names of all defined functions within current shell memory can be revealed using a **declare -F** command (uppercase "F"). Additionally, all defined functions within current shell memory can be listed using a **declare -f** command (lowercase "f").

Individual defined functions within current shell memory can be listed using the command **type** followed by the function name. Individual defined functions can be removed from current shell memory using the command **unset -f** and the function name.

Closing a Terminal window ends the shell session so any defined functions are removed.

Bash functions cannot return values with the **return** command as they do in programming languages such as C or Java but instead merely return the exit status of the last statement in the function.

function.sh

1. Begin a shell script by defining a function named "first" that will display a string whenever it gets called

```
#!/bin/bash

function first
{
  echo 'Hello from the first function!'
}
```

2. Next, define another function that will display the result of an arithmetical expression when called

```
cube5 ( )
{
  echo "5x5x5 = $(( 5*5*5 ))"
}
```

You can add a command in the **.bashrc** file to execute a shell script defining functions to be available whenever you start a shell session.

3. Now, simply add a call to the first function to execute its statements when the script gets executed

```
first
```

4. Save the script then make it executable and run the script using **source** to see output from the first function

```
mike@win-pc: ~
mike@win-pc:~$ source function.sh
Hello from the first function!
mike@win-pc:~$ _
```

5. Then, issue a **declare -F** command to see all defined functions in shell memory

6. Finally, enter **cube5** to call the other function in memory to execute its statements

Scripts executed with ./ run in a subshell so defined functions are not in the current shell memory.

```
mike@win-pc: ~
mike@win-pc:~$ declare -F
declare -f cube5
declare -f dequote
declare -f first
declare -f quote
declare -f quote_readline
mike@win-pc:~$ cube5
5x5x5 = 125
mike@win-pc:~$ _
```

Displaying Variables

Variables that are declared in a script outside any function definition are globally accessible to any function, so the variable values can be readily displayed and manipulated. Copies of those values can also be passed to functions in positional parameters:

vars.sh

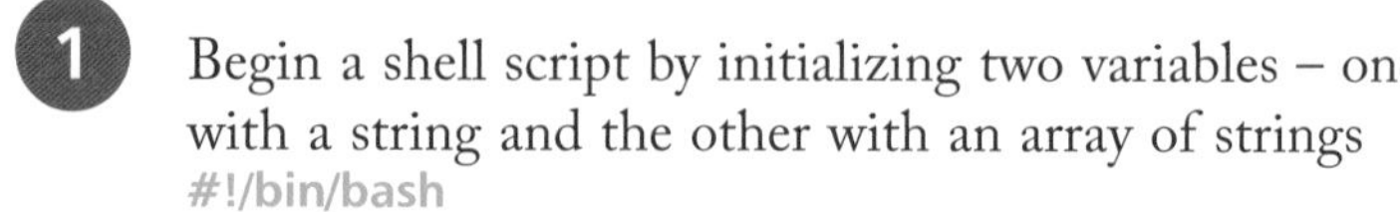

1. Begin a shell script by initializing two variables – one with a string and the other with an array of strings

```
#!/bin/bash

var='Bash in easy steps'
arr=(Alpha Bravo Charlie)
```

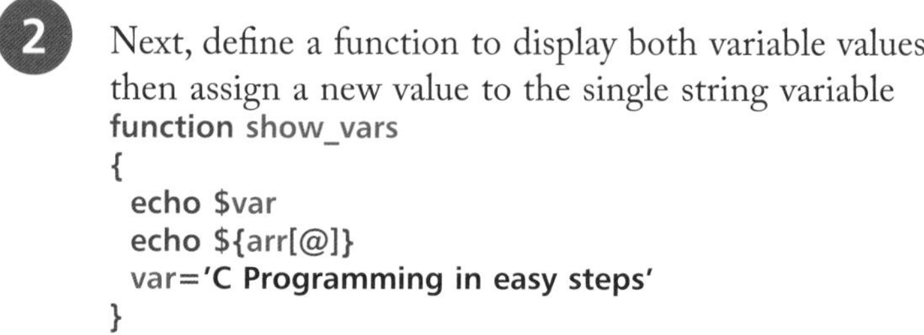

2. Next, define a function to display both variable values then assign a new value to the single string variable

```
function show_vars
{
  echo $var
  echo ${arr[@]}
  var='C Programming in easy steps'
}
```

The @ index operator that references all values of an array is described on page 118.

3. Then, add a call to the function to execute its statements

```
show_vars
```

4. Now, define another function to display all positional parameters then add a call passing a variable string value

```
function show_params
{
  str=$@
  echo $str
}
show_params $var
```

In this case, positional parameter **$1** will contain only the first word of the string.

5. Save the script then make it executable and run the script to see output from the functions

Note that the words in the single string get separated around each space break so are actually passed in parameters **$1, $2, $3** and **$4**. The **$@** parameter reproduces the spaces as it creates a values list. This can pass a copy of an array to a function for manipulation:

bubble.sh

1. Begin a shell script by defining a function to sort and display a copy of an array of values into ascending order

```
#!/bin/bash

function bubble_sort
{
  arr=$@
  for (( i = 0 ; i < ${#arr[@]}-1 ; i++ ))
  do
    for (( j = 0 ; j < ${#arr[@]}-1 ; j++ ))
    do
      if (( ${arr[j]} > ${arr[j+1]} ))
      then
        tmp=${arr[$j]}
        arr[j]=${arr[$j+1]}
        arr[$j+1]=$tmp
      fi
    done
  done
  echo "Original Order: ${nums[@]}"
  echo "Sorted Order: ${arr[@]}"
}
```

2. Next, initialize an array of unsorted integer values

```
nums=(3 8 20 25 12 7 32 1 16 29)
```

3. Now, call the function passing a copy of the array values

```
bubble_sort ${nums[@]}
```

4. Save the script then make it executable and run the script to see output from the function

```
mike@win-pc:~$ ./bubble.sh
Original Order: 3 8 20 25 12 7 32 1 16 29
Sorted Order:   1 3 7 8 12 16 20 25 29 32
mike@win-pc:~$
```

The bubble sort algorithm used here is not especially efficient but it is relatively easy to understand. It continues to loop, comparing the value in an element with that in the next element and swaps them if it is found to be greater, until all elements are in ascending order. The values of array elements can also be piped to a **sort -n** command for numerical sorting with

```
for i in ${nums[@]}
do echo $i
done | sort -n
```

Inputting Values

Input from the command line can be assigned to a script variable by specifying the variable name to the **read** command. This will pause awaiting input that will be assigned to the variable when the user hits the Return key. Input variable values can then be examined by conditional tests to ensure they are of the desired value type for manipulation by the program:

add.sh

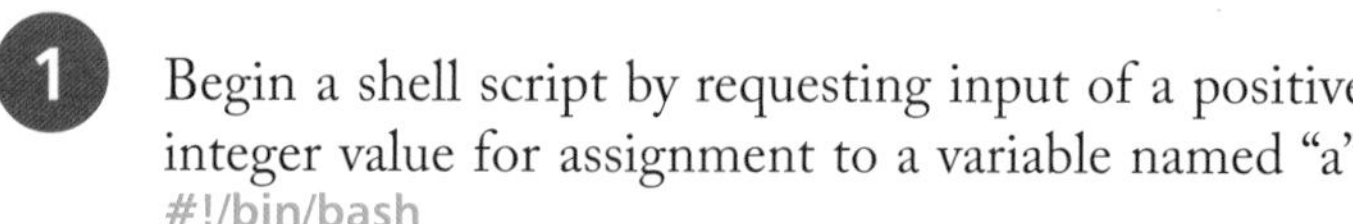

1. Begin a shell script by requesting input of a positive integer value for assignment to a variable named "a"

```
#!/bin/bash

echo -n 'Enter A Positive Integer: '
read a
```

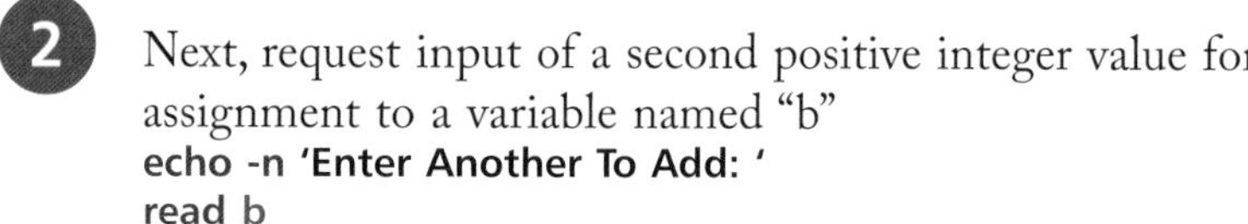

2. Next, request input of a second positive integer value for assignment to a variable named "b"

```
echo -n 'Enter Another To Add: '
read b
```

Scripts are implemented sequentially top-to-bottom, so functions must be defined before they can be called.

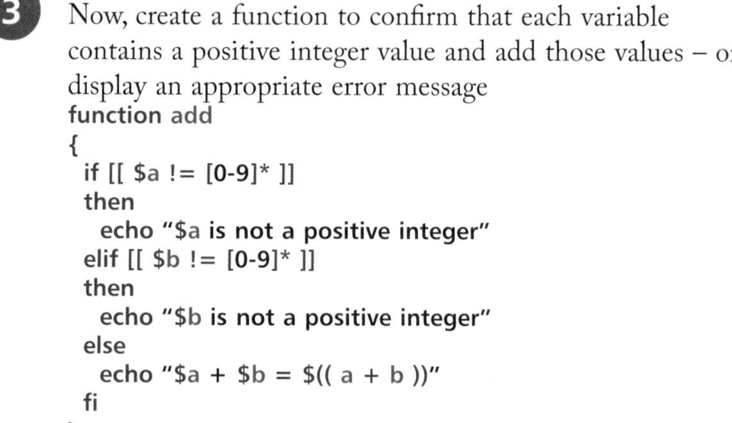

3. Now, create a function to confirm that each variable contains a positive integer value and add those values – or display an appropriate error message

```
function add
{
  if [[ $a != [0-9]* ]]
  then
    echo "$a is not a positive integer"
  elif [[ $b != [0-9]* ]]
  then
    echo "$b is not a positive integer"
  else
    echo "$a + $b = $(( a + b ))"
  fi
}
```

The conditional tests made in this function ensure each variable only contains any number of characters zero through nine.

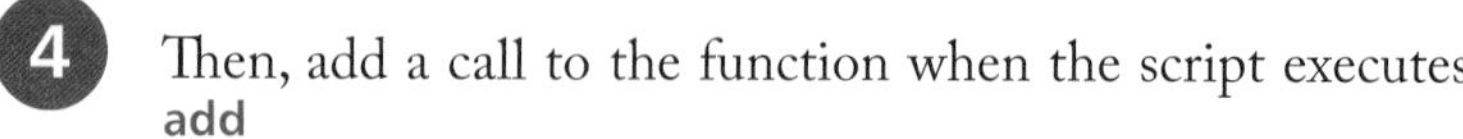

4. Then, add a call to the function when the script executes

```
add
```

5. Save the script then make it executable and enter values when requested to see their total or error messages

...cont'd

```
mike@win-pc:~$ ./add.sh
Enter A Positive Integer: 8
Enter Another To Add: 4
8 + 4 = 12
mike@win-pc:~$ ./add.sh
Enter A Positive Integer: 8
Enter Another To Add: X
X is not a positive integer
mike@win-pc:~$ ./add.sh
Enter A Positive Integer: 8
Enter Another To Add: -4
-4 is not a positive integer
mike@win-pc:~$
```

Input from the command line can also be specified as arguments to the script and assigned to variables using positional parameters:

#!
SH
sum.sh

1. Make a copy of the script listed opposite by issuing a command **cp add.sh sum.sh**

2. Next, remove all the lines listed in steps 1 and 2 opposite from the copy script

3. Now, edit the start of the copy script to assign the value of two command arguments to variables "a" and "b"

```
#!/bin/bash

a=$1
b=$2
```

4. Save the copy script then execute it with two argument values to see their total or error messages

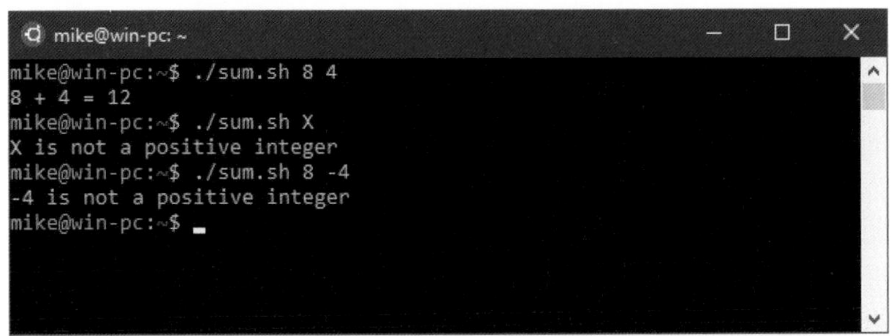
mike@win-pc: ~
mike@win-pc:~$ ./sum.sh 8 4
8 + 4 = 12
mike@win-pc:~$ ./sum.sh X
X is not a positive integer
mike@win-pc:~$ ./sum.sh 8 -4
-4 is not a positive integer
mike@win-pc:~$

Hot tip

This example can be improved by ensuring exactly two arguments are present – by changing the call to
if (($# == 2))
then add
fi

Providing Options

The positional parameters **$1, $2, $3, $4**; etc. are **readonly** so cannot explicitly be assigned values – they may only contain values specified as command arguments. They can, however, be manipulated by the **shift** command (except **$0** that contains the script run command). The **shift** command discards the initial value in **$1** then moves the value in each subsequent positional parameter down so that **1=$2, 2=$3, 3=$4**; etc. This can be useful to process multiple arguments specified to a particular option:

shift.sh

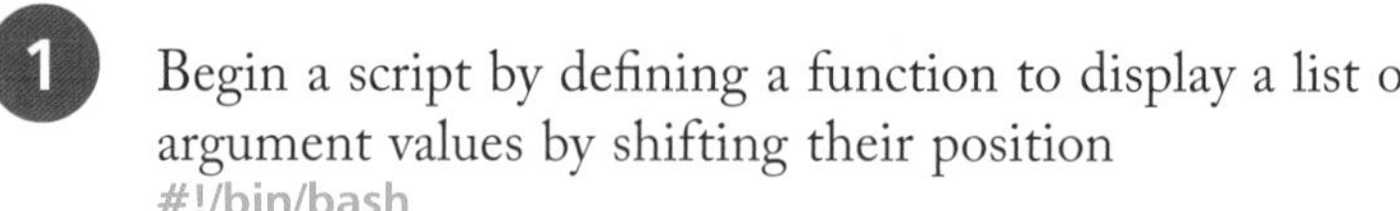

1. Begin a script by defining a function to display a list of argument values by shifting their position

```
#!/bin/bash

function process_args
{
  while (( $# > 1 ))
    do
      shift
      echo "Argument: $1"
    done
}
```

You can also specify an integer to **shift** to move multiple places, so that with **shift 2** then **$1=$3**.

2. Next, add a conditional test to call the function if a particular option has been specified

```
if [[ $1 = '-o' ]]
then
  process_args $@
fi
```

3. Save the script then make it executable and run it with multiple arguments to see each shifted value

```
mike@win-pc:~$ ./shift.sh -o 1 2 3 4 5 6 7 8 9 10
Argument: 1
Argument: 2
Argument: 3
Argument: 4
Argument: 5
Argument: 6
Argument: 7
Argument: 8
Argument: 9
Argument: 10
mike@win-pc:~$
```

The argument list specified to the script must be specified as an **$@** argument in the function call here – as functions see **$1** as the first argument in their own function call.

Bash provides a **getopts** command that allows you to easily recognize user options supplied to a script. This takes two arguments specifying a string and a variable. The **getopts** string can accept letters and the colon character. Each letter is a valid option, which if followed by a colon requires an argument. The option letter then gets stored in the variable (without the - hyphen prefix) and its argument, if applicable, gets stored in **$OPTARG**:

1. Begin a script by defining a function to display a message according to the value of a variable named "option"

```
#!/bin/bash

function process_options
{
  case $option in
    a ) echo "Selected $option" ;;
    b ) echo "Selected $option with argument: $OPTARG" ;;
    c ) echo "Selected $option" ;;
    * ) echo 'Usage: getopts [-a] [-b arg] [-c]' ;;
  esac
}
```

getopts.sh

2. Next, add a loop to specify valid options and handle each option by calling the function

```
while getopts "ab:c" option
do
  process_options
done
```

In this example you can specify **getopts -ab 8** to process both **-a** and **-b** case statements.

3. Save the script then make it executable and run it with various options to see them processed

```
mike@win-pc:~$ ./getopts.sh -a
Selected a
mike@win-pc:~$ ./getopts.sh -b
./getopts.sh: option requires an argument -- b
Usage: getopts [-a] [-b arg] [-c]
mike@win-pc:~$ ./getopts.sh -b 8
Selected b with argument: 8
mike@win-pc:~$ ./getopts.sh -c
Selected c
mike@win-pc:~$ ./getopts.sh -d
./getopts.sh: illegal option -- d
Usage: getopts [-a] [-b arg] [-c]
mike@win-pc:~$
```

You can suppress the automatic Bash error messages by inserting a colon at the beginning of the string, such as **":ab:c"** in this example.

Restricting Scope

The extent to which variables are accessible in a script program is called the "variable scope".

Global variable scope

Variables declared in the main body of a script, outside any function blocks, have "global scope". These are accessible globally throughout the script – both from within function blocks and from outside function blocks. A variable with global scope can therefore be overwritten by assigning a new value to that variable from anywhere in the script.

The **local** keyword can only be used in a script within a function block.

Local variable scope

Variables declared inside any function block, on the other hand, have "local scope". These are only accessible locally throughout the function in which they are declared – not from outside that function block or within any other function block. A variable with local scope can therefore be overwritten by assigning a new value to that variable only within the function in which it was declared.

Optionally, a function variable can be declared inside a function body with the **local** keyword to explicitly restrict its scope. This allows a local function variable to have the same name as a global script variable without conflict – the shell treats them as two distinctly different variables.

Parameter scope

Values passed as arguments to the script run command are accessible locally in the main body of the script in the positional parameters **$1**, **$2**, **$3**; etc. These have "local scope" within the script body so are not accessible from within function blocks – functions recognize different positional parameters.

A function cannot access arguments passed in the script run command unless a copy of them is passed as an argument in the function call.

Values passed as arguments in a function call are accessible locally in that function block in the positional parameters **$1**, **$2**, **$3**; etc. These have "local scope" within the function block so are not accessible from within the script body.

A copy of the arguments to the script run command can, however, be supplied to a function as an **$@** argument to the function call – as demonstrated in the example on page 158.

scope.sh

1. Begin a shell script by initializing two global variables

```
#!/bin/bash

str='Windows'
int=100
```

2. Next, display two script parameters (if available) and the global variable values

```
echo "Script parameters: $1 $2"
echo "Global String: $str"
echo -e "Global Integer: $int\n"
```

3. Now, add a function to overwrite one global variable; initialize a local variable; then display two function parameters (if available) and the local variable value

```
function call_me
{
  str='Linux'
  local int=200
  echo "Function parameters: $1 $2"
  echo -e "Local Integer: $int\n"
}
```

Explicitly declaring local scope for function variables is considered good practice as it prevents their modification elsewhere in the script.

4. Then, call the function – with one argument – and display the global variable values once more

```
call_me 'Al'

echo "Global String: $str"
echo "Global Integer: $int"
```

5. Save the script then make it executable and run it with two arguments to see the variable and parameter scope

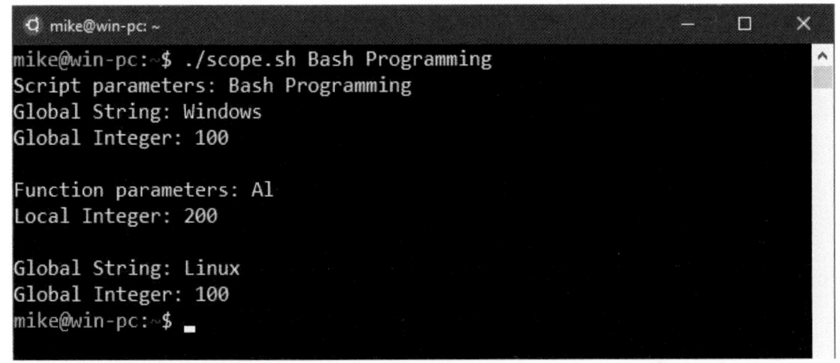

mike@win-pc: ~
mike@win-pc:~$ ./scope.sh Bash Programming
Script parameters: Bash Programming
Global String: Windows
Global Integer: 100

Function parameters: Al
Local Integer: 200

Global String: Linux
Global Integer: 100
mike@win-pc:~$

The function call passes only one argument so the **$2** parameter is not recognized.

Repeating Calls

A "recursive" function can be used to repeatedly call itself to execute the statements it contains. As with loop constructs recursive functions must make a conditional test that will at some point end the cycle. For example, to search through an array until a specified value is found:

linear.sh

1. Begin a script by filling an array with integers 1-64 and initializing two variables as a counter and a key to find

```
#!/bin/bash

for (( i = 1; i < 65; i++ ))
{
  (( arr[i-1] = i ))
}
i=1 ; key=8
```

2. Now, add a recursive function to iterate through the array elements until it finds the specified key value

```
function linear_search
{
  echo "Element value: ${arr[$i-1]}"
  if (( arr[i-1] == key ))
  then
    echo "Linear search found $key on attempt $i"
    return 0
  else
    (( i++ ))
    linear_search
  fi
}
linear_search
```

3. Save the script then make it executable and run the program to see the recursive function's linear search result

```
mike@win-pc: ~
mike@win-pc:~$ ./linear.sh
Element value: 1
Element value: 2
Element value: 3
Element value: 4
Element value: 5
Element value: 6
Element value: 7
Element value: 8
Linear search found 8 on attempt 8
mike@win-pc:~$
```

The integers stored in the array are 1-64 but stored in elements numbered 0-63.

The function must be called outside the function block, to begin the search, then from inside the function block each time the search does not find the key.

A linear search is not efficient on a large range of values – a recursive function can also make a more efficient binary search:

binary.sh

1. Begin a script by filling an array with integers 1-64

```
#!/bin/bash

for (( i = 1; i < 65; i++ ))
{
  (( arr[i-1] = i ))
}
```

2. Next, initialize variables as a counter; key to find; minimum; and maximum of a range of elements

```
i=1 ; key=8 ; min=1 ; max=${#arr[@]}
```

3. Now, add a recursive function to iterate through the array elements until it finds the specified key value

```
function binary_search
{
  mid=$(( (min+max) / 2 ))
  echo "Range:$min-$max Mid-point: $mid"
  if (( arr[mid-1] == key ))
  then
    echo "Binary search found $key on attempt $i"
    return 0
  else (( i++ ))
  fi

  if (( arr[mid-1] < key )
  then min=$mid
  else max=$mid
  fi
  binary_search
}
binary_search
```

The initial maximum range is the computed array length.

Change the key value to 50 in each example here to see a linear search make 50 attempts whereas the binary search needs just five.

4. Save the script then make it executable and run the program to see the recursive function's binary search result

```
mike@win-pc: ~
mike@win-pc:~$ ./binary.sh
Range:1-64 Mid-point: 32
Range:1-32 Mid-point: 16
Range:1-16 Mid-point: 8
Binary search found 8 on attempt 3
mike@win-pc:~$
```

Locating Bugs

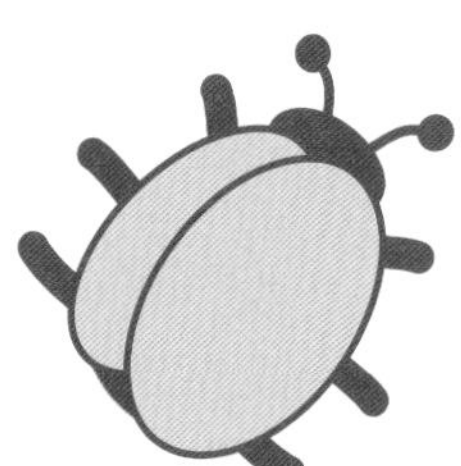

In Bash programming there are typically three types of error that can occur. It is useful to recognize the different error types so they can be corrected more easily:

- **Syntax error** – occurs when the interpreter encounters code that does not conform to the Bash shell language rules – for example, when a quote mark is omitted around a string. The interpreter halts execution and reports the error.
- **Runtime error** – occurs during execution of the program – for example, when a variable name is later mistyped. The interpreter runs the program and ignores the error.
- **Semantic error** – occurs when the program executes to its conclusion but performs unexpectedly in some way – for example, when order precedence is not explicitly specified. The interpreter runs the program and does not see the error.

Correcting syntax errors is fairly straightforward as the interpreter halts where the error occurs and describes the nature of the error:

syntax.sh

1. Create a script to output two strings, but with a quote mark omitted from the first string

```
#!/bin/bash

echo 'Bash in easy steps
echo 'End'
```

2. Run the script to see the interpreter report this syntax error then halt without executing any output commands

```
mike@win-pc:~$ ./syntax.sh
./syntax.sh: line 3: unexpected EOF while looking for matching `''
./syntax.sh: line 4: syntax error: unexpected end of file
mike@win-pc:~$
```

Simply add the missing single quote after the string on line 3 and run the script to see this syntax error corrected. To help track down other types of error scripts can be executed with a **bash -x** (expand) command, to display each line of the script with expressions expanded before execution:

3. Create a script to output two strings, but with the name of the variable different in each instance

```
#!/bin/bash
title='Bash in easy steps'
echo $titel
echo 'End'
```

runtime.sh

4. Run the script using **bash -x** to expand expressions – and discover that the variable has no value

```
mike@win-pc: ~
mike@win-pc:~$ bash -x runtime.sh
+ title='Bash in easy steps'
+ echo

+ echo End
End
mike@win-pc:~$
```

The **+** is the PS4 prompt that can be customized to show line numbers by adding **PS4='$LINENO: '** to your **.bashrc** file.

Simply correct the variable name so it has a value and run the script to see this runtime error corrected. Other types of error can be identified by executing scripts with a **bash -v** (verbose) command, to display exactly what input the shell is receiving:

5. Create a script to simply output the result of an arithmetical expression

```
#!/bin/bash
num=3
echo $(( num * 8 + 4 ))
```

semantic.sh

6. Run the script using **bash -v** to display the input to discover that default precedence is not producing the expected output of 36

```
mike@win-pc: ~
mike@win-pc:~$ bash -v semantic.sh
#!/bin/bash
num=3
echo $(( num * 8 + 4 ))
28
mike@win-pc:~$
```

Default operator precedence is left-to-right so **3x8=24 +4=28**, not **3x (8+4=12) =36**.

Add parentheses to group the expression as **$((num * (8 + 4)))** to explicitly specify precedence and so correct this semantic error.

Randomizing Numbers

Bash provides a **RANDOM** variable that generates pseudo-random numbers in the range 0-32767. An upper limit can be set using the **%** modulus arithmetic operator to specify a boundary – for example, to set a range of 0-9 using ((**RANDOM % 10**)). A lower limit can be set by adding to the result of that expression. For example, to set a range of 1-10 with ((**(RANDOM % 10) + 1**)):

random.sh

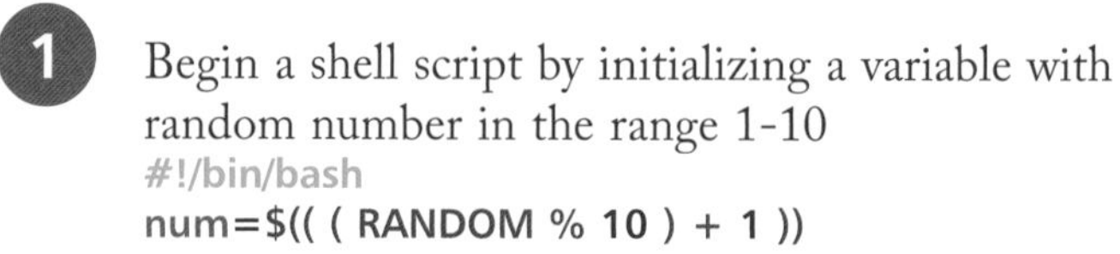

1. Begin a shell script by initializing a variable with a random number in the range 1-10

```
#!/bin/bash
num=$(( ( RANDOM % 10 ) + 1 ))
```

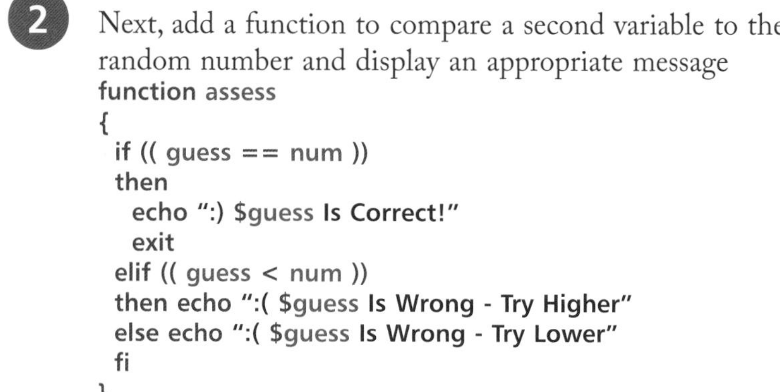

2. Next, add a function to compare a second variable to the random number and display an appropriate message

```
function assess
{
 if (( guess == num ))
 then
   echo ":) $guess Is Correct!"
   exit
 elif (( guess < num ))
 then echo ":( $guess Is Wrong - Try Higher"
 else echo ":( $guess Is Wrong - Try Lower"
 fi
}
```

The **RANDOM** variable should not be used for encryption but is suitable for trivial purposes.

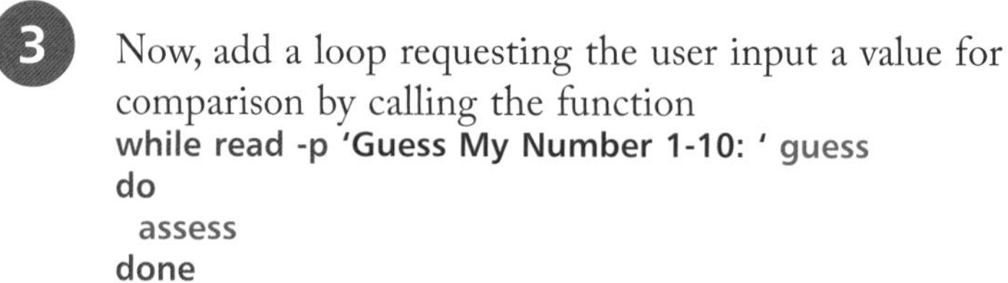

3. Now, add a loop requesting the user input a value for comparison by calling the function

```
while read -p 'Guess My Number 1-10: ' guess
do
  assess
done
```

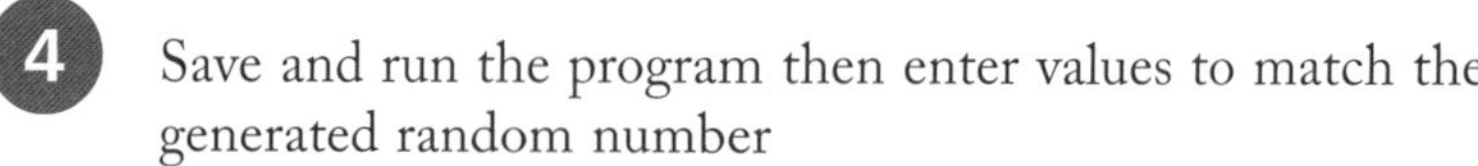

4. Save and run the program then enter values to match the generated random number

```
mike@win-pc: ~
mike@win-pc:~$ ./random.sh
Guess My Number 1-10: 3
:( 3 Is Wrong - Try Higher
Guess My Number 1-10: 7
:( 7 Is Wrong - Try Lower
Guess My Number 1-10: 5
:) 5 Is Correct!
mike@win-pc:~$
```

1. Begin a script by assigning the first argument to a variable if numeric and below 10, or supply a default value

```
#!/bin/bash
if [[ $1 = [0-9]* && $1 -lt 10 ]]
then a=$1 ; else a=6 ; fi
```

lotto.sh

2. Next, assign a second argument to a variable if numeric and greater than the first argument; or, supply a default

```
if [[ $2 = [0-9]* && $1 -lt $2 ]]
then b=$2 ; else b=59 ; fi
```

Here the *default values* select six numbers in the range 1-59 – to play the UK Lotto game or the New York Lotto game.

3. Now, add a function to select a quantity of numbers, specified by the first variable, from a randomized array of numbers in the range of one to that of the second variable

```
function lotto
{
  for (( i = 0 ; i <= $2 ; i++ ))
  {
    (( arr[i] = i ))
  }

  for (( i = 1 ; i <= $2 ; i++ ))
  {
    r=$(( ( RANDOM % $2 ) + 1 ))
    (( t=arr[i] )) ; (( arr[i]=arr[r] )) ; (( arr[r]=t ))
  }

  for (( i = 1 ; i < $1 ; i++ ))
  {
    str+="${arr[$i]} "
  }
  echo "Your Lucky $1 From $2 : $str"
}
```

4. Save and run the program with or without arguments to see it select a random unique series in a specified range

```
mike@win-pc: ~
mike@win-pc:~$ ./lotto.sh
Your Lucky 6 From 59 : 13 5 27 18 34 53
mike@win-pc:~$ ./lotto.sh 5 75
Your Lucky 5 From 75 : 30 43 3 71 52
mike@win-pc:~$ ./lotto.sh 1 15
Your Lucky 1 From 15 : 13
mike@win-pc:~$ _
```

Here, the supplied *argument values* select five numbers in the range 1-75 plus one number in the range 1-15 – to play the Mega Millions lottery.

Summary

- A function can be defined in a script using the **function** keyword or by placing **( )** parentheses after a function name.
- Commands in scripts executed using the **source** keyword are treated as if they had been typed at a command prompt.
- The **return** keyword in Bash functions merely returns the exit status of the last statement in the function.
- Variables declared in a script outside any function definitions have global scope so are accessible throughout the script.
- Values can be passed to functions as positional parameters by adding arguments to the function call.
- Input can be assigned to script variables by the **read** command or as positional parameters in command arguments.
- Positional parameters are read-only but can be manipulated by the **shift** command to process multiple arguments.
- The **getopts** command recognizes command letter options and stores associated arguments in the **OPTARG** variable.
- Variables declared in a script function have local scope so are only accessible from within that function block.
- Optionally, a variable may be declared with the **local** keyword to explicitly restrict its scope.
- Values passed to a script as arguments are accessible as positional parameters in local scope within the script body.
- Values passed to a function as arguments are accessible as positional parameters in local scope within the function block.
- A recursive function contains a statement that calls itself and must also provide a conditional test to end the cycle.
- Runtime and semantic errors can be located more readily by running the script with **bash -x** or **bash -v** commands.
- The Bash **RANDOM** variable generates a pseudo-random number in the range 0-32767.

10 Handy Reference

This section provides a summary of special characters, commands, date formats, and shell variables featured in this book.

Special Characters

Characters:	Description:	Example:
~	Home directory	**cd ~**
-	Previous directory	**cd -**
..	Parent directory	**cd ..**
/	Path directory separator	**cd /home/user**
./	Execute from this directory	**./bashscript**
?	Single-character wildcard	**ls doc.?**
*	Multiple-character wildcard	**ls *.txt**
[ ]	Wildcard set	**ls doc.[a-c]**
[!]	Wildcard negated set	**ls doc.[!a-c]**
{ }	Brace expansion	**echo {a..z}**
\	Escape next character	**\n**
;	Command separator	**pwd ; ls**
$	Variable substitution	**echo $SHELL**
$( )	Command substitution	**echo $(date +%H:%M)**
( )	Execute in subshell	**(echo $BASHPID)**
&	Execute as background job	**xcalc &**
' '	Strong quote	**echo "Literal $var"**
" "	Weak quote	**echo "Interpret $var"**

...cont'd

<table>
<tr><th>Characters:</th><th>Description:</th><th>Example:</th></tr>
<tr><td>( )</td><td>Group expression</td><td>2*(3+4)</td></tr>
<tr><td>|</td><td>Pipeline redirector</td><td>cat ballad.txt | more</td></tr>
<tr><td><</td><td>Input redirector</td><td>read < csv.txt</td></tr>
<tr><td>></td><td>Output redirector</td><td>echo Stored! > stored.txt</td></tr>
<tr><td>[@]</td><td>All array elements</td><td>${arr[@]}</td></tr>
<tr><td>#[@]</td><td>Array length</td><td>${#arr[@]}</td></tr>
<tr><td>#</td><td>Script comment</td><td># Line not interpreted</td></tr>
<tr><td>#!</td><td>Start shell script</td><td>#!/bin/bash</td></tr>
<tr><td>+ - * / %
++ --</td><td>Arithmetic operators</td><td>8 + 4</td></tr>
<tr><td>(( ))</td><td>Arithmetic expression operator</td><td>((8 + 4))</td></tr>
<tr><td>$(( ))</td><td>Arithmetic expression substitution</td><td>echo $((8 + 4))</td></tr>
<tr><td>== !=
> >=
< <=</td><td>Arithmetical expression
Comparison operators</td><td>if ((8 > 4))</td></tr>
<tr><td>&& || !</td><td>Logical AND, OR and NOT operators</td><td>true && true</td></tr>
<tr><td>[[ ]]</td><td>Conditional test operator</td><td>if [[true && true]]</td></tr>
<tr><td>-eq -ne
-gt -ge
-lt -le</td><td>Conditional test
Numerical comparison operators</td><td>if [[$num -ne 0]]</td></tr>
<tr><td>= !=
> <</td><td>Conditional test
String comparison operators</td><td>if [[$str != '']]</td></tr>
</table>

Commands A-D

Command:	Usage:	Description:
alias /usr/bin/alias	**alias** *name=command*	Define or display a shorthand name for a specified command
basename /usr/bin/basename	**basename** *path*	Print name with leading directory components removed from address
bash /bin/bash	**bash** **bash -v** **bash -x** **bash --version**	Explicitly invoke a new shell process Or provide detailed verbose output Or provide expanded output Or display version information
bg built-in	**bg** *%job*	Place specified job into background operation
break built-in	**break**	Exit immediately from a current **for**, **select**, **while**, or **until** loop construct
builtin built-in	**builtin** *command*	Explicitly execute the specified builtin command
bunzip2 /usr/bin/bunzip2	**bunzip2** *archive/s*	Decompress the specified archive or archives into individual files
bzip2 /usr/bin/bzip2	**bzip2** *file/s*	Compress the specified file or files into a single archive file
case keyword	**case** *word* **in** *pattern* **)** *statement/s* **;;** *pattern* **)** *statement/s* **;;** *pattern* **)** *statement/s* **;;** **esac**	Construct to selectively execute statement/s based upon word pattern matching
cat /usr/bin/cat	**cat** *file/s*	Print the content of the specified file or files to standard output
cd built-in	**cd** *directory*	Change the shell working directory to the specified directory, or to the home directory if none specified
chgrp /usr/bin/chgrp	**chgrp** *group file*	Change group ownership of the specified file to the specified group
chmod /usr/bin/chmod	**chmod** *mode file*	Change permissions mode of the specified file to the specified mode

Command:	Usage:	Description:
chown /usr/bin/chown	**chown** *user file*	Change user ownership of the specified file to the specified user
cksum /usr/bin/cksum	**cksum** *file*	Print the CRC checksum and byte count of the specified file
clear /usr/bin/clear	**clear**	Clear the Terminal screen, leaving the cursor at a command prompt
cmp /usr/bin/cmp	**cmp** *file1 file2*	Compare two specified files and report the location where they differ
comm /usr/bin/comm	**comm** *file1 file2*	Compare two specified files and print three columns of lines unique to file 1, lines unique to file 2, and lines common to both files
command built-in	**command** *command*	Explicitly execute the specified command
continue built-in	**continue**	Exit immediately from the current iteration only of a loop construct
cp /usr/bin/cp	**cp** *file/s destination*	Copy the specified file or files to the specified filesystem destination
cpio /usr/bin/cpio	*list* **| cpio -o >** *archive* **cpio -i <** *archive*	Copy a piped list of files directed out to a specified archive Or copy a list of files directed in from a specified archive
cut /usr/bin/cut	**cut -f** *number file*	Print the content of a column field number from a specified file
date /usr/bin/date	**date** **date +***format*	Display the current date and time Or display date and/or time components in a specified format
declare built-in	**declare -F**	Print the names of all functions in current shell memory

Commands D-F

Command:	Usage:	Description:
diff /usr/bin/diff	**diff** *file1 file2*	Compare two specified files and report unique and differing lines
dirname /usr/bin/dirname	**dirname** *path*	Print path with final component removed from the address
disown built-in	**disown** *%job*	Remove the specified job from the jobs table
do keyword	**do** *statement/s*	Start of statements block in a **for**, **select**, **while**, or **until** loop construct
done keyword	**done**	End of statements block in a **for**, **select**, **while**, or **until** loop construct
du /usr/bin/du	**du -k** *file*	Print the file size, in kilobytes, of the specified file
echo built-in	**echo** *argument/s* **echo -n** *argument/s* **echo -e** *argument/s*	Expand and print specified argument and add a final \n newline character Or expand and print specified argument without a final \n newline Or expand and print argument and interpret \ escape sequences
elif keyword	**elif** *statement/s*	Start of alternative conditional statements block in an **if** construct
else keyword	**else** *statement/s*	Start of alternative statements block in an **if** construct
enable built-in	**enable** *command* **enable -n** *command* **enable -n**	Enable a specified disabled shell builtin command Or disable a specified enabled shell builtin command Or print a list of all disabled shell builtin commands
esac keyword	**esac**	End of statements block in a **case** construct

Command:	Usage:	Description:
exit built-in	**exit**	Exit from the current shell and close sole user Terminal window
fc built-in	**fc** *command* **fc -l**	Open the specified command in the default text editor for editing Or list the last 16 commands in the shell history
fg built-in	**fg** *%job*	Place specified job into foreground operation
fi keyword	**fi**	End of statements block in an **if** construct
file /usr/bin/file	**file** *file*	Report the file type of the specified file
find /usr/bin/find	**find** *dir* **-type f** *file*	Locate the specified file within the hierarchy below the specified directory and print its path
for keyword	**for** *item* **in** *list* **do** *statement/s* **done** **for** *conditional test* **do** *statement/s* **done**	Iterate over a list and execute the specified statements for each occurrence of an item Or execute the specified statements on each iteration of a loop while a specified conditional test succeeds
function keyword	**function** *name* **{** *statement/s* **}** *name* **( )** **{** *statement/s* **}**	Define a function to execute the specified statements when called by the specified name Alternatively, define a function to execute the specified statements when called by the specified name Function calls may pass arguments to the function for reference via positional parameters **$1**, **$2**, **$3**, etc.

Commands G-L

Command:	Usage:	Description:
getopts built-in	**getopts** *string var*	Specify valid options in the string and place option letter without its - prefix in the specified variable
grep /usr/bin/grep	**grep** *pattern file*	Print each line of the specified file in which the specified pattern appears
groupadd /usr/sbin/groupadd	**groupadd** *group*	Add a new group account to the system
groupdel /usr/sbin/groupdel	**groupdel** *group*	Remove an existing group account from the system
groupmod /usr/sbin/groupmod	**groupmod -n** *N group*	Rename the specified group with new name N
groups /usr/bin/groups	**groups** *user*	Print a list of group accounts of which the specified user is a member
gunzip /usr/bin/gunzip	**gunzip** *archive*	Decompress the specified archive or archives into individual files
gzip /usr/bin/gzip	**gzip** *file/s*	Compress the specified file or files into a single archive file
hash built-in	**hash**	Print a hit list of recently executed program commands
head /usr/bin/head	**head** *file*	Print the first 10 lines of the specified file
	head -n *number file*	Or print the first specified number of lines of the specified file
help built-in	**help** *command*	Display a brief summary of the specified builtin command
history built-in	**history**	Print a list of all issued commands in the shell history
	history *number*	Or print the last specified number of commands in shell history
hostname /usr/bin/hostname	**hostname**	Print the name of the host system

Command:	Usage:	Description:
if keyword	**if** *conditional test* **then** *statement/s* **fi**	Construct to execute the specified statements when a test succeeds
	if *conditional test* **then** *statement/s* **else** *statement/s* **fi**	Construct to execute the specified statements when a test succeeds or to execute alternative specified statements when the test fails
in keyword	**in** *list*	Iterate over a list of items specified in a **for** construct or a list of patterns specified in a **case** construct
info /usr/bin/info	**info** *command*	Display the specified command documentation in Info format
jobs built-in	**jobs**	Print a list of all active jobs and display their job number and status
kill built-in	**kill** *process number*	Terminate the running process that has the specified process number
less /usr/bin/less	**less** *file*	Display contents of the specified file one screen at a time – that may be scrolled forwards and backwards
let built-in	**let** *name=value*	Assign the result of an arithmetic expression as a numeric value Replaced by **(( ))** arithmetic operator
ln /usr/bin/ln	**ln** *target linkname*	Create a hard link of the specified name to the specified target
	ln -s *target linkname*	Create a soft link of the specified name to the specified target
local built-in	**local** *name=value*	Create a variable of local scope of the specified name
logname /usr/bin/logname	**logname**	Print the name of the current user

Commands L-S

Command:	Usage:	Description:
ls /usr/bin/ls	**ls** **ls** *directory* **ls -a** **ls -i** **ls -l**	List contents of current directory List contents of specified directory List including files that start with . List contents and the inode numbers List contents in long format
man /usr/bin/man	**man** *command*	Display the specified command reference Manual page
md5sum /usr/bin/md5sum	**md5sum** *file*	Print or check MD5 128-bit checksum of the specified file
mkdir /usr/bin/mkdir	**mkdir** *dirname*	Create a directory of the specified name if none already exists
mkfifo /usr/bin/mkfifo	**mkfifo** *name*	Create a named pipe of the specified name
more /usr/bin/more	**more** *file*	Display contents of the specified file one screen at a time – that may be scrolled forward only
mv /usr/bin/mv	**mv** *file directory* **mv** *file name*	Move the specified file to the specified directory Or rename the specified file with the new specified name
nano /usr/bin/nano	**nano** **nano** *file*	Launch the Nano text editor in the Terminal screen Or launch the Nano text editor in the Terminal with the specified file open
passwd /usr/bin/passwd	**passwd** *user*	Prompt to set new password for the specified user – must be issued as root (using **sudo** command)
paste /usr/bin/paste	**paste** *file/s* **paste -s** *file/s* **paste -d:** *file/s*	Display lines of specified file/s in columns delimited by **\t** Tab character Or display one file at a time with each line in sequence on a row Or display lines of specified file/s in columns delimited by : character

Command:	Usage:	Description:
printf /usr/bin/printf	**printf** *"format " arg*	Print the specified argument in the specified format – **%s**, **%c**, **%d**, etc.
ps /usr/bin/ps	**ps**	Print a report listing all the current processes
pwd built-in	**pwd**	Print the current working directory
read built-in	**read** **read -p '** *prompt* **'**	Read a line from standard input Or display the specified prompt message then read standard input Input is stored in **REPLY** by default
readlink /usr/bin/readlink	**readlink** *link*	Print the name of the target file stored in a soft symbolic link
readonly built-in	**readonly** *name=value*	Initialize a variable with a specified value that cannot be changed later
reboot /sbin/reboot	**reboot**	Restart the computer – must be issued as root (using **sudo** command)
return built-in	**return** **return** *status*	Exit from a script reporting the status of the last executed command Or exit from a script reporting the specified status
rm /usr/bin/rm	**rm** *file* **rm** *directory*	Delete the specified file Or delete the contents of the specified directory prompting before each file deletion
rmdir /usr/bin/rmdir	**rm** *directory*	Delete the specified directory only if it is empty
sed /usr/bin/sed	**sed 's/***old***/***new***/'** **sed 's/***old***/***new***/g'**	Replace the first occurrence of the specified old string with new string Or replace each occurrence of the specified old string with new string

Commands S-U

Command:	Usage:	Description:
select keyword	**select** *item* **in** *list* **do** *statement/s* **done**	Generate individually numbered items for a specified list then execute the specified statement/s associated with the user's selected number
set built-in	**set -o** *option* **set +o** *option*	Set the specified option to ON Or set the specified option to OFF
	set -o noclobber	Prevent output redirection overwriting an existing file
	set -o emacs **set -o vi**	Set Emacs as command editor mode Or set Vi as command editor mode
shift built-in	**shift**	Shift positional parameters so **$2** becomes **$1**, **$3** becomes **$2**, etc.
shopt built-in	**shopt**	List shell options and display their current ON/OFF status
	shopt -s *option* **shopt -u** *option*	Set the specified option to ON Unset the specified option to OFF
sort /usr/bin/sort	**sort** *file/s*	Print a sorted concatenation of one or more files on standard output
	sort -r *file*	Print a reverse sorted concatenation of specified files on standard output
	sort *file/s* **-o** *file*	Output a sorted concatenation of one or more files to a specified file
source built-in	**source** *file*	Execute commands contained within a specified file in the current shell
stat /usr/bin/stat	**stat** *file*	Display current attribute status of the specified file
su /usr/bin/su	**su -**	Become the root superuser
sudo /usr/bin/sudo	**sudo** *command*	Assume root superuser status to execute the specified command

Command:	Usage:	Description:
tail /usr/bin/tail	**tail** *file* **tail** -*number file*	Print the last 10 lines of the specified file Or print the last specified number of lines of the specified file
tar /usr/bin/tar	**tar -cf** *archive file/s* **tar -xf** *archive*	Create a specified archive containing the specified file or files Or extract all files from the specified archive
tee /usr/bin/tee	**tee** *file*	Read from standard input then write that input to the specified file and also print it on standard output
test built-in	**test** *expression*	Evaluate the specified expression as a Boolean true or false value Replaced by **[[ ]]** conditional operator
then keyword	**then** *statement/s*	Start of conditional statements block in an **if** or **elif** construct
touch /usr/bin/touch	**touch** *file* **touch -t** *timedate file* **touch -d** *datetime file*	Update the access and modification times of the specified file to current time and date Or update the access and modification times of the specified file to a specified time and date
tr /usr/bin/tr	**tr** *old new*	Read from standard input and translate specified old characters to specified new characters then write the result on standard output
type built-in	**type** *command*	Describe how the specified command will be interpreted
unalias /usr/bin/unalias	**unalias** *name*	Delete the specified name from the list of defined aliases

Commands U-Z

Command:	Usage:	Description:
uniq /usr/bin/uniq	**uniq** *file/s*	Print the content of the specified file or files to standard output but omit any duplicated lines
unset built-in	**unset** *name*	Remove the definition of the variable with the specified name
	unset *name*[*number*]	Or remove the element of the specified array variable name at the specified index number
until keyword	**until** *conditional-test* **do** *statement/s* **done**	Execute the specified statements on each iteration of a loop while a specified conditional test fails – the loop ends when the test succeeds
unzip /usr/bin/unzip	**unzip** *archive*	Decompress the specified archive or archives into individual files
usermod /usr/sbin/usermod	**usermod -G** *group user*	Add the specified user to the specified group – must be issued as root (using **sudo** command)
vi /usr/bin/vi	**vi**	Launch the Vi text editor in the Terminal screen
	vi *file*	Or launch the Vi text editor in the Terminal with the specified file open
wait built-in	**wait**	Wait until all currently active child processes complete
	wait *pid*	Or wait until the specified process completes
wc /usr/bin/wc	**wc** *file*	Print the newline, word, and byte counts of the specified file
which /usr/bin/which	**which** *command*	Print the path address of the specified command

<table>
<tr><th>Command:</th><th>Usage:</th><th>Description:</th></tr>
<tr><td>while
keyword</td><td>while conditional-test
do
statement/s
done</td><td>Execute the specified statements on each iteration of a loop while a specified conditional test succeeds – the loop ends when the test fails</td></tr>
<tr><td>whoami
/usr/bin/whoami</td><td>whoami</td><td>Print the current username</td></tr>
<tr><td>xcalc
/usr/bin/xcalc</td><td>xcalc
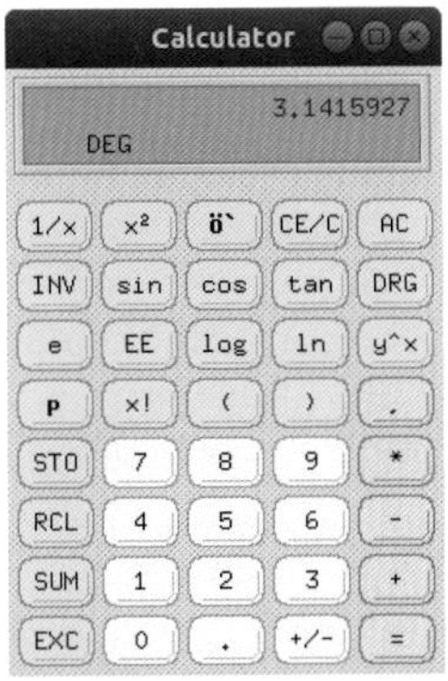
</td><td>Run a graphical scientific calculator that accepts keyboard input:

/ Divide
* Multiply
+ Add
- Subtract
= Equals
S Sine
C Cosine
T Tangent
Spacebar Clear</td></tr>
<tr><td>xeyes
/usr/bin/xeyes</td><td>xeyes

xeyes option color

</td><td>Run a graphical test application that follows mouse movement

Or run a graphical test application with RGB color option arguments:

-fg Pupil color (red)
-center Eyeball color (yellow)
-outline Outline color (blue)</td></tr>
<tr><td>zip
/usr/bin/zip</td><td>zip file/s</td><td>Compress the specified file or files into a single archive file</td></tr>
</table>

Date Formats

Format:	Description:	Example:
%a	Locale's abbreviated weekday name	**Tue**
%A	Locale's full weekday name	**Tuesday**
%b	Locale's abbreviated month name	**Feb**
%B	Locale's full month name	**February**
%c	Locale's date and time	**Tue Feb 4 13:30:08 2014**
%C	Century number (year/100 truncated)	**20**
%d	Day number of the month (01-31)	**04**
%D	Date in MM/DD/YY format	**02/04/14**
%e	Day number of the month (1-31)	**4**
%h	Locale's abbreviated month name (as **%b**)	**Feb**
%H	Hour in 24-hour clock format (00-23)	**13**
%I	Hour in 12-hour clock format (01-12)	**01**
%j	Day number of the year (001-366)	**035**
%m	Month number of the year (01-12)	**02**
%M	Minute number of the hour (00-59)	**30**
%n	A newline character	**\n**
%p	Locale's equivalent of a.m. or p.m.	**PM**

...cont'd

Format:	Description:	Example:
%r	Time in 12-hour format with suffix	**01:30:08 PM**
%R	Hour and minute time in 24-hour format	**13:30**
%S	Second in the minute (00-60)	**08**
%t	A Tab character	**\t**
%T	Time (as **%H:%M:%S**)	**13:30:08**
%u	Day number of the week (1-7) – where Monday is number 1	**2**
%U	Week number of the year (00-53) – where Sunday is first day of the week	**05**
%V	Week number of the year (00-53) – where Monday is first day of the week	**05**
%w	Day number of the week (0-6) – where Sunday is number 0	**2**
%W	Week number of the year (00-53) – where Monday is first day of the week	**05**
%x	Appropriate locale date	**02/04/14**
%X	Appropriate locale time	**13:30:00**
%y	Year number without century	**14**
%Y	Year number with century	**2014**
%Z	Time zone name or abbreviation	**EDT**

Shell Variables

Variable:	Description:	Example:
$	Process ID of the shell process (Read only)	**echo $$** **1234**
@	List of all passed positional parameters (Read only)	**echo $@** **One Two Three**
#	Total number of passed parameters (Read only)	**echo $#** **3**
0	Name of shell or script run command (Read only)	**echo $0** **./bashscript**
BASH_VERSION	Version number of Bash shell (Read only)	**echo $BASH_VERSION** **4.2.45**
BASHPID	Process ID of the shell process (Read only)	**echo $BASHPID** **1234**
EDITOR	Default editor of the shell	**EDITOR=nano**
HISTCMD **HISTCONTROL** **HISTSIZE** **HISTFILESIZE**	Number of the current history command Control command history options Number of history commands to display Maximum commands to store in history	**750** **HISTCONTROL=erasedups** **HISTSIZE=50** **HISTFILESIZE=500**
PATH	The path to search for commands	**echo $PATH** **/usr/bin:/usr/sbin**
PS1 **PS2** **PS3** **PS4**	Primary prompt string Line continuation prompt string Select option prompt string Debugging prompt string	**user@host:~$** **>** **#?** **+**
PWD	Current working directory	**echo $PWD** **/home/user/Desktop**
RANDOM	Generate random number 0-32767	**echo $RANDOM** **18643**
REPLY	User input for select options and the default variable for read command	**echo $REPLY** **typed input**
SHELL	Path address of the shell	**echo $SHELL** **/bin/bash**
TERM	Terminal type	**echo $TERM** **xterm**

Index

A

B

C

D

E

F

G

O

P

Q

R

S

T

U

V

W

X

Z